Be a Person
of value!

W9-AAZ-151

Praise for *Value-Added Selling*

"As competition and technology level the playing field, innovation in new products and SELLING VALUE are the two key differentiators that allow us to continue to grow. As the training lead for the largest division of the largest power tool, hand tool, and tool accessory company in the world, we train our sales teams to ALWAYS lead with value. Nowhere is the value selling model better explained, outlined, and laid out than this book. Paul Reilly and Tom Reilly have taken a timeless sales model and done a fantastic job of describing in detail how to identify value, talk about value, take credit for the value you bring, and most importantly not give away price. This should be required reading for every salesperson who wants to differentiate themselves from their competition. I highly recommend not only reading this book, but using it as a manual as you plan your territory and analyze your sales conversations."

—Dan Alia, North America National Training Manager,
Stanley Black & Decker

"I have been a big fan of Value-Added Selling for over 20 years—I am an avid believer in the three dimensions of value and the role of sales in developing the customer relationship and ultimately influencing the customer buying decision. The tools (i.e. VAS Call Plan & VAS Worksheet) that Tom and Paul have developed and refined over time help map the process and establish a more disciplined approach that in the end, when properly deployed, lead to a successful close. I have personally used the VAS model and experienced and as well witnessed countless "wins" as a result. The core material and message are timeless. I would highly recommend VAS to anyone."

—Ken Seymour, Senior Vice President Sales,
Folding Carton, WestRock

"Value-Added Selling philosophies from Tom Reilly Training have transformed our approach towards effective value capture and customer communication. This is critical at a time when businesses have dramatically changed how they evaluate, manage, and rank their suppliers. The value selling principles outlined in this book are a must read for all sales organizations and any sales person or manager."

—Gary Kleiner, Value Capture Manager, Parker Hannifin Corporation, Motion Systems & Fluid Connectors Groups

"Chase Plastics was selling around $67 million in sales revenue back in 2004 and prior to sending our entire sales force of 12 sellers to the Value-Added Selling seminar. Today we're a sales organization of 47 with sales revenues of $250 million. Each and every one of our sellers (young and old) has been through Value-Added Selling. Value-Added Selling is our mindset during each and every sales call we make. Like many companies we do not have the luxury of having the lowest prices in our industry. But due to Value-Added Selling we have the most effective sales team and margins within our industry"

—Kevin Chase, President, Chase Plastic Services, Inc.

"Nothing is more critical to a well-lived life than continuous learning. Reading well-written books is a huge opportunity to expand my perception of the world and how we all think and move. Tom and Paul Reilly have crafted a book that meets the criteria of being well written, full of practical information and thought provoking. It will be required reading for all our sales associates."

—Arthur B. Seifert, CPCU, RPLU, CIC, President, Glatfelter Program Managers

Copyright © 2018 by Tom Reilly and Paul Reilly. All rights reserved. Printed in the United States of America. Except as permitted under the United States Copyright Act of 1976, no part of this publication may be reproduced or distributed in any form or by any means, or stored in a database or retrieval system, without the prior written permission of the publisher.

3 4 5 6 7 8 9   QVS   23 22 21 20 19

ISBN   978-1-260-13473-5
MHID   1-260-13473-3

e-ISBN 978-1-260-13474-2
e-MHID   1-260-13474-1

This publication is designed to provide accurate and authoritative information in regard to the subject matter covered. It is sold with the understanding that neither the author nor the publisher is engaged in rendering legal, accounting, securities trading, or other professional services. If legal advice or other expert assistance is required, the services of a competent professional person should be sought.
—*From a Declaration of Principles Jointly Adopted by a Committee of the American Bar Association and a Committee of Publishers and Associations*

Library of Congress Cataloging-in-Publication Data

Names: Reilly, Thomas P., author. I Reilly, Paul (Sales training consultant), author.
Title: Value-added selling : how to sell more profitably, confidently, and
   professionally by competing on value, not price / by Tom Reilly and Paul Reilly.
Description: 4th edition. I New York : McGraw-Hill, 2018.
Identifiers: LCCN 2018007295I ISBN 9781260134735 (alk. paper) I ISBN
   1260134733
Subjects: LCSH: Selling. I Value added.
Classification: LCC HF5438.25.R45 2018 I DDC 658.85-dc23 LC record available
   at https://lccn.loc.gov/2018007295

McGraw-Hill Education books are available at special quantity discounts to use as premiums and sales promotions or for use in corporate training programs. To contact a representative, please visit the Contact Us page at www.mhprofessional.com.

VALUE–ADDED
SELLING

FOURTH EDITION

How to Sell More Profitably,
Confidently, and Professionally by
Competing on Value—Not Price

TOM REILLY | PAUL REILLY

New York Chicago San Francisco Athens London Madrid
Mexico City Milan New Delhi Singapore Sydney Toronto

To those who add value in what they do

Contents

PART III | VALUE-ADDED SELLING TACTICS

PART IV | SPECIAL TOPICS

Acknowledgments

As always, we thank Linda Huizenga whose work on this manuscript adds real value to the book. We are forever grateful to the folks at McGraw-Hill whose passion for this message and faith in the messengers make this work possible.

Introduction

"The man who does not read has no advantage
over the man who cannot read."
—Mark Twain

Everyone has habits—good and bad. Reading and professional study are habits, just like not reading and not studying are habits. Some habits change your life for the better and some change your life for the worse. One fact remains: our habits define the person we are. What impact do your reading and study habits have on your career? Here is a sampling of what we hear in our seminars:

"I'm too busy to read."

"I don't know what to read; there is so much out there."

"I don't like to read."

"When I come home from a long day, I'm too tired to read."

"I read so much work-related material I have no time for any other reading."

"I read a book once."

Reading is a positive habit for salespeople to have. Reading stretches the mind and expands one's vocabulary. It raises new questions and helps people discover new answers to old ones. Reading challenges rigid belief systems. It relaxes our mind while developing our analytical thinking skills. Reading makes people more interesting and allows them to be more empathic. Reading changes the person, and that experience becomes part of one's journey.

For these reasons and more, reading is the key to success in any profession. In fact, many great leaders in our society today are deep readers: Warren Buffet spends 80 percent of his workday reading.[1]

Bill Gates reads 50 books a year.

Elon Musk read two books a day, according to his brother. When asked how he learned to build rockets, Musk replied, "I read books."[2]

President Theodore Roosevelt's daily routine included reading an entire book in the morning before starting his formal duties as president.[3]

President John F. Kennedy read a legendary 2,500 words per minute and consumed six newspapers, cover to cover, with his daily breakfast.[4]

Mark Cuban reads three hours every day.[5]

J. K. Rowling has ignited a firestorm of young readers with her Harry Potter series. Her advice is as relevant for salespeople as it is for the youth: "Read as much as you possibly can. Nothing will help you as much as reading."[6]

In 2016, there were 674 million books sold in the United States.[7] How many of these did you read? If you're into trivia, about 23 percent of these were e-books.[8] Reading is just as important to success in sales as it is to quality leadership. Customers want to deal with knowledgeable and articulate salespeople. They want to buy from salespeople who empathize and understand buyers' needs and wants. Customers want to partner with salespeople who are on the right side of the growth curve. Reading sends a strong signal to others. It demonstrates a commitment to personal growth. It displays openness to new ideas. It reveals a desire for information that gives a competitive edge. Reading this book offers the opportunity and information to grow personally and professionally.

We are thrilled to bring you this fourth edition of *Value-Added Selling*. This new edition demonstrates our commitment to sharing with you the latest information available to keep you one step ahead of the competition. Value-Added Selling is a dynamic and evolving sales philosophy. It remains a content-rich message of hope, and we are proud to be its messengers. We are advocates for this enriching business philosophy because we know it works. For decades, we have witnessed firsthand the successes companies in every industry have enjoyed by practicing this pragmatic go-to-market strategy. Though the fourth edition reflects the realities of selling in the digital age, the history of Value-Added Selling is rich.

Its roots reach back to the 1970s when Tom began his sales career at a Fortune 500 chemical company. That experience of selling in a commoditized, price-sensitive market played a formative role in helping him shape a pragmatic sales philosophy. After enjoying success in manufacturing, Tom opened a distributorship in the laboratory supply industry in Houston, Texas. He likened this experience in distribution to customers choosing from a row of a half-dozen vending machines. He said, "Everyone in town sold the same stuff, and our great challenge was to figure out a way to get customers to insert their purchase orders into our vending machine." This experience proved to be a primer on how to compete without being the cheapest. He says today, "We were too small to compete on price. Imagine a corner hardware store attempting to sell cheaper than Home Depot."

Tom sold his company in 1981 to pursue a sales training career. For the first few years of training salespeople, he amassed a list of objections that salespeople brought to seminars. The most common objection was, "Your price is too high." It surfaced in many forms: "I can buy this cheaper from someone else." "I don't see your value." "I don't have the budget for what you're selling." All of these pointed to money as the primary obstacle. Sound familiar?

In 1984, Tom wrote the first edition of *Value-Added Selling* to help salespeople compete profitably and aggressively in price-sensitive markets. Since then, Value-Added Selling has become a global phenomenon. This message has touched salespeople in all corners of the world.

In 2013, Paul joined Tom Reilly Training as an associate and became a brand specialist on Value-Added Selling. Before joining Tom Reilly Training, Paul spent over ten years applying the principles of Value-Added Selling as a professional salesperson in the industrial and construction markets. He sold propane, tools and fasteners, and medical equipment. Although each one of these industries is unique, they shared a common challenge for salespeople: price sensitivity. When Paul experienced the power of Value-Added Selling firsthand, he decided that he wanted to become a standard bearer for this sales philosophy.

Much has changed since we released the third edition in 2010. Our economy has expanded. The United States' GDP growth rate (25 percent) is double the rate of inflation (13 percent) during that same era. This points to real economic growth. Imports have increased by 33 percent during that same period, and our trade gap continues to hover at 500 billion USD annually. In this same time period, the U.S. Dollar Index has increased 19.24 percent,[9] which creates additional headwinds for our exporting goods and services. Common sense tells us that the increase in imports is not from more expensive goods; it is from more of the same at lower prices. We are flooded with more and cheaper goods. The impact of this on selling price is a major challenge for U.S. businesses.

The top-line pressures of sameness, technology, and a culture of cheap present strategic and tactical challenges to the bottom lines of most organizations. "Sameness" is the commoditization of products and the convergence of services resulting from high levels of mergers and acquisitions, lack of innovation, and a failure to differentiate one's solution.

Technology has been a burden and a blessing. Though professional selling is a people business, technology has depersonalized buyer-seller relationships and made purchasing more transactional. Technology has given birth to a plethora of online sellers offering customers a misery of choices, in multiple colors and myriad sizes. A Google search for industrial supplies, agricultural products, construction equipment, computer and technology solutions, and business services yielded 43.1 million, 67.1 million, 80.3 million, 129 million, and 269 million hits respectively. Pew Research found in 2016 that 80 percent of consumers shop at least sometimes online with half of those shopping online weekly.[10] Technology has opened a Pandora's box of supply alternatives that has increased pressure on prices and muddied the waters of differentiation.

A culture of cheapness exacerbates price pressure. Value is now a euphemism for cheap—value pricing, value meals, and value investing. Advertisers use low prices to attract shoppers. When was the last time you watched a television commercial and heard car dealers brag about high prices? Though in 2017 only 10 percent of all retail was sold online,[11] with Amazon getting 44 percent of that, businesses are concerned about "the Amazon effect" on retailers, large and small, and B2B sellers.[12]

These strategic challenges for businesses present specific tactical challenges for salespeople. With the culture of cheap as the backdrop, the most common sales objection heard today remains, "Your price is too high." In our research, we asked several hundred salespeople to rank their top sales challenges. These are the top six concerns:

- Price-sensitive customers
- Inertia (see no reason to change)
- Communicating value
- Buyers that commoditize
- Differentiating
- Getting credit for value added

Five of the top six challenges focus on money-related issues. This is the challenge for salespeople—how to communicate their value and convince buyers that the salesperson's solution is the best way to go.

Much has changed since we released the third edition in 2010, yet much has remained the same. What remains the same is that buyers want value. They want to feel they are getting as good as they are giving. They want to feel like their suppliers understand their needs and respond accordingly. They want knowledgeable salespeople who can demonstrate and prove the value of their solution in the customer's world.

Our goals in this new edition of *Value-Added Selling* are to help you compete effectively and profitably in this market. We want to help you focus on the type of business that makes sense for your company, navigate these accounts effectively, communicate your value in unmistakable terms, stand out from the competition, deliver high-value solutions that make a difference for your customers, get credit for the value you help create, and fully leverage these relationships. In short, we want to help you confront the tactical challenges you face and emerge victorious for you and the customer.

You will see familiar ground in this edition. The underlying principles of Value-Added Selling are timeless truths that do not change. We have updated our research and changed some of the terms to reflect the realities of today's marketplace.

We've organized *Value-Added Selling* into four parts. Part I introduces you to the Value-Added Selling philosophy and provides you with valuable insight into what customers really want from suppliers. You will learn how to understand your value from the customer's perspective and to create sales tools that help you persuasively communicate your value to customers. Additionally, we share with you inside information from our studies of buyer preferences. Part I answers the question, "*Why* should I embrace the Value-Added Selling philosophy?"

Part II is the strategic side of Value-Added Selling. You learn that value-added salespeople employ 11 strategies to create value for the customer. This part answers the question, "*What* should I do to sell our value-added solution?"

Part III is the tactical side of Value-Added Selling. Here, you learn the steps of the value-added sales call: how to prepare, execute, and evaluate your selling activities. This part answers the question, "*How* do I make the value-added sales call?"

Part IV is a bonus—true value added. In this part, we discuss additional topics for value-added salespeople: selling to multiple decision makers, competing against online sellers, and engaging inside salespeople in the Value-Added Selling process.

These are some of the updates you will see in this new edition:

- **How to start and sustain a movement.** In this fourth edition, we look at how managers start and sustain a movement toward Value-Added Selling throughout the organization. Value-Added Selling is a unifying philosophy for the entire organization, and this action-oriented chapter helps managers operationalize this philosophy companywide.
- **Small-wins selling.** The small-wins philosophy has deep roots in social psychology that has migrated into the business world. Taking a small-wins approach keeps both the salesperson and buyer engaged. It focuses on the immediate, next best outcome to move along the sale. The new way to attain big results is to think small.
- **Critical sales path.** We have expanded our discussion on how the buyer's Critical Buying Path has a parallel path that the value-added salesperson travels. Your knowledge of this new material coupled with a small-wins approach will help you advance the sale with greater efficiency and effectiveness.
- **The pain proposition.** This addition to our section on customer messaging is based on extensive research on the

psychology of decision making. Buyers want to avoid pain at least as much as they want to achieve a gain. The success of this concept is one of the driving forces behind this revised edition.

- **Communicating with social media.** The use of social media is a major shift in purchasing behavior since the third edition of this book. It offers value-added salespeople one more way to surround customers with their messages of value.

- **Calling data.** Since the third edition of *Value-Added Selling*, we have conducted extensive research into the calling habits of effective salespeople. Contrary to a common belief, we found that cold-calling remains an effective way to initiate contact with prospects. We share with you the findings of this comprehensive calling habits study.

- **Handling objections.** Our latest price-sensitivity study revealed the top four reasons buyers object on price. Armed with this new information, we demonstrate how to craft your response to price objections.

- **Selling to multiple decision makers.** This chapter provides a broad context for team selling in a collaborative environment of multiple decision makers. This includes new information into current buying trends and who is involved in the decision process. We equip the reader with specific tools and actions to manage a complex sale with multiple decision makers.

- **Competing in an Amazon world.** Face-to-face selling remains a viable go-to-market strategy, though many salespeople feel helpless against online sellers. One of the most troubling objections salespeople hear is, "Why should I buy from you? I can buy the same thing online for less." This question (not objection) is really a gift for value-added salespeople. In this chapter, we provide the reader with strategies and tactics for selling against online sellers.

- **Value-added inside sales.** Value-Added Selling is a team sport. It requires the commitment of every department. In this chapter, we conduct a deep dive into the role inside sales plays in creating value for the customer and their outside sales counterparts. We also address the specific challenges facing inside salespeople. We have collected new data that forms the basis for the compelling need of including inside salespeople.

Our goal is to help you capture the most value from your reading and study of the fourth edition of *Value-Added Selling*. To this end, we suggest that you begin with a highlighter and an open mind. *Value-Added Selling* is a book to study, not just to read. To get the most value from this book, you will need to read and reread the passages you highlight. Understand the logic of this sales approach. Embrace the philosophy. Practice the strategies and tactics presented in these pages. Your value proposition for doing all of the above is to be able to compete aggressively and profitably as you deliver greater value to your customers. The real bonus is that you will like how it feels to work and live as a person of value. Enjoy your study.

Good luck.

Tom Reilly
Paul Reilly

THE VALUE-ADDED SELLING PHILOSOPHY

Part I introduces you to the Value-Added Selling philosophy. The strong appeal of Value-Added Selling has always been and remains its connection to foundational values and virtues like equity, honesty, synergy, excellence, and humility. In practice, this means treating people fairly, selling with integrity, working as a team, committing to high standards, and subordinating oneself to the mission. Who wouldn't want to be part of an effort like this?

Chapter 1 is a new chapter and explains how your company can start and sustain a movement throughout the organization based on the Value-Added Selling philosophy.

Chapter 2 explores value, your value add-itude, Value-Added Selling, characteristics of value-added salespeople, buyer preferences, the impact of discounting, and why salespeople fail to sell value. We have updated this chapter with the latest research in this area.

Chapter 3 is a new chapter and introduces you to the small-wins selling approach. This philosophy of incrementalism has proven successful in many fields, and salespeople can use a small-wins approach to create major victories.

Chapter 4 is a review and update of the Critical Buying Path. This cradle-to-grave view of the buyer's journey to finding value helps you understand the full scope of the buyer's needs. This enables you to communicate your value effectively.

Chapter 5 is a strategic overview of the Value-Added Selling Process. This model and your understanding of it serve as a foundation for the rest of the book. Your conceptual grasp of this sales process enables you to advance the sale in a step-by-step manner that parallels the buyer's Critical Buying Path. This step-by-step approach is called the Critical Sales Path.

Chapter 6 is a new chapter that explains the psychology of price shopping. We share some of the latest findings in the growing field of neuroscience and how they help us understand the mindset and decision making of buyers. Specifically, we explore how this information explains price-shopping behavior and how you can use this information in your sales efforts.

Chapter 7 defines and explains customer messaging and its impact on your selling. You learn how to create the collateral sales tools that make your message compelling. The emergence of social media as a sales tool has added a new dimension to customer messaging. You will also learn how to understand the customer's pain proposition and use its remedy as part of your communicating value.

CHAPTER 1

How to Start and Sustain a Movement in Your Organization

"Do you want to sell sugar water for the rest of your life, or do you want to come with me and change the world?"

With this question, Steve Jobs recruited Pepsi-Cola executive John Sculley to run the four-year-old company that he and his friend Steve Wozniak started in a garage. Jobs attempted initially to recruit the respected executive but failed in those early attempts. Then, Jobs challenged Sculley with the above question. Later, Sculley said: "I just gulped because I just knew that I would wonder for the rest of my life what I had missed." From 1983 to 1993, they worked together and delivered on the promise to change the world with their technology. And the movement they created continues to change the world today.

Few people have the opportunity to change the world the way these visionaries did, but you can start a movement—a value-added revolution—in your company.

At the end of this chapter, you will be able to:

- Explain the compelling need for organizational identity
- Define what a movement means to your organization
- Describe how movements go viral with clarity of purpose
- Explain how to start a movement in your organization
- Discuss how to sustain the movement once it starts

THE URGENCY FOR ORGANIZATIONAL IDENTITY

There is a pandemic identity crisis in business today. Many companies have lost their oneness. Consolidation through mergers and acquisitions has left many companies without a common culture. Like blended families, these companies end up being a little of this and a little of that. What they call culture is an amalgam of their disparate histories and sometimes incompatible values. The farther privately owned, entrepreneurial companies travel from the founder, the less they look like the original company. According to one survey, 56 percent of employees could neither describe nor embrace their company's culture. As some corporate management teams obsess on financial metrics, they distance themselves from the core values upon which their companies were founded. Other companies are confused about their place in their industries, as reflected in their go-to-market strategies: "Should we compete as a low-cost seller, as a value-added, total-solution provider, or both?" Most perform well as either a low-cost or value-added provider. Companies that attempt to do both fail.

The most immediate need for this chapter is to satisfy the myriad requests by our clients for a way to spread the value-added message throughout their organizations, at every level and in every department, from the shop floor to the top floor. They realize that Value-Added Selling is more than a sales course; it is a course of action—a new direction—for the entire organization. It is an integrated sales and operations process for designing and delivering value. Because it is a systems approach, organizational synergy (teamwork) replaces the functional silos that plague most companies. Because it is a process, Value-Added Selling focuses on the acquisition of new business and the retention and growth of existing customer relationships.

When an organization unifies around this common philosophy, it becomes a Value-Added Organization. To get a full return on Value-Added Selling, companies must become Value-Added Organizations, where all departments are focused on creating and delivering value.

Reorganizing and restructuring have become emotionally tagged organizational buzzwords in the past few decades. In many cases, these attempts fail because they focus on structures, processes, and systems but lack a cohesive set of values or a philosophical core. Becoming a Value-Added Organization is about reorienting, not reorganizing, though some of that may happen. Sculpting an organization with an orienting philosophy like value added is more than changing the way you do things. It changes the way people think and view the world. It is transformational change—it is a movement. Movements unify people and propel organizations.

WHAT IS A MOVEMENT

Every tsunami of change, great social cause, and watershed moment in history began as an idea that went viral and became a movement. The idea, a brainchild of one or two people, inspired a handful of early loyalists who became evangelists for the cause. Then they engaged a cadre of supporters that would make up the first and second waves of a movement that would shape history. We have seen this in all walks of life.

Gandhi suffered as he waged a nonviolent protest of the British government. His peace-movement philosophy became the foundation for the civil rights movement in the United States and the operating philosophy for Martin Luther King Jr. Nelson Mandela opposed apartheid and spent decades in prison. His resistance helped spawn democracy in South Africa and earned him a Nobel Peace Prize. In the United States, President John F. Kennedy inspired a movement among young people by challenging them to consider what they could do for their country. The result of that challenge became a movement called the Peace Corps. U.S. President Ronald Reagan envisioned a more unified Europe and challenged his contemporaries to "tear down that wall" that divided East and West. His vision reignited a conservative movement in the United States. Steve Jobs and Steve Wozniak envisioned user-friendly technology that changed personal computing. Herb Kelleher had a vision of a different type of airline and founded Southwest Airlines. His movement for low-cost air travel continues to fly and dominate today. Fred Smith had a vision of overnight package delivery and spawned a movement that became its own industry. His movement proved to be so profound that his abbreviated company name, FedEx, became a verb. Willie G. Davidson had a different view of motorcycles and bikers, and his vision for Harley-Davidson spawned a global movement for the biker lifestyle that attracts people from all walks of life. All of these movements began with the ideas of one or two people that ignited the passions of others.

These movement makers were not always heroes or readily accepted by others. From death to prison to public discord, many of these movement makers suffered. Their ideas were radical, threatening to many, and faced tremendous pushback. Some were disruptive to the point of dangerous. Yet, through courage and persistence, they prevailed. Their ideas lived and made history. Now, their inspirational stories are the grist of legend's mill.

You may not suffer life-and-death consequences from your movement to reorient your organization around the value-added philosophy, but you will experience pushback on your efforts. As you challenge the status quo, the status quo will challenge you. Guardians of the status quo are well-intentioned skeptics of anything new or disruptive. There will be those who just do not want to change because they resist all change. You may face peer pressure and ridicule from those who are personally threatened by your movement. It makes them painfully aware of their static interests. Remember, you are redefining success, you are shaking the foundation, and you are stepping out from the pack. Be prepared for this pushback, or your movement will fail.

GOING VIRAL WITH CLARITY OF PURPOSE

Every movement begins with a dream, vision, or notion. These ideas are big and small. They change the world or the way a department does something. In most cases, movement makers do not have to work hard to come up with an idea. It boils in a seething cauldron of passion, finding relief only in its expression. Movement means action, and movement makers do not wait patiently for the idea to take off. They launch it. With clarity of purpose, movement makers start and sustain their movements.

Movements (a new direction, reorientation, or revolution) take root from the seed of an idea. Clarity of purpose is the what, why, where, who, when, and how of your passion. What is your big idea? What burns inside you? What do you believe in so passionately that you want to tell others about it? What transformational change do you envision for your organization? What shared purpose will you submit to your team? Why is this important? Why now? Who should be involved? Where do we begin?

These questions can help you start and sustain any movement. Our focus is how you can start and sustain a movement to transform your company into a Value-Added Organization. A Value-Added Organization is in the business of creating value for everyone with whom it is connected. Everyone gains: buyers, sellers, stockholders, employees, environment, partners, and the community. With clarity of purpose, you must conceive and communicate your vision for this movement. Begin with these orienting questions and imagine what a value-added movement would mean to your organization:

- What would it mean if we adopted the value-added philosophy as our core operating philosophy?
- Can we compete based on our value?
- Why would we want to choose this path?
- What effect would this have on everyone involved?
- What prompted this vision, or what is driving this movement?
- Why now?

With clarity of purpose, frame this message in a way that will resonate with others. What begins with clarity of purpose will sustain your movement as constancy of purpose. You will surround your team with this true north of your movement.

ENGAGEMENT: HOW TO START A MOVEMENT

According to a Gallup study, two-thirds of employees are not engaged in their jobs. They merely show up for work.[1] Your movement can fix this problem.

As you prepare to launch your movement, there are some things you must know that will help you engage others. First, everyone wants to be a part of something bigger and better than themselves. That is why there are country clubs, motorcycle gangs, and everything in between. People long to belong. John Donne wrote, "No man is an island, entire of itself. Each is a piece of the continent, a part of the main." Charismatic leaders know and use this to their advantage. Because they are charismatic, they naturally draw others to them. Leadership charisma, coupled with the followers' need to belong, helps leaders recruit a close-knit group of supporters that are essential to any movement.

Second, people seek meaning from their work. People may show up for a paycheck, but they labor hard for the meaning they get from their efforts. There are few things as meaningful as shaping the landscape of the future by playing a vital role in a movement. Employees feel that they are doing something special and recognize that these opportunities do not come along often. We all know someone who left a good-paying job in pursuit of meaning from someplace. With millennials entering the workforce and seeking meaning in their careers, the sense of purpose from this movement will prove to be a powerful motivator for these employees.

Third, people compare themselves with others as a way to test how well they are doing. There is a field of study in psychology, social comparison theory, dedicated to the study of how and why people compare themselves with other people. This bandwagon effect becomes especially important as you tell your story to attract allies and to share successes that others are experiencing in the movement.

Fourth, it is not so much that people resist change as they resist being changed. When they are told, "This is what you will do," and it represents a significant departure from the status quo, people push back. When they are invited to join the process and become part of shaping history, they approach change with a different attitude.

Once you conceive of your idea and are prepared to communicate it, select your core group and expand your sphere of influence. Using Everett Rogers's *Diffusion of Innovation* model, identify your target group for this idea, and penetrate it as you would a market for a new product—in waves.

Wave One is close confidants. In marketing terms, these are innovators—the top 2.5 percent who welcome new ideas. If you are running a 100-person company, this will be your top management staff, maybe two to three inner-circle advisors. It is important that this group has operational knowledge of the business as well as knowledge of sales and marketing. Trust them to provide candid feedback on your idea. This close-knit group of advisors will help you shape, plan, and communicate your dream to the next layer of the organization. Share your vision with them, the compelling need for it, and the "doability" of the idea. Invite their feedback, especially perceived barriers. Ask them to help you sketch a plan to roll out this idea. Keep your planning conceptual and strategic at this point. Focus on these areas:

- What do we want to do?
- Why do we want to do it?
- How is this "doable?"
- What will it take to make it happen?

You will need to assess your organizational resources, systems, and structures to make sure that your movement will work with your infrastructure. You cannot become a Value-Added Organization if you offer no value added to the market. For example, you cannot brag about your technical expertise without on-staff experts to back up your claim. You cannot boast about your customer service when the average wait time to speak to a real person is five minutes. You cannot crow about your delivery success when you experience consistently high levels of backordered items.

Wave Two is top supporters and change agents. In marketing terms, these are early adopters—the next 13.5 percent of people who embrace new ideas. This next layer of managers, opinion leaders, and influencers make or break your efforts. In your 100-employee company, this is another 13 or 14 employees.

You have now engaged one-in-six employees to help you start a movement. This includes people who have operational, administrative, and marketing responsibility. Their perspective, input, and engagement are mandatory. Communicate your vision, translate it into a mission, explain why you are doing it and why now, roll out your strategic plan, and ask for their commitment.

Once you have secured their commitment, begin tactical planning with this group. They will drive change and help you lead this movement at lower levels in the organization. They know better than you how to get their people to execute. The action plan should have their fingerprints all over it. They will most likely select another group of supporters from the ranks who will act as opinion leaders—employees to whom others listen. These informal leaders can add either fuel to the fire or a bucket of water.

Wave Three is the rest of the company. In marketing terms, this will be the next two-thirds of the company that are responsible for the heavy lifting. For them to engage, you must communicate the vision and mission clearly and often. They must share your positive sense of urgency for action and optimism in the outcome. In communicating your vision, remember that employees do not necessarily get excited about a company's making more money unless they can see a direct benefit to themselves. They are more excited about being a part of something bigger than themselves and creating meaningful change; they are less excited about returning more money to the owner or shareholders.

The "why" of your movement and the "why now" are important in creating a positive sense of urgency. Use a blend of rational and emotional arguments to make your case for the "why" and "why now" of your movement. Humans are emotional creatures. We make emotional decisions. Neuroscientists have discovered through sophisticated brain imaging technology that 90 percent of the decisions humans make are driven by emotions.[2] This means 90 percent of the reasons others will accept or reject your movement will be emotionally based.

The power of story plays a major role in emotional connection. Big movements rely on big parallel stories and comparisons. Small movements rely on smaller stories to drive home the point. If you are trying to inspire a movement in your company, you are more credible if you tell stories of how other companies have done this versus retelling the story of how a major social movement changed the world. Scale affects the power of analogy.

As you communicate your vision and the mission that supports it, be clear about the metrics that you will use to measure your progress. This includes qualitative metrics like performance and behavioral changes, which are important in the early phases of the movement, and quantitative metrics that demonstrate productivity gains from your efforts.

Discuss perceived barriers openly and encourage input to dispel doubts. Help team members release their grips on doubt, uncertainty, and resistance. Build confidence in the group by demonstrating the doability of the movement. People rally around ideas that they believe they can implement. Share stories of others who have achieved similar things. Build confidence in your team by investing. When you commit resources (people, money, and time) to the movement, you inspire others to follow you. They know you are serious and willing to take a risk with you to make the dream a reality.

Congruence between your movement and your organization's values make a credible argument. Demonstrate how this movement respects and builds on the values that people signed up for when they joined your company. People reject change that violates their fundamental sense of what they stand for.

Every time you present your dream, drill down on the tactical application of it. If it is not tactical, it is not practical. Engage people at the ground level. As Wave-Two supporters help carry the message and the movement to Wave Three, first-level managers will define the behaviors they will expect from their employees who demonstrate their execution of the plan.

As you assign tasks, timelines, and responsibility, people take ownership of the process and the movement itself. Once they begin acting this way, the movement is the beneficiary of a powerful psychodynamic called cognitive dissonance. When people act in a certain manner, their attitudes conform to their behavior. It is a simple application of "We believe as we behave." Once the behavior and the attitude are in place, the process self-reinforces. They have internalized the mission. Belief drives behavior, which reinforces the belief. These evangelists take your vision and make it reality.

You have made your case, shared the dream, explained the urgency for action, and outlined the plan. Now it is time to close the deal. Invite this group to join you. Ask for their support. Ask for their commitment. Ask them to take ownership. Ask a Steve Jobs–type question: "Do you want to continue on the path we are on, or do you want to change our world?"

What about the remaining 16 percent of employees? This group will follow or resist. Some will leave; others will relent. You will not drive a movement with them. They will comply, with or without commitment. These laggards are the most resistant to change. They may complain, but the support of the other 84 percent overwhelms their resistance. At some point, they realize and accept the inevitability of the change, or they move on.

REINFORCEMENT: HOW TO SUSTAIN A MOVEMENT

Even though there is no one-size-fits-all strategy for starting and sustaining a movement, there are common denominators. Each situation is as unique as the movement itself. You start the movement with clarity of purpose and by engaging others. You sustain it with constancy of purpose, ongoing communication, and reinforcement.

To sustain your movement, take yes for an answer. This means two things. First, to change behavior (your qualitative benchmarks) you must initially reinforce the effort, not just results. To achieve the outcome you want, you must get people behaving in a desired way. This is a fundamental principle of behavioral psychology. If you focus on results too quickly, people get discouraged when they cannot deliver on your request. As the behavior becomes automatic, you begin to see the results you desire.

Second, employ a small-wins strategy to achieve big victories. You will read more about small wins in Chapter 3. The small-wins strategy has been employed in every significant social movement in the past several decades. When you construct your plan, list the immediate, next best outcomes that your people can achieve to make this movement a reality. Each of these next best outcomes is a small win and a step closer to total victory. You have the added advantage of experiential change. When people are part of the change process and experience these short-term successes, they are motivated to finish the job. Reinforce this motivation and action with ongoing communication.

One study reported that 76 percent of employees involved in a major initiative for their company found it highly motivating to hear about their progress.[3] Keeping employees in the communications loop enables them to monitor their progress vis-à-vis other teams. We have already established that people compare themselves with others.

Celebrating successes and heralding progress motivate employees. Encourage pride of ownership in a job well done. Let them bask in the recognition that their efforts are contributing to the movement. In addition to the intrinsic motivation for doing good work, some extrinsic rewards help. This includes monetary reinforcement and recognition programs that celebrate their contributions.

Reinforce the effort and sustain your movement by demonstrating your unwavering commitment. This means continuing to invest in ways that support the mission. It also means remaining faithful to the cause, especially during headwinds.

As a movement maker, it is not just about the quality of your efforts, it is also about the quantity and visibility of your personal commitment. Others notice how often you talk about the movement, how often you walk the halls, and how often you interact with them. Do not delude yourself into believing that you can delegate all of this to someone else. You must be a visible source of inspiration. People must hear and see you advocating often for the cause. Otherwise, they will feel you are being disingenuous—that you lack the personal commitment a movement requires. Your name and the movement must become synonymous. When someone hears one of the names, they think of the other. It is your movement that becomes their movement.

In sustaining your movement, use multiple sources of influence to surround followers with your message.

This means employing various communication channels to connect with them—direct contact, voice mail, e-mail, social media, written communication, specially designed collateral materials for your communications campaign, internal champions who will talk it up, outside experts that add credibility to the cause, feedback from customers on how the movement benefits them, supplier input and support, etc. You want to sustain the buzz throughout the movement.

At some point during reinforcement, you will begin to transfer ownership for the results as well as ownership for the process. During this ownership transfer, employees know that they have created something meaningful. They know that they are a part of something bigger than themselves. These loyalists are now advocates for the movement, champions for the cause, and guardians of the *new* status quo.

VALUE-ADDED SELLING REVIEW AND ACTION POINTS

1. There is a pandemic identity crisis today in business. Over half of employees do not understand their company's culture, and two-thirds are not engaged in their jobs.[4] You can use the Value-Added Selling philosophy to reorient your company around a common mission.

2. A movement is characterized by action. It is fundamental to the definition of the word. Your movement is a work in progress. You are a work in progress. Keep progressing. That is the purpose of the movement—forward motion. You are building a movement culture and a culture of movement.

3. Starting and sustaining a movement is a process. It is an evolution and maybe a revolution. Because it is an active process, you must be willing to challenge its viability at every step along the path. Ongoing evaluation of your position, efforts, and results will allow you to make course corrections and adjustments as needed. Every flight plan has checkpoints along the route to allow the pilot and navigator to adjust for the winds they did not anticipate. Adapting to the forces of change will keep you on course.

CHAPTER 2

Value-Added Selling

Value-Added Selling is a dynamic philosophy. It is evolving strategically and tactically as you read these pages, but the philosophy itself is stable. This chapter introduces you to the Value-Added Selling philosophy and its rock-deep-roots principles.

At the end of this chapter, you will be able to:

- Define the purpose of a business
- Discuss the meaning of value
- Define Value-Added Selling
- Discuss your value add-itude
- Describe the characteristics of value-added salespeople
- Recite what buyers really want from sellers
- Explain the real impact of discounting on your company
- Know important price facts
- List the reasons why salespeople fail to sell value-added solutions

WHAT IS THE PURPOSE OF A BUSINESS

When we ask this question in seminars, the most common response echoes the words of Adam Smith: "To make money—hopefully lots of it." Some people quote Peter Drucker, "The purpose of a business is to get and keep a customer." Still, others will say, "The purpose of business is to beat the competition." Phil Knight, cofounder of Nike, wrote in *Shoe Dog*, "For some, I realize, business is the all-out pursuit of profits, period, full stop, but for us business was no more about making money than being human is about making blood. . . . It's a basic process that enables our higher aims, and life always strives to transcend the basic processes of living. . . . We wanted, as all great businesses do, to create, to contribute." This is much closer to our idea of what a company is all about. We submit that the purpose of a business is bigger than making money, creating customers, or beating competitors. This is another way of saying, "The *why* of business must be bigger than the *what* of business." We argue that the purpose of a business is to create value. Our proposition is simple: if your purpose is to create value, the profit will follow. Our proposition raises two questions:

- What is value?
- For whom do you create value?

We will answer both of these questions in the next section.

WHAT IS VALUE

Two things determine value: what someone *gives up* and what that person *gets* in return. This ratio of inputs and outcomes is a true measure of value. Customers assign value to something as they answer this question: "Is the product or service a fair exchange for what I give up in time, money, and energy to acquire and use it?" In Value-Added Selling, price is what buyers pay and value is what they receive.

Equity plays a major role in one's perception of value. To get as good as you give is good value. To get better than you give is great value. For this reason, people make relative value decisions. They weigh sacrifice against gain to determine value. Buyers sacrifice precious resources when they purchase from you. In turn, they expect a fair exchange. They want you to invest as heavily in them as they invest in you.

In Value-Added Selling, there are special value considerations:

- **Value is personal.** Like beauty, value is in the eye of the beholder. It's the buyer's perception of value that counts. More precisely, it is his or her perception of equity that registers as value in their minds. You really don't know what value is until you first hear it from the buyer. If you want to determine what someone really values, observe what he or she is willing to sacrifice to acquire it.

- **Value is bigger than price.** Value is an outcome, result, or return on investment. First comes the investment, then comes the return. The yield of your solution determines its value more than the price to acquire it. Buyers who obsess on price must be educated to think in terms of return on investment. To paraphrase William James, the father of American psychology, where value is the thing sought after, the thing of supreme value is cheap, whatever the price one must pay for it. Value trumps price in his terms.

- **Value is a long-term concept unless you sell precious metals or gems.** Value generally comes from what the product or service *does* more than what it *is*. The intrinsic value of gold, diamonds, etc. is the exception. Its worth comes from *being* more than *doing*. If you maintain a long-term focus of value, it gives you the forum to discuss everything you do for the buyer and its impact on his world.

- **Perceived value describes the look and feel of things.** It is largely sensory: how something looks, sounds, feels, smells, and tastes.

- **Performance value describes the outcome of your solution.** It is what the product, service, or company does for the buyer. While perceived value fuels buyer expectations, performance value affects buyer satisfaction.

Now to the second question: For whom do you create value? In Value-Added Selling, everyone wins—buyer and seller. How can it be a good deal for the buyer if the seller does not win? How can it be a good deal for the seller if the buyer does not win? In the zero-sum game of win-lose, the loser (buyer or seller) will abandon the relationship as soon as possible. So much for long-term gain. In his book *The New Economics*, W. Edwards Deming wrote, "The aim proposed here for any organization is for everybody to gain—stockholders, employees, suppliers, customers, community, environment—over the long term." That everyone gains is a noble pursuit in business. Because

Value-Added Selling is built on a foundation of equity, all must benefit from the relationship. Putting the customer first does not mean putting yourself last.

Value is more than a cheap price. A cheap price for a product that fails to perform is lousy value at any price. In his book *Value-Added Purchasing*, Dr. Eberhard Scheuing wrote, "Looking only at a product's acquisition cost is like looking only at the tip of an iceberg. Below the surface of the acquisition cost lie the treacherous costs of owning and using the product." To summarize our definition of value, there is a formula that we use in our seminars to illustrate this.

$$Price + Cost + Utility + Impact = Value$$

Price is the acquisition number—the initial, up-front payment. Cost is the total cost of ownership, usage, and disposal of something—sometimes called TCO (total cost of ownership). Utility is what the solution does. Impact is the effect of the solution on the customer's business. The combination of these four variables is the value of your solution. In this model, you can see that price plays a minor role in the determination of value. Remember this as we dig deeper into the value of your solution.

WHAT IS VALUE-ADDED SELLING

Value-Added Selling is a business philosophy. It's a process of proactively looking for ways to enhance, augment, or enlarge your bundled package for the customer. Value-Added Selling is a need-satisfaction model of selling built around these principles:

- Promise a lot and deliver more
- Contribute and extract maximum value to and from this relationship
- Sell to the customer's needs, not against the competition

Notice the key words in this definition: *philosophy, process, proactively,* and *bundled package.*

Value-Added Selling is a philosophy, not just a book, a speaker, a seminar, or this year's company theme. Value-Added Selling must be rooted deeply in your psyche as the way you want to conduct business. It's a maximum-performance philosophy of excellence in all that you do. The value-added philosophy, which is at the core of this model, offers sage advice to its practitioners: Do more of that which adds value and less of that which adds little or no value. This is why Value-Added Selling is an orienting philosophy for your company. Imagine if everyone bought into the movement and began living this philosophy at work.

Value-Added Selling is a process, an ongoing and integrated sales/operations model for designing and delivering equitable, value-added solutions. As you will read in future chapters, this is a team sport for your organization because the sales force can only promise what operations delivers.

As a philosophy, Value-Added Selling is proactive. Being proactive means being conscientious, taking ownership, and acting accountable for creating satisfied customers. Proactive, Value-Added Selling is pre-emptively seizing control of the sales conversation and guiding it down a path of value, not price. It's everything you do before price becomes an issue. It's all the value you build in on the front end so that price is less of an issue on the back end. You can't wait for the buyer to raise a price objection and then decide to practice some Value-Added Selling on the buyer.

Value-added salespeople sell a three-dimensional, bundled package. These three things are the product, the company, and themselves. We refer often to the three dimensions of value throughout this book.

In the early 1990s, two Fortune 100 companies asked buyers how much value the company's salespeople brought to the table. These companies discovered that their salespeople delivered 35 to 37 percent of the value added that buyers received. How much value do you deliver to your customers? There is another dimension to this question. How much value do you contribute to your company? Are you a value-added salesperson to your organization?

Our Best Sales Practices research (BSP) studied more than 100 top salespeople from different industries including construction, industrial, packaging, and food service. These salespeople had to be in the top 10 percent of their sales force in gross sales and/or profit. In addition to extensive testing and sales manager interviews, our research team contacted more than 600 of their customers to interview them. One question we asked was, "When you make a buying decision, how much of that decision is weighted on the product, the company that supplies the product, and the salesperson with whom you deal?" Here is what they told us:

- 57 percent of the buying decision was because of the product.
- 18 percent of the buying decision was because of the company.
- 25 percent of the buying decision was because of the salesperson.

This tells us that the same product from the same company from two different salespeople is two different solutions altogether. Buyers attach value to the salespeople with whom they do business. Are you weighing this heavily on your buyers' minds? If you're not selling your personal value, you're discounting the 25 percent that buyers say you're worth.

If you were to leave your company tomorrow and go to work for a quality competitor, how much business would you take with you? If you answer, "Not much," then it's safe to assume that you're not delivering significant value to your customer. In Value-Added Selling, salespeople are a big part of the solution.

Albert Einstein offered sage words that apply to salespeople. In 1955, William Miller of *Life Magazine* interviewed Albert Einstein and asked him to comment on success. Einstein's responded "Try not to become a man of success, but rather try to become a man of value. He is considered successful in our day who gets more out of life than he puts in. But a man of value will give more than he receives." When we share that story in our seminars, we challenge salespeople with this question, "Would your customers and company describe you as a person of value?"

WHAT IS YOUR VALUE ADD-ITUDE

It's not a typo. How do you define value? From which direction does your definition of value flow: outward from you to the customer, or inward to you from the customer? In other words, are you seller focused or customer focused in your definition? Value-added sellers define value from the customer's point of view.

Customer-Focused Value

Customer-focused value is viewing what you sell as value received, not just value added. It's processing your solution as the buyer processes it—seeing it through buyers' eyes. It's their problem, their need, their money, and a solution with which they must live. The sale *should* be more about the customer than the seller. Customer-focused salespeople say, "Why can't we sell what they want to buy?" Contrast that to those who retort with their own definition of value: "Why can't they buy what we want to sell?" From whom would you rather buy?

Seller-Focused Value

Traditional sellers define and sell value in their terms. This is seller-focused value. Some sellers have a field-of-dreams mentality: "If we sell it, they will buy it." or "If we don't sell it, they don't need it." This is a seller-focused approach to business, a variation of the old Henry Ford-ism: "You can have any color car you want as long as it's black."

Arrogance abounds in seller-focused value: "We sellers know what's best for you, the buyer." Seller-focused companies practice a tarnished Golden Rule of business: "We treat everyone the way *we* want to be treated." It sounds good, but it is still the seller who determines how people want to be treated. That is seller-focused thinking. A better way to say this is, "We treat customers the way *they* want to be treated."

A variation of this seller-focused attitude is, "We treat everyone the same way." Again, this sounds good on the surface. After all, it appears fair and democratic to treat everyone the same. Make no mistake about it: treating everyone the same is for the expediency of the seller, not the buyer. The seller is fundamentally saying, "We treat everyone the same. No one gets special treatment from us."

Value-added salespeople sell products by solving problems, satisfying needs, and serving people. These words change the optics of selling—solving, satisfying, and serving. They are customer-focused words. These words describe a sales philosophy that focuses on creating value for customers and sellers. Value-added salespeople sell as a function of doing these other things.

A fundamental principle of Value-Added Selling is that if you define and sell value in customers' terms, they pay for it with a higher selling price. If you define and sell value in sellers' terms, you pay for it with a bigger discount.

VALUE–ADDED SALESPEOPLE CHARACTERISTICS

According to a study that appeared in the *Harvard Business Review*, only 12 percent of salespeople are rated as "excellent" by customers. That is why we chose the top 10 percent of salespeople for our BSP research. The first question we asked end users was, "In a word, how would you describe this salesperson?" The answers were fascinating. We received more than 1,000 separate responses to this question. We submitted these responses to a sorting technique we call *content analysis*. We laid out these responses and studied them for patterns. Ten categories or patterns emerged. Here is how customers described top-achieving salespeople. These descriptors read as solid benchmarks for anyone who aspires to become a value-added salesperson.

Knowledgeable

In all the studies of salespeople we've conducted over the past 20 years, knowledge consistently ranks number one in customer preferences for salespeople. Buyers want to deal with salespeople who know their stuff. One director of purchasing told us that he depends on his supplier salespeople for 60 percent of the industry knowledge he gains. This includes knowledge in these categories: product, company, industry, and customer.

Professional Demeanor

"The consummate professional" is how one customer described his top-achieving salesperson. Professionalism includes how you carry yourself, dressing the part, and integrity. Customers also described professionals as passionate and persistent but not pushy.

Thorough

Are you good at details? Top achievers in our study are. They handle details for their customers so the customers can focus on results. Thoroughness includes efficiency, which means there is not a lot of wasted effort on their part. They practice the value-added philosophy: Do more of that which adds value and less of that which adds little or no value.

Results Oriented

Customers had a simple definition of results orientation: "They save me time and money." "They find me inventory when I need it." Creating results is a key success dynamic in most jobs; in professional selling, it's critical.

Problem Solvers

This includes researching problems, finding solutions and making things work. These salespeople are more focused on making a difference than simply making a sale. They are not merely selling products; they are solving problems and creating value.

Relationship Oriented

Are you easy to work with? Do you accommodate the customer? Are you personable? These are ways customers described the top-achieving salespeople in our study. Later in the book, we detail significance of this aspect of professional selling. We can tell you this much now: it is the critical success dynamic for anyone who desires to make sales a career.

Customer Focused

Top-achieving salespeople provide a powerful example of what it means to be customer focused. Customers describe this as having a "whatever-it-takes attitude" for serving. Seeing things from the customer's perspective and understanding buyer needs are important parts of being customer focused. Buyers also used these two words to describe top achievers: our *advocate* and personal *liaison* with their companies.

Responsive

Responsiveness means "timeliness with information" and "getting back to me when I need him." Accessibility was another way that customers described these salespeople. This means being able to contact the salesperson at all times of the day and night.

Good Communicators

Good communicators listen openly. In our study, we discovered that these top salespeople spent 60 percent of their time listening on sales calls. Being a communicator also means keeping customers informed of new products, innovative solutions, and even bringing bad news as it occurs. One customer said, "I need to hear it—good or bad."

Reliable

Are you dependable? Top-achieving salespeople follow up and deliver on promises. This is the number one way they earn trust with customers. Follow-through and consistency reassure buyers they are dealing with professionals.

This list begs the following question: How many of these words would your customers use to describe you? If you're looking for a benchmark to model, this list of 10 descriptors is a great place to start. It is no accident that the first half of this list are more professional competencies and the second half more interpersonal skills. Professional selling requires this blend of task focus and people orientation. You can be as aggressive as you want in pursuing a piece of business if you balance it with an equally strong measure of empathy.

Implicit in these descriptions of top-achieving salespeople are the values and virtues of Value-Added Selling.

- Excellence—value-added salespeople give it their all. They hold themselves to high standards and put their best work on display for the world to witness.
- Equity—value-added salespeople believe in and practice fairness. A win-win outcome is their true north. They know that if it's not a good deal for both of them—buyer and seller—it's not a good long-term deal for either of them.

- Humility—value-added salespeople practice the most paradoxical virtue in business. This means they are willing to view things from another's perspective and subordinate themselves to the greater good of serving others. Why is this paradoxical? Because they embrace humility, they capture value from the value they create for customers.
- Integrity—value-added salespeople embrace this fundamental value as good business. They know that trust is a solid foundation upon which to build a lasting relationship with customers.
- Synergy—value-added salespeople value the power of "we." They know that they are part of a team of individuals that design and deliver value-added solutions. They are more focused on creating value for the team than a job for themselves.

WHAT BUYERS REALLY WANT

Buyers want more than a cheap price. Over the years, we have conducted a number of studies of buyers and users of products. We have studied all sectors of industry: manufacturing, distribution, and the service industry. From our research, we've concluded that most of the price objections salespeople encounter are self-inflicted wounds.

When we asked buyers to rate price on a 10-point scale (10 meaning that price is important), they rated it 7.2; salespeople rated price 8.3. Who's making a bigger deal out of the selling price, the buyer or the salesperson?

In a study we conducted in our Value-Added Selling seminars, 72 percent of salespeople and their managers admitted they would discount if confronted by a price objection.

Separately, in our BSP research, 45 percent of top-achieving salespeople even admitted that they would discount for their best customer. In the control group of 1,769 salespeople and their managers, 58 percent said they would discount. What's important to keep in mind is that this control group was participating in a Value-Added Selling seminar. They were predisposed to denying their discounting tendency.

Salespeople who expect price resistance generally find it. If you begin the sales call by anticipating a price objection, you unwittingly create one. Asking questions that put the focus on price encourages buyers to shop price. You would be amazed at the number of salespeople who ask a prospect, "Is price important in your decision process?" Who would say no to this question?

In our salespeople and manager survey, we asked what they felt their customers would tell them is an acceptable price-range differential for a better total solution for their needs. They told us they believed customers would pay an average of 9.3 percent more for a better overall solution. And yet, this same group said they would give away 7.46 percent of that acceptable differential if the customer asked for a cheaper price. Who do you think is creating much of this price misery? Salespeople, of course.

In another study, we asked decision makers to consider a scenario where three salespeople offered similar solutions: "If one salesperson showed greater long-term savings, would you pay a higher acquisition price for the solution?" All survey respondents said they would pay more for a documented, long-term savings proposal.

Only one-in-six shoppers is a true price shopper—someone who considers only price. One-in-six is a value-added shopper—price is a low priority. For the remaining two-thirds of buyers, price is *an* issue but not *the* issue. This means 83 percent of your customer and prospect base are open to the value-added argument. Why waste time on price shoppers when you don't own the other 83 percent?

So, if they don't want a cheap price, what *do* they want? Good question. Here is what we discovered in our BSP research.

Buyers said they would pay 11.4 percent more for a better-quality product than they currently use and 9.9 percent more for better service than they currently receive. Another way to view these numbers is: three-fourths of these buyers said they would pay more for better quality, and two-thirds would pay more for better service. When we asked which was more important, cost or price, 67 percent of buyers rated cost (total cost of ownership) as more important than acquisition price.

Then, we offered them a list of 24 variables (8 product, 8 company, 8 salesperson) to choose from, and they told us which 12 were most important to them. By frequency distribution, here is their ranking of the top 12 preferences:

TOP 12 LIST
1. Quality and performance
2. Customer service
3. Knowledgeable salespeople
4. Product availability
5. The supplier stands behind what it sells
6. Supplier ease of doing business
7. Salesperson follow-through on promises
8. Trustworthiness of the salesperson
9. Product durability
10. Salesperson accessibility
11. Acquisition price
12. Technical support

Before you complain about price objections, ask how your solution compares with items 1 through 10. Your knowledge, follow-through, trustworthiness, and access are more important to the customer than price. There are 10 things more important to buyers than acquisition price. Buyers care more about equity than acquisition price. They want to get as good as they give. Buyers turn to price when they perceive an inequity in what they're giving versus what they're getting. Concentrate on delivering more than you promise and more than the buyer expects—you will live with fewer price objections.

ARE YOU CUTTING YOUR PRICES, OR ARE YOU CUTTING YOUR THROAT

Do you think it makes sense to cut your prices to sell more products? When deciding whether to cut your prices, be sure that you're not cutting your throat. Is a low-price strategy prudent? Is all business good business, regardless of the price?

Let's first examine the psychological impact of price-slashing. How do existing customers perceive your price-cutting strategy? They could interpret it as a tacit admission that your prices were too high all along, and you've been gouging them. They may resent it and reject you. Your strategy backfired. It may even create speculation that additional price cuts are imminent. Our research found that 45 percent of executives believed that a price discount would lead to subsequent discounts.

This speculation causes a wait-and-see attitude in the marketplace, and it goes like this: "Let's wait and see if the prices will go even lower than they are now." Remember electronic calculators, DVD players, computers, and cell phones? By the same token, volatility in the stock market has created this wait-and-see attitude on Wall Street. Investors wait in the wings for buying opportunities.

By lowering your prices, you're setting a dangerous precedent. You're telling buyers that lower prices are possible. If they hold out long enough, perhaps they'll get an even better deal. Most automobile buyers embrace this attitude. Who pays full sticker price for a new car? Nobody. The reason is that no one has to. The precedent has been set. Auto price wars began decades ago, leaving plenty of casualties along the way.

Cutting your prices also gives the impression that your company, personnel, and products are not as good as the competition. You're positioning yourself as number two, three, or four. Inadvertently, you're telling the buyer that you're not as valuable as the competition, and your only defense is to quote a cheaper price: "Our strongest advantage is our price." What's the impact of this on employees? Workers start believing that their quality is lower than the competition's quality. They are less motivated to produce high-quality products. You've created a self-fulfilling prophecy that further diminishes your position in the marketplace.

How does cutting price influence you as a salesperson? Your confidence in your company and product begins to wane. How do you think you would fare in a competitive sales situation in which quality is the single criterion? Is it possible that you've psyched yourself out and you feel noncompetitive? If so, the buyer knows it. It's written all over your face.

How does price cutting affect your motivation? Do you feel as excited about serving this customer when he or she gets bargain-basement pricing? Have you ever taken a piece of business and regretted it afterward? Maybe you even resented the customer because you felt that you got the short end of the deal.

Consider the pragmatic implications of lowering your prices. Your profit margins erode, which generally means there is less money for research and development, bonus programs, quality control, and administrative support. When you begin shaving resources because of reduced profit margins, you weaken your long-term competitiveness. You create a situation in which you will be less competitive in the future. Consequently, you'll need to cut your prices again to stay in the game. How long can that go on before you're out of business?

For years, people have justified cutting their prices with the assertion that they could make it up through increased volume. If you're selling at 97 cents on the dollar, you can't make it up in volume. With its existing resources, your company may not be able to handle the extra volume needed to compensate for the reduced profit margin. Extra volume could mean hiring more people and purchasing additional equipment to accommodate the volume. More personnel and equipment challenge the already-suffering profit margins. You've created a chain reaction. Lowering prices means you must sell more volume, which means you must invest in greater resources, which means lower margins, which means you must generate greater volume, which means even greater demands for resources, and so on ad infinitum.

If you're still unconvinced that lowering your prices can have undesirable consequences, consider this: How much more do you need to sell to compensate for the loss in your gross margins? Figure 2.1 presents a hypothetical example.

FIGURE 2.1 **Profit Impact of Discounting**

How much you must increase sales to earn the same profit when discounting

		Current Gross Margin						
		10%	15%	20%	25%	30%	35%	40%
Price Discount	5%	100%	50%	33%	25%	20%	17%	14%
	10%		200%	100%	67%	50%	40%	33%
	15%			300%	150%	100%	75%	60%
	20%				400%	200%	133%	100%
	25%					500%	250%	166%
	30%						600%	300%

If you operate on a potential gross margin of 40 percent and decide to discount by 10 percent, you must increase your unit sales by 33 percent to earn the same gross profit dollars. If you discount by 20 percent, you must increase sales 100 percent—i.e., double your sales—to maintain your profit dollars. If you discount by 30 percent, you must increase sales by 300 percent, i.e., quadruple sales—to maintain your profit dollars. That seems like a lot of work just to offer a discount.

Figure 2.2 demonstrates how raising prices affects profitability.

FIGURE 2.2 **Profit Impact of Raising Prices**

Amount of business you can lose when raising prices and maintain the same profit dollars

	Current Gross Margin						
	10%	15%	20%	25%	30%	35%	40%
5%	33%	25%	20%	17%	14%	13%	11%
10%	50%	40%	33%	29%	25%	22%	20%
15%	60%	50%	43%	38%	33%	30%	27%
20%	67%	57%	50%	44%	40%	36%	33%

(Price Increase — left axis)

If you operate on a potential gross margin of 40 percent and decide to raise prices by 5 percent, you can withstand an 11 percent loss of business and maintain the same profit dollars. A price increase of 10 percent can withstand a 20 percent loss of business while maintaining the same profit dollars. Be clear on what we are proposing here. We are not suggesting that you look for ways to lose business by raising prices. We are pointing out that changing the price, whether up or down, affects your profitability and your business.

If you still remain skeptical, consider this. For a company with average return on sales (according to the S&P 500 index average rate of return for the past 90 years), every bottom-line dollar you retain because of more prudent pricing decisions is like adding 10 dollars to the top line. So, if you are able to retain an additional $10,000 on the bottom line because you are selling value versus cutting price, it is like adding $100,000 in sales to the top line. Can you use an additional $100,000 in sales this year?

PRICE FACTS

Based on our research and experience, we've compiled a list of important facts to consider relative to price. Use this insight to make better
decisions:

- In the absence of all other information, brand name is still the
  best indicator for quality. If you sell brand-name items, buyers
  perceive greater value in your product because of the quality.
  Quality and time are two things that generally trump price.
  Quality enables buyers to sleep well at night knowing they
  bought the best. When the buyer needs something in a hurry,
  price is a low priority.
- Market leaders can easily charge more than the competition.
  If your prices are within 10 percent of the industry average,
  you'll have little trouble maintaining your share of the pie.
  Our most recent studies show that buyers are willing to pay 9
  percent more for a better overall solution.
- Some sellers use a decoy product pricing strategy to drive sales
  to a preferred option. They will offer three options—one high-
  priced item, one low-priced item, and one mid-priced item.
  Buyers typically choose the mid-priced item.
- If you charge more, people perceive greater value. Conversely,
  there is a reverse trend toward low-priced goods. If your
  products are too cheap, people don't want them. They assume
  something must be wrong with them.
- Buyers are more price sensitive about the *necessities* in life than
  the *niceties*. If it's a frill and they want it, buyers don't balk.
  On the other hand, when buying commodities, buyers are
  more concerned with price. When was the last time you heard
  someone complain about the price of a new Mercedes or Rolex?

We've trained salespeople from companies that are the cheapest in
their industries. They ask, "How do I sell against greater value? What
can I do to compete with a company that offers better service and
quality?" Isn't it ironic that they want to know how to compete with
you, the value-added salesperson, while you want to know how to sell
against price?

You could summarize by saying the greater the perceived value you bring to the sale, the fewer price objections you encounter. Invest your selling time in seeking ways to add value versus cut price. The fundamental question you must ask is, "Am I cutting my price, or am I cutting my throat?"

WHY DON'T SALESPEOPLE SELL VALUE ADDED

With such compelling information, it makes sense to ask why salespeople don't sell value added. The promise of greater profitability, coupled with positioning your solution as the value-added solution, is enticing. So, why don't salespeople stick to their guns and hold the line on their prices? Here are several reasons:

Fear

Fear is the number one reason salespeople discount. Some salespeople fear losing the order. Others fear that the buyer may perceive them as greedy if they charge too much for their goods and services, though no one can tell me how much is too much. Guilt is the other side of this coin. Some salespeople feel guilty charging higher prices than their competition charges, and they fear the buyer's reaction. Guilt is a cheap emotion that exacts a great price on salespeople.

Lack of Confidence in What They Sell

Some salespeople don't believe their solution is any better than the competition's. They feel unjustified in charging more than the competition. These salespeople need to do some in-depth soul-searching. They should study their product's features and benefits and their company's value-added services. They should also study the competition's vulnerabilities. If you conclude, after studying, that you're no better than the competition, you could be working for the wrong company. If you're not sold on your value added, how can you sell customers on your value?

Lack of Skills or Knowledge

No one has taught these salespeople to sell value added. They need training in the principles, strategies, and tactics of Value-Added

Selling. Selling value added requires knowledge and skill. If this is your problem, reading this book should provide immediate relief.

Projection

This is one of the more common reasons salespeople cut price. If a salesperson is a price shopper in his or her own life, that salesperson will get more price objections than the average salesperson. Why? This salesperson projects his or her feelings onto the buyer by rationalizing, "I shop price. Doesn't everyone?" He or she assumes that price is important to everyone. If one-in-six shoppers is a price shopper, one-in-six sellers is a price seller. You sell price because you buy price.

Mixed Management Signals

Managers support Value-Added Selling as long as it serves their purposes. If capacity drops for a month or two, management gets nervous and may decide on a short-term, volume-sales mentality: Sell more at a lower price, and make it up in volume. This confuses customers and frustrates salespeople. If you're a manager reading this, you must display the courage of your convictions. You cannot expect your salespeople to hold the line on prices if you change your mind and blow with the wind.

Sales Stockholm Syndrome

The Stockholm syndrome describes an early 1970s bank robbery in Stockholm, Sweden. The robbers took hostages and held them captive for several days. The captives formed an attachment to, and identified with, their captors. The captives even defended the robbers later in court. Salespeople run the risk of contracting the *sales Stockholm syndrome*, which means they overidentify with customers to the point that they find it difficult to charge full prices to their friends and confidants.

Salespeople understand this maxim: "If you expect price to be an issue, it will be." If you begin your sales call expecting to hear a price objection, you will hear one. Unwittingly, unconsciously, or inadvertently, you will create your own monster. You may not always get what you want, but you generally get what you expect. If you turn on your sales radar and program it to detect price sensitivity, it won't take long to elicit that price objection from the buyer.

VALUE-ADDED SELLING REVIEW AND ACTION ITEMS

1. Ask and answer this question, "What is the purpose of a business?" Is your personal business philosophy more about making money or about creating value for your customers and your company?

2. To sell value added successfully and profitably, you must enlarge your definition of value. Price is what buyers pay; value is what they receive. You must educate buyers that the value of something is more than its price or cost; it includes the long-term impact value of what you sell— what it does for the buyer.

3. A customer-value focus means you define value in buyer terms, not seller terms. If you define value in buyers' terms, they pay for it with a higher selling price. If you define value in sellers' terms, you pay for it with a bigger discount.

4. Sell all three dimensions of value: the product, your company, and yourself. The same product from the same company from two different salespeople represents two different solutions. The concept of selling all three dimensions of value serves as the foundation for communicating your value, presented throughout this book.

5. Remember, as a value-added salesperson, you earn the privilege of selling your products and services by solving, satisfying, and serving your customers.

6. To increase your value as a salesperson, study. Invest in your own personal research and development. You are the product over which you have the most control. Build your knowledge base and gain proficiency in the professional competency areas and relationship skills that will differentiate you from all other salespeople.

CHAPTER 3

Small-Wins Selling

Have you ever had a goal so big you weren't sure how to get started? Salespeople experience this challenge whenever they pursue a large, complex opportunity that could take years to realize. These large, complex opportunities feel like a never-ending scavenger hunt, where each clue leads to another clue, and another, and another. Salespeople meet a new contact, which leads to another meeting, which leads to gaining another level of approval, which leads to product testing, etc. When salespeople pursue large, complex opportunities, they feel like they are always chasing down the next clue. All the while, salespeople experience multiple setbacks, stalling their progress.

Some salespeople manage large, complex opportunities well, while other salespeople get lost in the weeds. Some salespeople push through setbacks, while other salespeople get discouraged and quit. Some salespeople eat an elephant one bite at a time, while others try to consume the whole thing in one sitting.

Successful salespeople break down large, complex opportunities into manageable small wins. They win big opportunities by designing and pursuing success in small steps. Along the path to success, there are a series of small wins that move the sale forward. These small wins keep salespeople focused, motivated, and engaged. Small wins give salespeople a sense of control.

Focus is one of the greatest challenges salespeople face. Today, salespeople are inundated with distractions. Distracted salespeople achieve focus by simplifying their sales approach. They focus on the immediate, next best outcome. They don't distract or discourage themselves with everything they need to achieve.

Small wins keep people motivated. Sales is one of the few professions where succeeding only once in 10 tries is still considered successful. Most people cannot handle this level of failure and uncertainty. Salespeople face more setbacks than successes. These constant setbacks can lead to frustrations and self-doubt, and a frustrated salesperson rarely performs at his or her best. Salespeople need something to build their confidence and get back on track.

There is a better way for you to manage large, complex opportunities. Big opportunities excite, inspire, and eventually frustrate salespeople. Balance your excitement by focusing on small wins. Celebrate each small win to keep yourself inspired. Reduce frustration by properly setting your own expectations. Realize that it's not one or two small wins that lead to success, it's the aggregate. Behind every big victory, there is a series of small wins.

In this chapter, you will learn how to apply a small-wins approach to keep you focused, motivated, and engaged. At the end of this chapter, you will be able to:

- Define small wins
- Describe the benefits of a small-wins approach
- List examples of small wins
- Detail small wins from previous success
- Apply the small-wins approach to account planning
- List three ideas to manage salespeople using a small-wins approach
- Describe what gets in the way of achieving small wins

WHAT IS A SMALL WIN

In the January 1984 *American Psychologist* (vol. 39), Karl Weick wrote about redefining the scale of social issues and how to create change. In his article "Small Wins: Redefining the Scale of Social Problems," he argued that large-scale change doesn't happen through large, significant events. Instead, big change happens through a series of small, moderately significant events. On the surface, social problems like equal rights, environmental regulation, and unemployment are too big to manage. Big problems must be broken down so problem solvers can focus on overcoming the smaller, more manageable challenges.

Weick defines a small win as a "concrete, completed outcome of moderate importance. By itself, one small win doesn't mean all that much. But a combination of small wins can attract allies, deter adversaries, generate momentum, and lower resistance to subsequent proposals. A small win is a controllable opportunity that produces a visible result."

Although Weick is defining small wins in the context of social change, the concept can be broadly applied to include most changes, including sales. The same methods used to redefine social change can help salespeople redefine their large, complex opportunities to more manageable outcomes.

By itself, one small win doesn't mean much. One meeting, a product demonstration, or a single proposal does not guarantee long-term success in an account. Expecting one small win to deliver the desired results is the equivalent of expecting one workout to deliver your desired health. It's the combination of several small wins that leads to big change.

Small wins attract allies. In Value-Added Selling, we call allies internal champions. Consider how a new product gains traction within an account. Initially, a salesperson will sell the idea to one decision maker to try the product. The first successful outcome provides proof for other decision makers. Other departments start using the new product and enjoy successful outcomes. Each decision maker that has a positive experience with the product promotes it to other decision makers. Now you have a group of allies selling the product for you. This group continues to promote your solutions, generating additional momentum while protecting you from adversaries.

A jigsaw puzzle is a perfect analogy for small wins. Imagine putting together a 1,000-piece puzzle. Puzzles can be frustrating and overwhelming. But each piece of the puzzle represents a small win. Each connection produces a visible outcome that demonstrates progress.

Weick mentions that one small win by itself may seem unimportant. By itself, connecting two puzzle pieces might seem unimportant. But when several pieces are connected, you generate momentum. In fact, Karl Weick mentions that a combination of small wins lowers the resistance to subsequent proposals. Once you achieve a small win, the next small win becomes easier. You generate momentum.

When putting together a puzzle, each subsequent puzzle piece becomes easier to place. Since puzzles are easier to complete as you place more pieces, the puzzle seems more difficult and time-consuming in the beginning. Likewise, in a large, complex sale, the initial small wins seem more difficult. Be aware of this, but don't be frustrated by it. With a small-wins approach, it will naturally take more time and effort in the beginning, but once the earlier pieces are in place, the process will become easier.

Not all puzzle pieces are created equal, and neither are small wins. Some small wins generate more progress and momentum than other small wins, just like some puzzle pieces generate more progress. For example, finding the edge pieces will help you establish the border. Completing the border will give you a head start. Some puzzle pieces have special colors or symbols, making them easier to place in the puzzle. Once you build off these specialty pieces, it's easier to generate momentum. These small wins create momentum and are considered leveraging points because of the increasing impact they have on your success.

Identify the leveraging points in the sales process by analyzing your previous successes. In each success ask yourself, "What small wins had the greatest impact or generated the most momentum?" Then ask, "What were the small wins that led to this leveraging point?"

Puzzles are not completed in a logical, linear format. You don't start at the top and work your way down, from left to right. You'll place several pieces together and then find another section to piece together. Likewise, small wins aren't always linear. They are achieved in the real world, where there are many dynamics at play. Small wins do not always happen in a predictable order. Instead of obsessing over perfect order, ask yourself, "Are we moving in the right general direction? Are we moving closer toward our goal, or further away from it?"

Once you achieve a series of small wins, you've built a foundation. When you experience failures or setbacks, you don't have to start over. Instead, you start at the previous small win. For example, when putting together a puzzle, you might leave the puzzle for a day or two, or get stuck, or you can't find the missing piece. These temporary setbacks don't cause you to start over. Instead, you start again where you left off. The same is true for setbacks in the complex sale. Each small win strengthens your foundation of success. A temporary setback or stall doesn't mean you need to start over. You start at your previous small win. Consider the small wins listed below:

- You completed an initial meeting with the operations manager.
- The engineer and operations manager agreed to a trial.
- The engineer included your solution in the specification.
- You met with procurement and established the budget based on your solution.

These small wins build a foundation. If your procurement contact leaves the organization, you don't have to start over. You have built a foundation of small wins, and you already have several puzzle pieces in place. There will be setbacks and stalls, but during these setbacks, remind the buyer (and yourself) of the momentum you have already generated.

In the previous example, the procurement contact leaves the organization. In your initial meeting, remind the new procurement contact of the momentum generated:

"Mr. Buyer, it's great to meet you. Let's spend a few minutes reviewing where we are on this project. We have met with the operations managers and engineer to conduct a trial. Our trial performance exceeded both the engineer's and operations manager's expectations. Our performance then prompted engineering to include our solution in the specification. Also, we have gained budgetary approval for the solution." With small wins, you don't need to start over, just review your momentum.

It's important to define what a small win is not. A small win is not asking for an initial meeting, it's having the actual meeting. A small win is not making a request for additional information, it's receiving the customer information. A small win is a complete, implemented outcome. A small win is outcome-based, not effort-based. Effort is a critical component of any small-wins approach, but don't confuse effort with outcome.

THE BENEFITS OF A SMALL–WINS APPROACH

Small wins keep salespeople focused. Salespeople are pulled in multiple directions. With mobile devices, social media, and 24/7 accessibility, salespeople are distracted from their intended course. In today's selling environment, the need to stay focused has never been greater.

Clarity and simplicity lead to focus. With a small-wins approach, you identify the immediate, next best outcome. Then you only focus on achieving that outcome. Think about your biggest sales opportunity. How many outcomes must you achieve to get the desired result? It can be an overwhelming number. Now consider only the immediate, next best outcome. It's manageable and attainable. Don't worry about the tenth outcome. The tenth outcome doesn't matter until you complete the first nine.

Small wins keep you motivated. In their groundbreaking book *The Progress Principle*, Teresa Amabile and Steven Kramer identified what really keeps employees motivated and engaged.[1] They analyzed nearly 12,000 journal entries taken from 238 employees at seven different companies. Participants journaled about their day-to-day activities over several weeks (9 to 38 weeks). After reviewing the data, the authors found that employees were the most motivated and most engaged on the days that they made progress in meaningful work. Self-efficacy and accomplishment are critical in any profession, especially in sales.

Consider how a small-wins approach will impact a salesperson's motivation. The salesperson begins pursuing a massive opportunity that will take several years to materialize. Over that three-year period, the salesperson faces several setbacks. If the salesperson views every setback as a failure, he or she gives up. Too often, salespeople associate a short-term setback as a long-term failure. By focusing on small wins, salespeople stay motivated. Again, the best way to manage a long-term, value-added sale is to break it down to manageable pieces, just like the jigsaw puzzle—one piece at a time.

Small wins beget more small wins. Achieving small wins generates momentum, which increases motivation. Most salespeople know what it's like to "be on a roll." That feeling of success makes sales a rewarding profession.

Jim Collins wrote about this in his timeless book *Good to Great*. Collins analyzed what caused good companies to transform into great companies. One contributing factor was generating self-sustaining momentum. He referred to this momentum as the flywheel effect. Collins describes a flywheel as a 30-foot-diameter wheel weighing 5,000 pounds. To initially move the wheel requires a lot of effort (like an initial small win), but eventually the momentum becomes self-reinforcing. When referring to those companies that went from good to great, Collins mentions that big results and groundbreaking transitions do not happen all at once. They are a culmination of all the previous events that led to the transition. In the same way, as a salesperson, your transition from where you are to ultimate success is due to a culmination of small wins.

IMPLEMENT A SMALL-WINS APPROACH

For a small-wins approach to succeed, salespeople and management must buy in to the concept. If management buys in but salespeople refuse to focus on small wins, the process fails. If salespeople buy inbut management doesn't have the patience to see it through, the process fails. A small-wins approach requires commitment throughout the entire organization.

Identifying Small Wins

You cannot achieve a small win until you identify the ultimate goal. At first glance, the big win can be exciting, motivating, and for some, overwhelming. The first step is to identify your big goal and then shrink it. Identify the series of small wins that will lead to your ultimate success.

Identify the small wins based on your dynamic selling environment. Ask yourself, "From initial contact to contract, what is the series of immediate, next best outcomes that I need to achieve?" Make a list of all the small wins.

Once you identify the series of small wins, create a plan to achieve them. Plan your week using this small-wins approach. Begin every week by asking yourself, "What action do I need to take this week to achieve my small win?"

You can also identify small wins by analyzing previous successes. Review your organization's greatest sales successes. Your greatest success usually means biggest net profit or revenue. Break down the success by detailing the small wins. It's critical to analyze the initial small wins that generated momentum. These first few small wins are often overlooked or forgotten.

The goal during this exercise is quantity. The more small wins you uncover, the better. After reviewing several successes, ask yourself, "What are the common small wins?" Although each opportunity requires unique small wins, you will notice overlap. These overlapping small wins help guide your effort.

Small wins are not always achieved in an orderly, linear fashion. Don't obsess over the perfect order. When gauging your success of a small-wins approach, ask yourself, "Are we getting closer to our ultimate goal, or are we moving further from it?" This is the acid test to gauge the effectiveness of your approach.

Avoiding Small Losses

Identify small losses you want to avoid. In every sale, there are small wins that generate momentum toward your desired outcome, and there are also small losses that impede your progress. In *The Progress Principle*, the authors found that small losses and setbacks had a more powerful impact than small wins. In other words, negative events impeded progress more than positive events contributed to progress. This is the frustration of a missing puzzle piece.

You can only avoid small losses you are aware of. Take a minute to analyze your failures. Think of lost opportunities and identify the small losses and setbacks that impeded progress. For example, you couldn't secure a meeting with a key decision maker, the engineer would not endorse your solution, or you only met with a procurement buyer. Identify small losses that led to the failure or impeded your progress. Then develop a plan to avoid or overcome these small losses. Value-added salespeople know what they want to achieve, and more important, what to avoid.

Coaching Salespeople Using a Small-Wins Approach

If salespeople report to you, coaching them is your number one priority. Coaching your sales team using a small-wins approach is conceptually simple. You teach salespeople to focus their time, energy, and effort on achieving the immediate, next best outcome. You also coach them on how they must achieve that outcome. For salespeople, this approach requires steady commitment. As a sales leader, this approach requires patience and restraint.

A small-wins approach requires both a long-range vision and short-term focus. For managers, this delicate balance can be frustrating. On the surface, a salesperson might not display his normal sense of urgency. He appears to be spending an inordinate amount of time getting started. A small-wins approach requires more time and effort in the beginning. Remember, small wins will, as Weick said, "attract allies, deter threats, and lower resistance to subsequent proposals." Getting started is more difficult and time-consuming; finishing happens faster—just like the puzzle. Managers must be patient in the beginning and encourage the salesperson. The salesperson needs reassurance that he is on the right path, in spite of the difficulty.

Let's take a closer look at the puzzle analogy and how it relates to a sales manager's role. Imagine a group of students having to put together a puzzle. The students are given four hours to complete the puzzle, and the teacher is evaluated on the student's ability to achieve this goal.

Each puzzle piece represents a small win. The students first organize the puzzle by laying out the pieces. Then they start organizing and connecting various puzzle pieces. All the while, the time keeps ticking by. An hour passes, and the puzzle is only 10 percent completed. Two hours pass, and it's only 30 percent completed. Three hours pass, and the puzzle is only 50 percent completed.

Does the teacher have the patience and restraint to give the students time to finish, or will the teacher jump in and redirect their efforts? How often do sales managers jump in and redirect their salespeople?

Anyone who has ever put together a puzzle knows that the first half takes more time and energy than the second half. Every manager should realize that front-end small wins take longer and seem disorderly. The manager's role is to keep salespeople focused and motivated, not to immediately jump in and redirect their efforts.

Motivating employees is a challenge. Motivation is more than a rah-rah speech at your monthly sales meeting. True motivation is internal. The key to motivating salespeople is getting salespeople to motivate themselves.

Ask your salespeople to detail a list of small wins they plan to achieve. Discuss how they will achieve these small wins. Conduct a barrier analysis to reveal potential roadblocks and to create a backup plan.

Meaningful work is highly motivating. Managers should focus on helping salespeople achieve small, meaningful wins. Celebrate successes, coach them through small losses, and find a way for them to progress.

Help Your Customers Achieve Small Wins

Your customers are like you in so many ways. They are also trying to achieve a goal. Their goal might be different, but it's a goal nonetheless. They also have a 1,000-piece puzzle they are trying to complete. Helping your customers achieve progress leads to greater loyalty and a better overall customer experience.

To help your customers achieve small wins, ask yourself the following questions:

- What are this organization's goals?
- What are the departmental objectives associated with these organizational goals?
- What are the small wins that will lead to these departmental goals?
- How can I help this department achieve these small wins?

Organizations will partner with salespeople who help them achieve their organizational goals. Customers measure the impact of salespeople by the value they create, not the price they charge. The more small wins you help your customer achieve, the less important price becomes.

WHAT PREVENTS SALESPEOPLE FROM FOCUSING ON SMALL WINS

In seminars, we ask salespeople the following questions:

- What gets in the way of you calling on high-level decision makers?
- What gets in the way of you holding the line on pricing?
- What gets in the way of you asking for a customer's commitment?

The response is nearly always the same for all three questions—fear. Salespeople fear upsetting their lower-level contacts, losing the business, or destroying relationships. The salespeople's fear motivates them to focus on safe, lower-risk activities. For example, salespeople know they should hold the line on pricing and talk to other decision makers, but they don't. Why? Fear. They fear losing the order.

When listing small wins, identify the perceived risk of each small win. Once you do this, discuss ways to mitigate risk. In risk-filled situations, it's natural to dwell more on what you stand to lose versus what you stand to gain. Acknowledge this tendency and focus more on the gain. Remind yourself of the greater risk, doing nothing and getting nothing.

Salespeople operate in a high-energy field; consequently, they are impatient. A strong sense of urgency coupled with their competitiveness doesn't always help with a small-wins approach. In an effort to close a sale or reach a goal, the salesperson might skip a few steps or try to jump ahead.

For example, the salesperson knows she should demonstrate a new product to gain buy-in before quoting the solution. However, she is close to hitting her monthly number, so she skips this step and works directly with procurement to get a purchase order. The salesperson's urgency to close was more compelling than her commitment to the small-wins approach.

Managers also push salespeople and challenge them to produce results. Although managers are trying to drive business results, it can drive the wrong behaviors. Managers are driven (and evaluated) by results. Therefore, they drive their teams to produce accordingly. Managers need to demonstrate their commitment to small-win behavior instead of big-win results. Initially moving a heavy flywheel is difficult, and then it becomes easier. Initial small wins are just like the initial turns of a flywheel. In the early stages, commitment and patience are going to be critical. It's tempting to skip steps early in the process, trying to show greater progress and gain results. However, skipping steps at the beginning of a small-wins approach can lead to a more difficult road toward the finish. Both managers and salespeople need to temper their urgency with patience. The commitment to a small-wins approach has to be greater than the temptation to skip ahead.

VALUE-ADDED SELLING REVIEW AND ACTION ITEMS

1. A small win keeps salespeople focused and motivated. A small win is a concrete, implemented outcome of moderate importance. A small win is outcome-based, not effort-based. One small win doesn't generate much progress, but a series of small wins will generate momentum.

2. Implement a small-wins approach through a small-wins audit. The first step is to identify a long-term, account-specific goal. Dream big. Then ask yourself, "From initial contact to contract, what is the series of immediate, next best outcomes that I need to achieve?" Make a list of these outcomes, and then focus your time on achieving the next best outcome.

3. Identify the small losses that impede your progress. Small losses can have greater impact than small wins. Know which small wins to focus on and which losses to avoid.

4. If you are a manager, use the small-wins approach to coach your sales team. Focus their time and energy on small wins. Give them time to achieve small wins (be patient), coach them when they are off track, and celebrate small successes to build confidence and keep your team motivated.

CHAPTER 4

The Critical Buying Path

From its mouth near Dinar, the Great Menderes River snakes its way throughout southwestern Turkey for approximately 363 miles until it empties itself into the Aegean Sea near the ancient port of Miletus. As the crow flies, it spans a distance of approximately 180 miles. The ancient name for this river was Maiandros (Maeander) and is the root of our word *meander*. Aerial photos of this river illustrate the circuitous route it travels. Some salespeople would argue that many customers follow a similar path when they attempt to satisfy their needs.

Some buyers have simple needs; others have complex needs. Some buyers paradoxically treat simple needs as complex, while other buyers treat complex needs as simple. Understanding the buyer's needs is important to determine if your solution is the right fit. Understanding how buyers engage their needs and make buying decisions is vital for how you frame your message and communicate your value.

This chapter offers you a different way to study and approach the buyer's needs. Teaching buyers how to make better long-term buying decisions benefits both buyers and sellers.

At the end of this chapter, you will be able to:

- Discuss the importance of understanding your customer's journey
- Describe your buyer's decision-making style
- Explain a major obstacle to good buying decisions
- Define the full scope of the buyer's needs
- Discuss the buyer's Critical Buying Path
- Identify benchmark steps along this path
- Assess your value vis-à-vis the buyer's needs

- Frame a compelling value story about your impact on the buyer's world

THE NEED TO UNDERSTAND YOUR BUYER'S JOURNEY

A thorough understanding of the buyer's needs is the first step you take on your Critical Sales Path. In our study of 254 B2B salespeople, we asked them about the challenges they face in getting new business. One-in-five said that understanding the buyer's needs was a challenge. The inference is that 80 percent feel they understand the buyer's needs. That sounds optimistic, but it flies in the face of our meta-analysis of customer research. Approximately three-in-four customers feel that salespeople do not understand their needs or buying process. One study found that only one-in-five salespeople truly understand the customer's needs. We can infer from this that either salespeople underestimate the importance of understanding the buyer's needs or this is a blind spot for salespeople. Either way, buyers see a bigger problem here than salespeople perceive. There is another consideration that has an impact on the customer's buying decision: How many buyers really understand their needs?

Your understanding of the buyers' world—their needs, wants, desires, operating environment, decision making, and the full impact of their decisions—can help you identify where you can add meaningful value, communicate this value effectively, and deliver a value-added solution.

BUYING PARADIGMS

How buyers perceive their needs tells you how they will evaluate your solution. Understanding their buying paradigms—the way they view their needs and make buying decisions—determines how you proceed with the sale. Do they see their needs as simple or complex? Do they want a long-term solution or a short-term fix? Some buyers are willing to do a deep dive exploration of their needs, while others are content with swimming at the surface. For some buyers, emotion trumps reason, while other buyers try to make purely rational buying decisions. In some organizations, conflicting agendas and egos complicate the process. Power-base distribution often dictates whether they will make a logistics, financial, or technical decision. With all these pressures, buyers generally choose one of two buying paradigms: they either satisfice or maximize.

Satisfice

Nobel Laureate Herbert Simon, psychologist and economist, introduced the term *satisfice* to describe a decision-making style that opts for an outcome that is merely *good enough*.[1] It is a combination of *satisfy* and *suffice*. Those who satisfice choose adequacy over optimal solutions. Part of Simon's argument for satisficing is that we lack adequate cognitive resources to predict with sufficient precision and reliability the probability of outcomes of complex decisions. In other words, people can't possibly know everything they need to know to make these types of decisions. Other reasons people satisfice are that they lack information, time, money, or the will to make complex decisions. They simplify and choose expediency and sufficiency.

The outcome of satisficing is that buyers dumb down their needs and value-strip the options they are evaluating. For salespeople, this means buyers simply look at price. They ask these types of questions: "What can we live with?" "What minimum standards can we accept?" "What's the cheapest way to fix this problem?" Implicit in each of these questions is the answer for the value-added salesperson: you must help them sophisticate, not complicate, the decision process. Cognitive psychologists may argue that our perceptual filters are designed to screen out the *noise* so we can get to the heart of the matter. Complex decision variables are not *noise*. They are relevant because they affect the outcome, which translates into value. To sophisticate the decision process means to teach buyers to maximize.

Maximize

To maximize is to opt for the best possible outcome. It answers these questions: "What is the best way to approach this situation?" "What is our ideal outcome?" "What is our best-case scenario?" Maximizers choose potential over good enough.

Maximizing involves weighing all decision variables along a timeline that extends well into the future. These input variables include needs that are synergistic, connected, and whole. This is an important training point for Value-Added Selling. While some buyers may dumb down or isolate their needs, to maximize they must view them holistically because they are more interdependent than independent. Encouraging buyers to consider all their needs, think long term, and dream about ideal outcomes is a good first step on this royal road you travel to provide value-added solutions.

SILOS ARE A MAJOR OBSTACLE TO GOOD BUYING DECISIONS

In 1971, Walt Kelly published his famous *Pogo* cartoon "We have met the enemy and he is us." At times, humans are their own worst enemies. Years ago, an attendee in one of our seminars asked, "Whose customer is it? I'm in operations. Is it my customer, the sales force's customer, or *our* customer?" This rhetorical question required only a smile of acknowledgment.

A silo is a tall cylinder that is used to store material and safeguard its contents from outside elements. Organizational silos are similar in that they isolate their members from other people. They are called turf wars, power struggles, sibling rivalries, family feuds, political infighting, and so on. Silos are classic us-versus-them battles, and they are as old as Cain and Abel. Silos exist when one group of employees views another group of employees as separate, or worse, as the enemy.

Silos exist in organizations when one group is alienated or isolated from other groups. Consequently, they do not communicate. These silos can be functional, divisional, or geographic. Functional silos exist when one department operates as a separate entity, independent of other departments. Silos reflect a failure of systems in organizations. Each silo has a separate focus and operates independently.

Engineering and finance have different organizational functions. One works with technology and the other with money. When departments fail to communicate, it widens this chasm. When purchasing fails to communicate with engineering or production or operations, it is as if purchasing is buying for itself instead of for another entity.

Divisional silos exist when different groups within the company pursue different markets, operating as quasi-separate companies. Divisional silos are complicated by the fact that they also contain functional silos within these separate divisions. A purchasing group for one division is different and separate from the purchasing group in another division. Even though these divisions may serve related markets in the same industry, they still operate independently of each other. Many times, they are unaware of what other divisions do or whom they should contact with questions or opportunities.

Geographic silos exist when groups are separated by space. The corporate office is in one city, and the branches are in other cities. Purchasing for a large global corporation may be centralized in one location, and those who use the product work somewhere else. This is a problem when purchasing responds to supply requisitions but never talks to the people in the field who request and work the product.

Offices located in different cities are separate organizations. These agencies understand the organization's needs as they are spelled out in the requisition. They may know what they need but not *why* they need it. For example, the Houston office purchases for a mine in Wyoming, and there is little physical contact between the two. From a procurement perspective, consolidating purchasing in one location may sound like a great way to leverage purchasing dollars, but at what cost to efficiency and effectiveness? These silos create supplier issues as well, as salespeople attempt to penetrate these accounts to meet with all levels of decision makers and influencers.

Some silos are benign. They exist simply because two separate units fail to communicate. Others silos are malignant because one unit may passively or even actively sabotage another unit. Withholding information is different from lobbing hand grenades over the cubicle walls separating units, but it is still sabotage.

Silos exist because management allows them to exist. Some executives like management by conflict. They create competitive environments where departments compete for precious resources. Some managers allow silos to exist because they are in denial: "We don't have that problem in our company." Yes, they do. If an organization has more than one layer of management, more than one department, and a fuzzy mission, it has silos. Silos also exist because mid-level managers focus more on winning turf battles than creating value for customers.

The second reason silos exist is because management does not communicate clearly and often its commitment to serving customers.

Companies have one mission—to create value for customers, which in turn allows them to extract value from those customers. Anything other than that is a distraction. Silos are distractions. Companies cannot create value for customers or for the company when team members are more interested in creating a position for themselves than value for the team.

Turf wars are so common that a company is an anomaly if it does not have them. The American Management Association surveyed top executives and found that 83 percent of them had silos in their companies, and 97 percent of them believed that silos were hurting their organizations.[2] Companies have silos, especially when they think they do not.

IndustryWeek magazine found that silos are the top obstacle to growth.[3] Companies cannot win battles against the competition when their employees waste energy battling each other. In fact, a smart competitor only needs to watch these turf battles send business the competitor's way. Just as negativism is a complete waste of a perfectly good imagination, organizational silos are a waste of a perfectly good competitive spirit. With all of the competition organizations face, do they really need competitors inside their own walls? Silos kill competitiveness.

Silos are honest-to-goodness profit piranhas. Inefficiencies, mistakes, and miscommunications chew away at the bottom line. The indirect cost of missed opportunities is forgone value that can never be recaptured. Silos lead to employee disengagement, which Gallup estimates costs U.S. businesses between $450 and $550 billion annually. Companies do not have that kind of money to waste. Silos unleash a chain of viral negative consequences that will kill business.[4]

Silos lead to employee and customer dissatisfaction. Unhappy employees create unhappy customers. Silos breed mistrust, suspicion, and frustration. Good employees leave. Customers run for the exits, as they feel like the neglected child of dysfunctional parents. Silos destroy operational efficiency. IBM found that employees spend 25 percent of their time seeking information that someone in the company already has discovered.[5] Too bad they do not communicate.

Sales is not the enemy. Operations is not the enemy. IT is not the enemy. Management is not the enemy. Customer service is not the enemy. The credit department is not the enemy. HR is not the enemy. If you are a distributor, your factories are not the enemy. Purchasing is not the enemy. Customer silos make it difficult for salespeople to navigate the decision process. We cover this more fully in Chapter 27 on selling to multiple decision makers.

As a salesperson, you can work with customers whose organizations are siloed. Get connected. Talk to employees at all levels in the organization. Ask questions that call into play the broad needs of their organization—purchasing needs, manufacturing needs, technical support needs, administrative needs, and so on. Advise one department what you are doing with other departments. Arrange for task-force meetings that include multiple disciplines. When discussing your solution, include an impact statement of how your solution creates value for other departments. Be clear that your solution is a total solution for their organization. Encourage cross-functional communication between your company and the customer's organization.

Value-Added Selling has always been a team sport. The sales force may sell the first experience with your company, but it is the total experience that brings customers back. Salespeople can promise only what operations delivers. The whole organization must embrace this mission to create value for customers; otherwise, you will have silos in your organization. Silos are barriers for Value-Added Selling; they obstruct you from getting full value for your investment.

Abraham Lincoln said, "A house divided against itself cannot stand." Though his reference was more serious than organizational turf battles, his words are a poignant reminder of the dangers of infighting.

THE FULL SCOPE OF BUYERS' NEEDS

Buyers have a choice of how they want to view their needs. They can view them as *impact area needs* or *process needs*. These impact areas include things like logistics needs, IT and technical needs, training needs, service and support needs, administration needs, financial needs, operations and manufacturing needs, and sales and marketing needs. Your solution may have an impact on any or all of these areas. Purchasing needs to shore up the logistics of a transaction, while manufacturing is more concerned with how well a solution performs in the system, and sales and marketing is more concerned with how that solution makes it easier to take to their markets.

The compartmentalizing of needs by function, department, or location contributes to the problem of silos. *Process needs* are more linear, fluid, and sequential. This approach to needs helps companies avoid silos. This process-oriented view of needs provides us with the model for the Critical Buying Path.

THE CRITICAL BUYING PATH

In 1985, Michael Porter wrote in his book *Competitive Advantage*, "Competitive advantage cannot be understood by looking at a firm as a whole. It stems from . . . many discrete activities. . . . Every firm is a collection of activities that are performed to design, produce, market, deliver, and support its product. All of these activities can be represented using a value chain." He was describing a process of inbound and outbound activities in which companies engage to create value. He was building on an idea that was taking root to view an organization's value creation as a dynamic process. At about this same time, supply chain management gained popularity because of the technology available to coordinate logistics. Toward the end of the 1990s, customer journey mapping gained popularity as a way to understand the customer experience. We began our work on the Critical Buying Path when it became obvious to us that salespeople needed a comprehensive understanding of the buyer's cradle-to-grave needs in order to contribute maximum value to the relationship.

The Critical Buying Path (CBP) is the sequence of steps buyers go through from need to satisfaction. More specifically, it is the sequence of steps buyers go through from the moment a need *exists* (not surfaces) up to and including reordering or disposing of a product you haven't even sold them yet. When Tom first introduced this concept in his 1993 book *Value-Added Sales Management*, he defined it as a "buying and usage process." Today's definition is broader because we have witnessed how companies have enlarged the concept to add value at every step along this path.

Think of the CBP as a process of complete need satisfaction. It is bigger and broader than the buyer's supply chain; it is a supply chain on steroids. Supply chains typically satisfy logistics needs for buyers. The scope of the CBP includes all ways you can add meaningful value.

In addition to being a sequence of events and a process that flows toward complete need satisfaction, the CBP is a cradle-to-grave flow of interconnected activities, needs, and solutions. To interrupt the flow—as by satisficing—robs the buyer of the opportunity to achieve something great. *Sequence*, *process*, and *flow* describe something that is ongoing—a continuous relationship with a supplier versus a transaction-based relationship.

Your buyers have a CBP whether they know it or not. Even the most commodity-minded price shoppers have a CBP if they would slow down the decision making and consider the possibility. The CBP encourages buyers to view their needs as dynamic and evolving. This suggests your Value-Added Selling strategy: help buyers understand the full scope of their needs; then they can appreciate the impact of your value-added solution. Buyers who embrace this concept make better long-term buying decisions and maximize the value they receive from their supply partners. The CBP turns a *satisficer* into a *maximizer*. As buyers thoroughly understand their needs, it is more difficult for them to value-strip your solution and reduce the buying decision to price only.

As you study the buyer's CBP you develop a broader and deeper understanding of his needs. You become customer focused as you begin to see your solution as value received, not just value added. You engage the buyer more in the process; you stretch his time horizon; you enlarge the discussion from core-commodity, logistic needs to total needs; and you ensure all influencers get their say. By understanding the buyer's CBP, you will see a model emerge for assessing your value added and a framework to communicate your value and differentiate your solution.

The CBP has three stages or categories of needs: Presale Planning, Acquisition/Transition, and Postsale Usage. Within each of these three stages or broad categories of needs are subcategories of needs that are steps along the CBP. The more of these steps you identify, the greater the possibility of your adding meaningful value.

Presale Planning

The Presale Planning stage begins the moment a need exists. The buyer may be aware or unaware that he or she has a need. Early account penetration can help you uncover this need and shape the decision process to favor your solution. The buyer's dominant need during this stage is for information. Our buyer survey found that buyers' need for information is an opportunity area for salespeople to add value. These are just a few of the questions a buyer might ask in this stage:

- What do we need?
- Why do we need it?
- What's available and from whom?
- Which is the best alternative and why?

You may discover that subcategories of needs—the steps along the CBP—include things like *studying* (conducting an internal needs assessment, forecasting, establishing buying criteria like solution parameters and budgets), *sourcing* (meeting with potential suppliers, observing product demonstrations, testing, and requesting proposals) and *selecting* (committee meetings and deciding). The specific activities for this stage depend on the buyer and her needs. It can vary from one buyer to another.

Acquisition/Transition

The Acquisition/Transition stage begins when the bid is awarded, contract signed, or order placed. It includes everything that the buyer must do to prepare to use or transform the product into value. The buyer's dominant need during this stage is for smooth, seamless, and painless transitions to your solution.

As in the Presale Planning stage, there are subcategories of needs or steps along the CBP. They may include things like placing orders, preparing people and facilities, and receiving and redistributing goods. Just like the Presale Planning stage, the specific activities or category of needs depends on the customer. Some may have several preparatory activities they must conduct; others may simply wait for the goods.

Postsale Usage

The Postsale Usage stage begins when the customer transforms your solution into value and extends into the future for complete need satisfaction. The buyer's dominant needs at this point are maximum performance and economy.

As in the previous two stages, there are subcategories of needs or steps along the CBP. They may include activities like using your product, reselling your product, getting service and repair, receiving technical support, reordering parts, and even disposing of your product once it no longer meets their needs.

See Figure 4.1 for an illustration of how the CBP flows from need to satisfaction, including sample benchmark activities along the path. This path will change from customer to customer, even though some customer segments will have similar paths.

HOW TO USE THE CRITICAL BUYING PATH IN VALUE-ADDED SELLING

Using the CBP is one of the most customer-oriented approaches to selling. Your role changes as the buyer's needs evolve along the path. We cover this more deeply in Chapter 5, "The Value-Added Selling Process." From diagnostician, to promoter, to supporter, to satisfaction specialist, your role evolves parallel to the evolution of customer needs.

In the early phases of the sale, the Presale Planning stage, you ask the buyer to share with you her decision process: "Would you walk me through your project start to finish?" "Please tell me about your approval and decision process?" "Who will be affected by this buying decision?" "What does a long-term success look like for this project?" The purpose of these types of questions is to get buyers talking about the steps they will go through in studying their needs, deciding who they want to work with, using your product, and extracting the most value they can from their supply partners. Simply, you want the buyer to detail the steps along her CBP.

Armed with that information, there are a number of things you can do. First, as you lay out the buyer's activities along the path, ask these questions: "How do we bring value to the customer at each step along the path?" "Are there things we do that add cost but no value along this path?" "Are there things we should be doing to add value along this path?" This internal audit of your value added exposes the efficacy of your solution. You may need to make some changes.

Second, you can ask buyers what they would like to see you do at each step along the path to bring them meaningful value.

Presale Planning

The customer needs information.

Sample activities may include:
Study
Design
Budgeting
Testing

Acquisition/Transition

The customer needs smooth, seamless, and painless transitions to your solution.

Sample activities may include:
Procurement
Receipt of goods
Redistribution
Installation

Postsale Usage

The customer needs maximum performance, great service, and economy.

Sample activities may include:
Usage
Maintenance
Service
Reorder

Steps along the Critical Buying Path represent critical buying and usage activities for the customer and a potential impact area for you to add value.

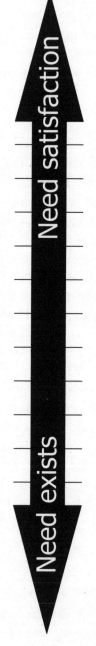

Need satisfaction

Need exists

FIGURE 4.1 Sample Critical Buying Path

Third, the CBP provides you an infrastructure to present your value-added solution. You can lay out on paper or demonstrate with a visual aid how your company supports the buyer at each step along the path, "Ms. Buyer, in our early meetings you described for me the path you will travel to satisfy your needs. Each of those benchmark steps gives us the opportunity to demonstrate how our value added has a real impact on your business. For example . . ." At this point, you would begin your chronology of value as it relates to the buyer's CBP.

Your ability and willingness to frame your value added within this customer-focused context is a key differentiator strategy. As others are selling products, you are demonstrating a comprehensive value delivery system that supports the buyer at every critical step along her path. You have sophisticated, not complicated, the process. You have demonstrated your customer-value focus. You have proven your long-term worth to the buyer. Now it is time to turn this buyer into a customer.

Fourth, the CBP provides you with a way to determine and document your value-added impact throughout the Postsale Usage stage. This provides topical discussion points for your follow-up sales calls. In Part II, you will learn about the importance of this defensive selling activity.

VALUE-ADDED SELLING REVIEW AND ACTION ITEMS

1. Buyers and sellers must have an in-depth understanding of the buyer's needs, wants, and desires and the context in which buyers make their buying decisions. This enables both to design a value-added solution.

2. Myriad forces influence buying decisions: objective buying criteria, emotions, egos, and so on. Buyers make two types of buying decisions: they satisfice, opting for something that is merely good enough, or they maximize, seeking the best way to solve a problem. To sell your value added, you must help buyers get into the maximize mindset.

3. A major obstacle when making value-oriented buying decisions is organizational silos. Salespeople help buyers tear down silos when the salesperson becomes a conduit that feeds valuable information to all parties.

4. Buyers needs are complex and interconnected. To satisfy all these needs, they go through a sequence of events from the moment a need exists through complete satisfaction. This is called the Critical Buying Path.

5. Your understanding of this CBP helps you understand value added as value received. This is customer-oriented selling at its best. Armed with this information, you can present a compelling argument for why your solution is *the* value-added solution for this buyer. It also gives you a way to check on the efficacy of your value creation.

CHAPTER 5

The Value-Added Selling Process

In Chapter 4, you read about the Critical Buying Path. You learned how to sophisticate the buyer's decision process. You want to encourage buyers to make long-term, value-oriented buying decisions. Many of the problems salespeople encounter come from a short-term, transaction-oriented mentality, either on their part or on the buyer's part. This transactional approach means that buyers and sellers go from deal to deal and from order to order. They view each other as a necessary cost of doing business.

In Value-Added Selling, buyers and sellers view each other as partners. Value-Added Selling is a philosophy and a process. It's more than a sales call. It's a way to contribute maximum value to, and extract maximum value from, the customer. Because Value-Added Selling is a process that parallels the buyer's Critical Buying Path, you must align your activities with those of the customer.

This chapter is about the process of Value-Added Selling—the steps you go through, the strategies you employ, and the parallel sales activities that mirror the buyer's Critical Buying Path.

At the end of this chapter, you will be able to:

- Define the Value-Added Selling Process
- Describe the strategic significance of your activities
- Differentiate between offensive and defensive selling
- Name the four groups of Value-Added Selling strategies
- Define and discuss the Critical Sales Path

WHAT IS THE VALUE-ADDED SELLING PROCESS

Traditional, seller-focused approaches to selling concentrate on the act of acquiring new business: filling the pipeline, pitching the product, and closing the deal. Most of the strategies and tactics that salespeople learn for this approach center on writing orders.

Because Value-Added Selling is customer focused and principled in equity, its strategies and tactics concentrate on maximizing the value that the salesperson contributes to and extracts from the relationship. This automatically expands the time horizon beyond the acquisition point, offering you more opportunities to add value with your product, your company, and yourself. Value-added salespeople understand the buyer's needs from the moment these needs exist, up to and including complete need satisfaction. Thus, value-added salespeople have a cradle-to-grave view of the buyer's needs.

Value-Added Selling mirrors the process that buyers follow to make better long-range buying decisions. The Value-Added Selling Process begins with the salesperson developing an in-depth understanding of the buyer's needs, wants, and concerns. This insight into the buyer's priorities helps the salesperson view his or her solution as value received, not just value added. The process continues through the buyer's purchasing, receiving, using, and eventually disposing of the product that the salesperson is attempting to sell.

This expanded view of the sales process means that the salesperson's job is not limited to chasing new business and writing deals. It includes activities such as helping the buyer achieve smooth transitions, assuring customer satisfaction, maximizing product or service performance during usage and development, and fully leveraging the relationship.

Value-added salespeople define their role in broad terms. They wear many hats. One is business acquisition and development, but it's not the only hat. They specialize in customer satisfaction, logistics support, applications, expediting, disposal, transitions, and training, to name a few.

The way to become a value-added salesperson is to determine the path your buyer follows and seek ways to add value at every step along that path.

STRATEGIC OVERVIEW

During your study of the Critical Buying Path you learned that buyers' critical activities fall into one of three main stages or categories: Presale Planning, Acquisition/Transition, and Postsale Usage. As the buyer's needs evolve and expand throughout this process, the salesperson's role changes and evolves depending on where the buyer is. Value-added sales activities parallel and support the buying activities.

During planning, the buyer's greatest need is for information. The salesperson provides information. During acquisition, the buyer's greatest need is for smooth and seamless transitions. The salesperson assures a smooth transition. During usage, the customer's greatest need is for maximum performance and economy. The salesperson reinforces customer satisfaction by helping the customer achieve maximum performance and economy. See Figure 5.1, "The Value-Added Selling Process."

In the Presale Planning stage, the salesperson is in the *offensive* selling mode—the business acquisition mode. *Offensive* selling is pursuing new business. During the Acquisition/Transition and Postsale Usage stages, the salesperson is in the *defensive* selling mode—the business retention mode. *Defensive* selling is protecting, reinforcing, and growing existing business. Although defensive selling is not part of most sales training, it is a unique and critical part of Value-Added Selling. Every viable sales culture must have both dynamics at work—offensive and defensive selling.

Value-Added Selling is a blend of offensive and defensive selling strategies. Within these two selling modes, there are four major groups of sales strategies. While all of these strategies parallel the buyer's critical activities, the first two groups represent *offensive* selling, and the last two groups characterize *defensive* selling.

Focusing

Focusing is identifying viable sales opportunities, penetrating the account thoroughly, and "customer-izing," or developing an in-depth understanding of the buyer's needs. Analytical and diagnostic skills play an important role here, as the salesperson embarks on fact-finding missions and behind-the-scenes study and research.

FIGURE 5.1 The Value–Added Selling Process

Presale Planning (Information)	Acquisition/Transition (Smooth Transitions)	Postsale Usage (Economy and Productivity)
During Planning, the buyers' greatest need is for information. They study their needs, source a solution, and select the best alternative. Their critical activities include needs assessment, setting priorities and objectives, establishing budgets, etc.	During Acquisition/ Transition, the buyers' greatest need is for smooth, seamless, and painless transitions. Their critical activities include placing orders, receiving goods, redistribution, handling credits, returns, etc.	During Postsale Usage, the customers' greatest need is for maximum performance, productivity, and economy. Their critical activities include usage and disposal.

Offensive Selling Mode Pursuing new business		Defensive Selling Mode Protecting existing business	
Focusing	Persuading	Supporting	After-Marketing
Account Selection Account Penetration Customer-izing	Positioning Differentiating Presenting	Process Support Relationship Building	Tinkering Value Reinforcement Leveraging
During this phase of the sales process you identify viable sales opportuni- ties, qualify these opportunities, pen- etrate the accounts thoroughly, and develop an in-depth understanding of the customer's needs, wants, and concerns. You take this information and brainstorm a solution. *You're in the diagnosti- cian role.*	This is the phase of the sale where you polish your image, create distance between you and the competition, and convince the customer that your product or service is *the* value-added solution. *You're in the promoter role.*	During this phase of the sale you follow up to ensure that the customer expe- riences smooth transitions to your solution, receives special attention as needed, and builds strong relationship ties. *You're in a ser- vice and logistics support role.*	This is the sale- after-the-sale: the phase when you look for ways to continue to add value, get credit for what you do, and grow your business. You're an advocate for the customer and liaison for your company. You help monitor their inventory and usage. *You're in the growth mode.*

© 2018 Tom Reilly Training

Persuading

Persuading is a process of influencing, not arguing someone into submission. It is positioning—crafting an image of your total solution for the buyer, differentiating the solution, and presenting a compelling reason to buy. In focusing, the salesperson plays more of a diagnostic role; in persuading, the salesperson is more of an influencer.

Supporting

Once the buyer has placed the order and is waiting to receive the goods, the salesperson switches to defensive selling activities. Supporting, this third group of strategies, includes process support and relationship building. The salesperson's logistics skills and people skills play an important role at this stage of the Value-Added Selling Process.

After-Marketing

After-marketing, the fourth group of strategies, is the sale after the sale. It's defensive selling at its best. After-marketing includes tinkering, value reinforcement, and leveraging. This means looking for ways to re-create value for the customer, gaining recognition for the impact of your solution, and increasing your business with existing customers. The salesperson's follow-up, creativity, and initiative are instrumental at this point.

In the course of the Value-Added Selling Process, the salesperson evolves from diagnostician to influencer to expediter to customer satisfaction specialist. Your activities parallel your customer's activities. This is customer-oriented selling at its best. Before determining your next step, you must first determine where your customer is in the buying and selling process.

THE CRITICAL SALES PATH

Value-Added Selling involves offensive and defensive selling strategies. The blend of these two groups of strategies is a key differentiator for this sales philosophy. The Value-Added Selling Process describes the 11 strategies that value-added salespeople employ to design and deliver value-added solutions for their customers. It is the *what* they must do to advance the sale. The Critical Sales Path (CSP) is the sequence of steps that value-added salespeople take to execute the 11 strategies. It is *how* they must execute to advance the sale, the activities (behaviors) that drive the sales process along the CBP.

Our definitions of *strategy* and *tactics* will clarify this for you. *Strategy* is an aerial view of the sales process, and *tactics* are the ground-level activities that support the strategies. The following examples add additional clarity.

Account selection is strategy number one. The strategy question that the value-added salesperson answers is, "Am I chasing the right business?" The tactical side of this includes writing a definition of a high-value target account, compiling a list of these account characteristics, adding names to this list, and confirming that this account meets the selection criteria.

Account penetration is strategy number two. The strategy question that the value-added salesperson answers is, "Am I talking to all the right people?" The tactical side of this includes compiling a list of decision makers and influencers, finding others who can refer people to them, using social profiles to identify contacts, securing appointments, meeting with them, understanding their priorities, and so on.

Customer-izing is strategy number three. The strategy question that the value-added salesperson answers is, "Do I understand my customer's needs, wants, and fears?" The tactical side of this includes making a list of questions for each level of decision maker, interviewing different people, doing behind-the-scenes research, and so on.

Positioning is strategy number four. The strategy question that the value-added salesperson answers is, "Am I projecting the image of a value-added supplier?" The tactical side of this includes describing on paper what image the salesperson wants to project, collecting materials that support this image, surrounding the customer with this image, and so on.

Differentiation is strategy number five. The strategy question that the value-added salesperson answers is, "Have I differentiated our status as a value-added supplier?" The tactical side of this includes describing on paper the differentiating image that the salesperson wants to project, collecting materials that support this image, surrounding the customer with this image, and so on.

Presenting is strategy number six. The strategy question that the value-added salesperson answers is, "How compelling is my argument for our solution?" The tactical side of this includes preparing a sales message that mirrors the customer's needs, preparing a presentation that maximizes the perceived value of the solution, creating examples of performance value, and designing proof sources that have merit with the customer.

Supporting is strategy number seven. The strategy question that the value-added salesperson answers is, "How painless have we made it for the customer to implement our solution?" The tactical side of this includes order confirmation, expediting shipments, introducing cross-functional teams, and so on.

Relationship building is strategy number eight. The strategy question that the value-added salesperson answers is, "How is my personal and professional relationship with the customer?" The tactical side of this includes trust-building activities like consistent follow-up, listening more than talking on sales calls, delivering on promises, appropriate entertainment, and so on.

Tinkering is strategy number nine. The strategy question that the value-added salesperson answers is, "Are we working as hard to keep the business as we did to secure the business?" The tactical side of this includes identifying barriers to world-class service, monitoring the viability of one's solution, seeking ways to improve the product, and so on.

Value reinforcement is strategy number ten. The strategy question that the value-added salesperson answers is, "Are we getting credit for all of our value added?" The tactical side of this includes preparing no-charge invoices, conducting regular performance reviews, asking value-reminding questions, and so on.

Leveraging is strategy number eleven. The strategy question that the value-added salesperson answers is, "Are we maximizing our value?" This means contributing and extracting the most value to and from this relationship. The tactical side of this includes identifying new opportunities to create value, studying the buyer's inventory needs, asking for referrals, and so on.

The CSP also serves as a coaching guide for managers. The strategic questions for each of these 11 strategies provide a framework to conduct opportunity reviews. You will see these questions at the beginning of each chapter in Part II. Connecting tactics to these strategic questions will add focus and purpose to the salesperson's activities.

VALUE-ADDED SELLING REVIEW AND ACTION POINTS

1. Buyers advance through various steps in planning, acquiring, and using a product or service. This Critical Buying Path offers you a model for adding value. Your Value-Added Selling Process should parallel your buyer's buying path.

2. Your sales activities are divided into two modes: offensive and defensive selling. Offensive selling is pursuing new business, while defensive selling is protecting and growing existing business.

3. The Critical Sales Path is the tactical application of the Value-Added Selling Process. It is the step-by-step approach of your sales activities that drives the sale forward with a series of small wins.

CHAPTER 6

The Psychology of Price Shopping

For the past five years, we have invested our professional study time in the emerging field of neuromarketing. This fascinating field is the nexus of neuroscience, marketing, behavioral economics, and psychology. Researchers have been mapping the human brain to gain deeper understanding of humans' perceptual and cognitive processes. One of the outcomes is a better understanding of the decision-making process. For salespeople, this insight is vital to understanding how customers make decisions.

A traditional view of economic decision making is that humans are calculating machines that seek to maximize the utility of their outcomes. Yet, humans persist in making decisions that fall short of their expected utilities. Some other force must be at work. That force is human nature.

Richard Thaler, professor of behavioral science and economics at the University of Chicago Booth School of Management and co-author of *Nudge: Improving Decisions About Health, Wealth, and Happiness*, explains that humans lack the mechanical structure and predictability of robotic calculating machines. Humans do not lack the capacity to make rational decisions, but they do not spend a lot of time thinking about their decision-making process. Though Thaler represents the best of contemporary thought, his comments reflect a seventeenth-century scientist and thinker, Blaise Pascal, who said, "The heart has reasons that reason cannot understand."

Humans operate as feeling and thinking systems within the subjectivity of their personal experiences and the stark objective reality of their world. This dualism of emotion and reason explains human behavior. It even explains why and how sometimes really smart people make dumb decisions. In his book *Predictably Irrational*, Dan Ariely writes that while standard economics shows that human beings are rational, we are often far less rational in our decision making. We have found in our work that buyers often make predictably irrational decisions, especially when it comes to price. That's what this chapter is all about.

To navigate the choppy waters filled with price-sensitive buyers, you must understand what drives buyers' behavior and how they make decisions. Armed with this information, you have a fighting chance. Will you convert all price shoppers to value-added buyers? No. Will you convert some? Yes. The information you receive in the next few pages will help you with your conversion rate.

At the end of this chapter, you will be able to:

- Describe the internal and external forces that help shape decisions
- Discuss the specific characteristics of price shoppers
- Name ways you can change the conversation with price shoppers to guide it down a path of value and not price

THE PSYCHOLOGY OF DECISION MAKING

After studying scores of textbooks, journal articles, and scientific studies, we have come to this conclusion: humans are pleasure-seeking, pain-avoiding, cognitively biased, emotional, and irrational decision makers that prefer simple, surefire solutions that generally result in trade-offs. Like all motivated behavior, buying decisions are the result of dynamic internal and external forces acting on the individual. Internal forces include emotional and cognitive dynamics. Sometimes these are referred to as affective and deliberative forces, respectively. Emotional forces excite as cognitive forces assess. This dual process network of emotion (feeling) and cognition (thinking) ideally works together in an integrated way, acknowledging the reality (context) in which the decision maker operates and respecting the subjectivity of the individual's emotions. Here is what we know about humans:

- **Humans are pleasure-seekers.** They love pleasure and hate pain. Because pain is a more powerful motivator than gain, people work harder to avoid pain than to pursue a gain. Along the same lines, losses loom heavier than gains. People have a bias for certainty. They prefer a bird in the hand to the two in the bush. Accordingly, people forgo potentially bigger future gains for a certain immediate gain. Additionally, people risk bigger potential losses to avoid a sure-thing immediate loss. Even if the gain is small and certain, they will take the immediate gain. Even if the long-term losses are greater, they will risk absorbing those long-term losses against the certainty of the immediate, known smaller loss.
- **Negative emotions are powerful.** They are a more powerful source of energy than positive emotions because they have greater operational value. Consequently, memories for negative events are stronger than memories for positive events. This plays an important role in survival of the species. It is more important to recognize and recall threats than to remember the tastiest berry on the tree.
- **Humans run on autopilot most of the time.** They make automatic decisions 85 to 90 percent of the time. Automatic decisions are driven by emotions. In the hierarchy of emotions, fear is at the top of the list. Fear is the most powerful motivator, and the greatest fear is of the unknown. Fear is so powerful that it even trumps greed. Buyers are more concerned with making a mistake than they are with getting it right.
- **Humans have a status quo bias.** They like things to remain fairly stable. Change is uncomfortable, but people must adapt to change to survive. Often, they resist. It is not so much that people hate change, but rather that they dislike being changed. Change that emanates from within is a more powerful source of energy.
- **Humans are social creatures.** They depend on others for learning and safety. One of the most fundamental human emotions is the need to fit in—to be a part of something greater than self. This is one reason that social media is

growing in popularity. Anyone can go online and validate his or her point of view by appealing to like-minded individuals.

- **People like the idea of choice but dislike choosing.** Consequently, they use mental shortcuts called heuristics. Humans are wired for simplicity. It is more efficient for the brain to make quick decisions that require little processing. This is why buyers use heuristics. A cheap price, as a decision variable, is an example of the mental shorthand. Contrast, novelty, past experiences, and so on provide the decision maker with a quick and efficient decision-making process.

- **Humans have a temporal bias for "now."** For most people, immediate gratification takes too long. This, coupled with a bias for certainty, makes it difficult for people to appreciate fully the long-term benefits of a proposal. Centuries before the advent of neuroscience, Adam Smith wrote, "The pleasure which we are to enjoy ten years hence interests so little in comparison with that which we may enjoy today." This is why the small-wins approach is so effective when proposing new ideas to customers. In this approach, you present an immediate, doable course of action that results in a short-term gain.

- **Humans have an arbitrary sense of fairness.** This colors their perception of equity. What may seem fair to one person can be perceived as patently unfair by another person.

- **Decision biases affect choice.** As you read in a previous chapter, some people maximize and choose the best possible alternative; other people satisfice (settle) for something merely acceptable.

- **Perception matters.** Some people process their realities with a big-picture view. Others process their realities with a detailed view. This accounts for some people being able to process multiple variables at once and understand the dynamic relationship among these variables.

- **People are stuck on their own ideas.** People value their discoveries, insights, and ideas more than what they are told and sold. People care more about their motives to decide than your motives for them to decide. This is called confirmation bias, and people gravitate toward information that confirms what they already believe.

No one makes decisions in a vacuum; people make decisions in the broader context of their world. The internal forces of emotion and cognition operate within the decision maker. The decision maker lives and decides in the context of a bigger world. Contextual factors are external to the individual, influencing the outcome of the decision. In business, there is no escaping these external forces. To fully understand the buyer's needs, wants, and fears, salespeople must understand the context in which buyers make decisions—the incentives and pressures that they face. Their decision-making climate can have a profound effect on the buyer and his or her choice.

THE PSYCHOLOGY OF PRICE SHOPPERS

The central fallacy of price shopping is that a cheap price is the best price. To paraphrase renowned economist Henry Hazlitt, assuming that a cheap price is sufficient to achieve overall cost effectiveness is the same illusion that adding water to milk creates more milk. As most salespeople know, oftentimes a cheap price is too big a cost to bear.

Much of what we wrote about shoppers in general applies to price shoppers in particular. There are three areas that demand closer scrutiny: temporal bias, tunnel vision, and viability. Your understanding of these three areas will help you have better conversations with your customers and make better seller decisions.

Short-Termism

Short-termism is a chronic cognitive bias. And it's been that way for a while. Instant gratification has its roots in the garden of Eden when Adam succumbed to temptation and accepted a bite of the forbidden fruit. In 1936, noted economist John Maynard Keynes observed that investor time horizons were "three months or a year hence."[1] Day traders have invaded the stock markets, motivated by their short-term view of the financial markets. A 2017 article in the *Economist* describes a McKinsey and Company study that found 73 percent of corporations are short-termists.[2]

Price shoppers are short-term thinkers. They have a temporal bias for immediacy. They live in the here and now. The expediency of the present drives their decisions. This means they focus on acquisition versus ownership costs. In Critical Buying Path terms, they are stuck in the first phase—the Presale Planning phase. Fear and greed play a major role in this decision. Fear causes people to play defense—to hoard and hunker down. Fear of missing a buying opportunity drives some to opt for a cheap price. Fear of making a mistake by overpaying is another consideration. People have finite resources and cannot afford to squander them on unequitable outcomes. The fear of being taken advantage of raises a trust concern.

Delay discounting is the study of impulsivity and certainty as they relate to perceived loss and gain. There is an emotional tendency for people to opt for a lesser, more certain, more immediate reward than to wait for a larger, less certain, longer-term gain. It is the opposite of delayed gratification: The longer you must wait for the reward, the more you discount its value. People value a gain that is certain more than a gain that is less certain, even if it is bigger. For salespeople, this means that the price difference between your product and that of your competition is a known, short-term gain. The value of the long-term gain of your solution is less certain, and hence less desirable, even if it's bigger than the discount difference between you and the competition.

To illustrate this to seminar participants, we employ a simple take-the-money-and-run game with attendees. We offer them the choice of $1,000 cash today or $1,200 in one year. That is a 20 percent gain over one year. This is far better than any reasonable investment people can make. Over 90 percent of the people to whom we offer this take the money and run because it is now and certain. This is one reason why buyers are seduced by discounts.

Loss aversion also plays a role. People fear a certain loss so much that they will take higher future risks to avoid a known, short-term loss. This is the logic behind people continuing to put money in a slot machine. Their inner dialog goes something like this: "I can't afford to walk away now. I've lost too much to get up right now. I'll put a few more dollars in the machine to see if I can regain my loss." If your price is higher, the price difference between you and the competition is perceived as a certain loss. The buyer views paying more as a loss.

So, the buyer will forgo a potentially bigger, future gain (your value added) to avoid the certain, immediate loss.

Another way to view loss aversion is opportunity cost. Opportunity cost represents the indirect costs and missed opportunities when one chooses a course of action. Buyers often view the price difference between one seller and another as an opportunity cost and ask themselves, "What other ways could we spend or invest that money if we did not choose the more expensive alternative?" Those forgone alternatives are the opportunity costs of the more expensive alternative. What price shoppers fail to acknowledge is that there is an opportunity cost for purchasing a cheaper alternative with less value. By choosing the cheaper alternative, they forgo all of the value that the more expensive and better alternative offers. They forgo the opportunity to capture that value. This is "opportunity value."

Discounts are often presented and viewed as deals. Deals trigger an addiction-like rush in people. It is the stuff of which feeding frenzies and bargain hunting are made. Deals trigger a scarcity response in people. Their inner dialog may sound like this: "If I don't act now, I'll miss out on a great deal." Fear and greed working together are a formidable foe.

Price Shopper Tunnel Vision

Tunnel vision describes a condition characterized by a narrow field of view, limited peripheral vision, or a single-minded concentration on one thing. People demonstrating tunnel vision have a constricted point of view and focus exclusively on a single point. They are often described as having a one-track mind. It's easy to see how price shoppers can fall into this pattern. They narrowly focus on a single issue when purchasing: price.

Though it sounds like a visual defect, we are really describing a cognitive bias. Price shoppers choose to focus narrowly on this single issue to the exclusion of other, relevant concerns. This means they oversimplify needs, narrowly define purchasing success, and value-strip solutions. Small thinking about their needs characterizes their decision process. They fail to consider comprehensive needs and the totality of a solution. This one-dimensional buying decision frustrates sellers and deprives the buyer's organization of a total solution.

Another way to view this narrow-minded thinking is that the buyers are claiming that there is nothing special about their needs or situation because they are willing to settle for a generic or commodity-type solution. An effective response to this mindset is, "Mr. Buyer, I'm sure there are some salespeople who will tell you there is nothing special about your situation and attempt to sell you a one-size-fits-all solution, but that's not us. We believe every customer we deal with is special and demands that type of attention. Therefore, we create solutions that fit the customer, not shape the customer's situation to fit the product."

This policy may be directed by upper management, constricted by limited funds, or misguided strategy by purchasing agents who believe this is a way to cut costs. Organizational silos account for some of the behavior as well. When purchasing fails to communicate with others in the organization, buyers lack insight into the impact of their decisions. Our research shows that one-in-six shoppers fit this one-dimensional buying paradigm. These are price shoppers—those who consider price only as their primary decision variable. They ignore or underrate the layers of value that sellers offer. More important, they undervalue their total organizational needs.

Price Shopper Aggravation and Viability

The third characteristic of price shoppers is that the aggravation factor in dealing with them is higher. They complain more. They return goods more often. They pay late. Is this the foundation you want to build your business on? We submit that selling to price shoppers is like being bitten to death by ducks. Every quack represents another concession they demand from their sellers. It pays to remember the old saying, "If it walks like a duck, looks like a duck, and quacks like a duck, it's probably a duck." The challenge for salespeople is to take a longer-range view of the customer and consider the whole relationship. They need to ask themselves, "Is this a viable opportunity?"

CHANGING THE CONVERSATION

Are salespeople doomed to succumb to price shoppers? No. You can have better conversations with buyers and even redirect some of them down the path of value versus price. Will it work in every situation? No. It will work some of the time, and that makes the effort worthwhile. There are three things you can do to change this conversation.

Sell the Concept

Earlier you read that Value-Added Selling is a conceptual sale. A conceptual sale represents a fundamentally different way of viewing and doing things. A product sale is more concrete, sensory, and tangible. A conceptual sale is more abstract, cognitive, and intangible. Conceptual selling is arguing a case much bigger and more fundamental than a mere product. It means selling a new idea, an emerging technology, a partnership, or a better way to do something. In most cases, it is selling the first step of change, and most people are uncomfortable with change, especially one-dimensional buyers. You are challenging them to think in terms bigger than their one-dimensional focal point.

The types of concepts that value-added salespeople sell include taking a longer-range view of things, considering a broader view of the impact of a decision on an organization, and understanding the total cost of acquiring and owning something. Adam Smith gave us a preview of this thinking a couple of centuries ago in his *Wealth of Nations*: "The real price of everything, what everything really costs to the man who wants to acquire it, is the toil and trouble of acquiring it." We would add that the real price includes ownership and disposal of something that the buyer is considering. Further, total cost is the real cost of any commodity. Price is a transactional product feature. Total cost includes acquisition, ownership, usage, and disposal. Price shoppers make short-term, one-dimensional, product-feature decisions.

There are many other concepts that salespeople sell, but our focus at this point is to help buyers make long-term, comprehensive buying decisions that maximize the value of the solution they receive from sellers. The most expedient way to do this is to employ the small-wins strategy that you read about in Chapter 3. This is the *immediate next best outcome* approach. When asking the other person to consider something new, break down that acceptance into the immediate, next best outcome. Ask yourself this question: "What is the most immediate, next best outcome this person must achieve to move toward the ultimate goal?"

This could include a discussion of the long-term consequences of a decision, designing an impact statement for how the decision will affect the rest of the organization, agreeing to a cross-functional team meeting to introduce all the players to each other, touring the seller's facilities to demonstrate logistics support, and so on.

Once you have established the immediate, next best outcome and the buyer agrees to it, take yes for an answer. This means accept the progress you are making. Change is a slower process than most salespeople desire. Accept this and work with the system, not against it.

Stretch the Time Horizon

You have read multiple times in this book that price shoppers are short-term thinkers. Encouraging them to think and plan longer term is a conceptual sale and a prerequisite for their making a value-added buying decision. Short-term conversations with buyers include topics like price, compliance to product specs, inbound logistics, and payment options. Long-term conversations include topics like total cost, usage of the product, transformation into value, return on investment, and replacement. Changing this conversation into a long-term discussion is a two-step process.

Step one is to ask questions that cause the buyer to think long term. Here is a sample list of these types of questions:

- If you were to fast-forward a year or two from now, what would cause you to say that you made a great decision to partner with us for this project?
- What does success look like on this project?
- Would you please walk me through your project start to finish?
- Once implemented, what are your long-term concerns for this project?
- What return are you seeking on your investment?
- Long term, how do you see us creating value for you?
- How do you see this contributing to your long-term growth, efficiency, and profitability?

Step two is to stretch the time horizon by demonstrating how you help them long term. Present long-term solutions. For example, you could demonstrate how you will help them plan, implement, and capture the most value from your solution. In planning your approach, ask these questions.

- How do we help the customer plan and design the right solution?
- How do we help the customer implement, install, or adapt our solution?
- How do we help the customer capture the most value from our solution?

You will notice that your answers to these questions walk the buyer down the Critical Buying Path. Buyers' acknowledgment of their Critical Buying Path is a small win and a big step on your journey to help them make a better, value-added buying decision.

Enlarge the Discussion

Humans are biased for simplicity. Even though humans have the mental capacity to make complex computations, they still prefer simple decisions. To paraphrase Barry Schwartz, who wrote *The Paradox of Choice*, we like the idea of choice, but we just hate choosing. This bias for simplicity plays a role in tunnel vision. One-dimensional decisions are simpler. Enlarging the discussion beyond a single decision variable paves the way for your broader discussion of your total value. This process includes three steps.

Step one is to penetrate the account fully. This is Value-Added Selling strategy number two. Talk to a lot of people. Engage multiple influencers and decision makers. Make sure their agendas are included in the final decision. Be the information hub. When you possess this clearinghouse of information, you can infuse your presentation with relevant organizational value for the buyer.

Step two is to ask questions that call into play other decision variables. Price shoppers are small thinkers. They oversimplify their needs and value-strip buying alternatives to the core-commodity, naked product. This means they settle for something just good enough to get by. Use the need-satisfaction model of selling to enlarge the conversation about their needs, and then you can present your solution. For example, ask questions that cause the buyer to think bigger:

- Can you describe the full scope of this problem?
- Who all is affected by this problem?
- What is the full impact of this problem on your organization?
- How do you define value on this project?
- Beyond the product, what do you need from your partners?
- What are your mission-critical issues for this project?
- What is your greatest concern on this project?
- What is your total cost for this project?
- How do you assign cost throughout your life cycle on this project?
- How would this help you better serve your market?
- How would a broader partnership with our company help you swell your bottom line?

Once you have enlarged the discussion on the buyer's needs, expand your discussion of benefits. Once again, you sell a three-dimensional solution: product, company, and you. Answer these three questions in your presentation:

- Why this product?
- Why our company?
- Why me?

In your attempt to change the conversation, you will discover that selling conceptually, stretching the time horizon, and enlarging the discussion are three intertwined strategies. Selling conceptually often involves a long-term perspective and broader field of view.

VALUE-ADDED SELLING REVIEW AND ACTION ITEMS

1. Humans are pleasure-seeking, pain-avoiding, cognitively biased, emotional, and irrational decision makers that prefer simple, surefire solutions that generally result in trade-offs. Humans operate as feeling and thinking systems within the subjectivity of their personal experiences and stark objective reality of their worlds. This dualism of emotion and reason explains human behavior. Knowing this helps you understand the buyer as a person who is trying to reconcile this dualism.

2. Price shoppers are characterized by their short-termism. They operate in the here and now. They are also characterized by their tunnel vision—their tendency to simplify their decisions to a single variable, price. We have determined that the aggravation factor of dealing with price shoppers is high. They complain more, return goods more frequently, and pay late. These characteristics contain the seed of the solution for selling to them.

3. You can successfully change the conversation with price shoppers by selling conceptually, stretching the time horizon, and enlarging the discussion. Often these three strategies work in concert to help buyers make better, long-term, value-added decisions.

CHAPTER 7

Customer Messaging

You've got eight seconds and 31 words to grab the buyer's attention! You have 10 minutes—at most—to make your best case.

We live in an ADD chaotic world. We get news in sound bites, consume fast food, and read book summaries. We fly coast-to-coast at 500 miles per hour, communicate globally in real time, and run the mile in three minutes and forty-three seconds. We text and drive, gas and go, and eat on the run. We do everything fast. We are a distracted and hyperactive culture.

These distractions cost U.S. businesses a whopping $650 billion annually in lost productivity. People experience 56 interruptions per day, spend 28 percent of their days dealing with these interruptions, switch activities every three minutes, and face a minimum 600 marketing exposures every day.[1] The noise level in the buyer's head is deafening. All of that is your competition.

Marketing is more than a department; it's every way you communicate with your customers. It includes brochures, ads, websites, trade-show booths, journal articles, social media presence, how your folks answer phones, how your drivers drive (especially if your name and logo are on the company vehicle), the look of your proposals, your packaging, the look of your invoices, point-of-sale pieces, and so on.

This chapter is about your communications with customers. It's about how you shape your message for specific customers, the documentation you need to support this message, and the campaign you design to surround customers with your value story.

At the end of this chapter, you will be able to:

• Define customer messaging

- Discuss why it's important to launch a customer messaging campaign
- Identify and list your value added
- Design collateral support materials to communicate your value
- Communicate your value through social media
- Incorporate the buyer's pain proposition into your messaging

WHAT IS CUSTOMER MESSAGING

Customer messaging is the ongoing conversation you have with your customers. It's the *what* and *how* you communicate. Customer messaging is the marketing side of sales. It is your planned communications campaign. Controlling these conversations for customer interface is vital to your marketing and sales efforts. A breakdown in communications confuses and frustrates customers. Consistency is key. It's imperative that everyone involved in customer communications understands and communicates the same message.

Your marketing department could spend millions of dollars to position a brand, and with a single confused sales presentation or imprudent discount, you negate that branding effort. Customer messaging must be strategic and coordinated. When it is properly designed and executed, this campaign preps the battlefield of the customer's mind for your sales efforts.

Using the ideas in this chapter will result in message clarity, congruence, and synergy. The focus will be tactical (field level), customer-centric message campaigns. Ongoing, multiple exposures make up your campaign. The outcome of these planned and managed conversations is to surround customers with compelling messages of value.

Once you're clear on the value-added messages you want customers to hear, you can take these messages to the market. How you broadcast these messages is limited only by the edge of your imagination. Here are some examples of how companies surround customers with their messages of value: printed messages on invoices, recorded phone messages, web-based communications, trade journal ads, customer bills of rights, awards brochures, shipping documentation, e-mail blitzes, case studies, value worksheets, and sharing social media content. To begin your campaign, you must be clear on your value added.

VALUE ADDED

Let's begin with a definition of value added. According to the U.S. Department of Commerce, value added is the difference between raw material input and finished product output.[2] On a practical level, it's everything you do to something from the moment you buy it, sell it, and service it. Value added is both quantitative and qualitative.

Quantitative value added is easy to sink your teeth into and to get your arms around. It's visible, tangible, observable, measurable, objective, quantifiable, substantive, and performance based. It stands on its own merits. You can attach a dollar value to it.

It's what you *do* for the customer. It includes cost containment, increased market share, greater efficiency, and competitive gain. Your toll-free phone number, personalized delivery, customer training programs, extended warranty, replacement parts, and 24-hour maintenance have quantifiable gain for the buyer. Quantitative value makes it easier to sell your solution.

Qualitative value added is more difficult to get your arms around. Compared with quantitative value added, it's more subjective and intangible—not easily measured. It offers more style than substance, perceived and felt, but not quite as objective. Some people call it soft-dollar value because it makes the buyer feel good about your product, your company, and you. It's more of who you *are* than what you *do*.

Qualitative value added describes the number of locations and the facilities available to the buyer, the management philosophy of your company, the goodwill you've created with customers, the product's brand name, your company's reputation, your company's depth and breadth of resources, the number of years your company has been in business, your knowledge as a salesperson, and how your stuff looks when it arrives.

While quantitative value added stands on its own merits, qualitative value added implies a benefit. Qualitative value added produces a warm and fuzzy feeling for buyers. They view qualitative value added as a security blanket or cushion. It enables them to get a good night's sleep. What's that worth? Customers know it's important, but they may find it difficult to nail down. To paraphrase a customer's quote in our survey, it is the look and feel of things. Qualitative value gets people excited about your solution; it builds expectations. Quantitative value satisfies the customer's more tangible needs; it performs for the customer.

Your Value Audit

One method for determining your value added is to study all three dimensions of value: your product, your company, and you. First, in addition to its perceived value, what is your product's impact value on the customer? Identify the impact of your value by considering how your product enhances or improves the following for the customer: profitability, operational efficiency, productivity, performance, quality, safety, ease of use, waste reduction, uptime, durability, consistency, reliability, operating costs, warranty, serviceability, convenience, compliance to specifications, and timeliness, to name a few.

How does your product add value to your customer's product? Does this product synergy increase competitiveness, attractiveness, and end-user acceptance? How do customers perceive your product, as an investment or an expense? Our BSP results tell us that the product is 57 percent of the reason why buyers choose an alternative.

Second, separate from the product dimension, what value added does your company offer the customer? Make a list of the value added your company provides. This list contains both quantitative and qualitative value added. It includes literature, reputation, industry leadership, facilities, technical support, location, systems, depth and breadth of inventory levels, shipping policies, ordering options, ease of doing business, distribution channels, field support, online support, electronic commerce, free delivery, hours of operation, customer loyalty programs, disposal, trade-in policy, and so on.

Third, the next dimension of value is you—what you do for the customer. The easiest way for you to arrive at your value added is to refer to the Value-Added Selling Process explained in Chapter 5 and determine how you add value at each step along the path.

In the Presale Planning stage, for instance, you may add value by conducting an in-depth needs analysis, providing a live demonstration of your product, studying the buyer's needs and brainstorming a solution, locating hard-to-find items for the buyer, and submitting a professional proposal.

In the Acquisition/Transition stage, you may add value by assuring smooth, painless, and seamless transitions to your product. Your value-added activities could include confirming order status, expediting, tracking back orders, providing training for employees, following the supply chain, and helping with credits and returns.

In the Postsale Usage stage, you add value by following up to assure maximum performance and economy from your product. This postsale support, coupled with helping customers' businesses grow, will differentiate you from all other salespeople with whom your customers meet. Present this chronology of value added as an example of how your support parallels customers' needs.

A second method for determining your value added is illustrated in the above example. Study your solution from the customer's Critical Buying Path. How does your solution (all three dimensions of value) support the customer and add value at every step along the way?

A third method for determining your value added is a freestyle brainstorming exercise. To begin this exercise, make a list of all the value added you offer your customer. Write down as many as you can think of. Go for quantity. You can always revise and edit. This includes the quantitative (what you do for customers) and qualitative value (who you are). Seek input from different disciplines in your company. Each discipline and employee brings a unique source of value to the customer. You can include your customers in this exercise too. Survey them to determine which value-added services contribute the most to their bottom lines. You may find some surprises here. This menu of value added describes a feast for the buyer.

CUSTOMER MESSAGING TOOLS

There are a number of tools that you can use to surround the customer with your message of value. The following list contains some of the more common ways we have seen salespeople and their companies communicate their value to customers. Your company's website plays a major role in communicating value. There is an entire discipline in marketing today that is dedicated to analyzing the content of your communications. Sales and marketing must work together to create the most relevant information customers want and the most powerful messages to communicate your value-added position in the marketplace. Here are some examples to use in your messaging campaign.

The VIP List

The primary use of this information from your value audit is to construct a VIP (value in purchasing) list. The VIP list is made up of all the information from the previous exercises. It is *the* fundamental selling tool for value-added salespeople and your first customer messaging tool. The VIP list is a menu of your value, an inventory of what makes you special, and a portfolio of assets. Think about that last word—assets. Isn't that what partners bring to relationships?

You use this list to communicate your total value to the buyer. You could turn this compilation into a brochure, a handout on your company letterhead, a website page, a sheet in your proposals, or a collateral literature piece to combat price objections.

One salesperson uses this list as a supplier performance appraisal. Twice a year, he audits his company's performance against the VIP list to ensure that the customer receives all the value on the back end that he promised on the front end.

Another salesperson gives the VIP list to his buyer to use as an internal sales piece to sell others in the buyer's company on the salesperson's value added. He had discovered that his internal champion did a better job of selling for him when armed with a support piece explaining his company's value added.

One salesperson conducted a value audit and presented his findings as a list of 30 value-added extras to her best customers. She asked these loyal customers, "Which of these are most important to you?" She then trimmed the list to 10 and it became her VIP list. When attracting new customers that look a lot like her existing customers, this list comes in handy for communicating her value. It's already been field tested by her best customers.

Managers can use this VIP list as a training tool. One of our clients conducts a VIP list exercise every January to ensure his sales force understands the depth and breadth of his company's value added. He begins with a blank flipchart page, and his salespeople fill that page and several others with examples of their value added during the sales meeting. This is one way to keep his salespeople focused on their total solution. Also, it's a great tool to use with new hires to cut their learning curve for the company's value-added solution and to brace them for handling price resistance. The only limitation to your using the VIP list is the edge of your imagination. There are as many ways to use this list as there are salespeople.

The Elevator Speech

The elevator speech has been around for so long in sales that it is largely attributed to Anonymous. Salespeople have used this simple messaging technique to get appointments, networking events, website content, getting past gatekeepers, and opening sales conversations with customers. Like the VIP list, the only thing that limits your use is the edge of your imagination.

There are varying opinions of what makes up an elevator speech, and we prefer a simple format that meets our criteria for 31 words or less. You want this to be a quick attention-getter. Anything that is too long loses the buyer's attention. In as few words as possible, answer these three questions:

- Who are we?
- What do we do?
- To whom do we sell?

Here are a couple of examples.

Franklin Scientific is a full-line distributor of laboratory supplies and equipment. The primary markets we serve are universities, biotech, clinical labs, pharmaceutical, R&D, and government laboratories. (26 words)

Tom Reilly Training specializes in teaching salespeople and their managers how to compete aggressively and profitably based on their total value, not price. (23 words)

In both cases, these elevator speeches would encourage the buyer to ask, "How?" That's the point. They are interest-generating, simple explanations of what companies do. Now, compare that with this elevator speech.

Hays technology is a global partner in the content-analysis industry offering analytics in a cohesive and integrated methodology to maximize innovative design parameters that produce valuable outcomes for our client partners that seek to understand the clickstream activity of online buyers of multiple applied technologies. We know that in theory, theory and practice are the same, but in practice they are not, so we pursue pragmatic adaptations of complex data sets and simplify them into simple and coherent solutions. (79 words)

Huh? The really sad part is that someone in marketing communications must approve of something like this. Remember, humans are wired for simplicity.

The Customer Bill of Rights

The third customer messaging tool is the customer bill of rights. This is the experience you plan to deliver to your customers and an important part of your messaging campaign. It's the promise you make, your covenant with customers. Promises influence expectations. Customer expectations play a major role in customer satisfaction.

All employees must be clear on these promises since they help create customer expectations. How your employees deliver on these expectations affect customer satisfaction. Having a clear standard for serving customers and communicating its importance internally is the first step in this process. You can create this with a customer bill of rights. The customer bill of rights answers this question: What six things do our customers have a right to expect when doing business with our company?

Here is a sample bill of rights constructed by the employees of a small manufacturing company in Southeast Missouri.

> Our customers have a right to expect a quality product and prompt service.
>
> Our customers have a right to expect accuracy in our quoting and our billing.
>
> Our customers have a right to expect knowledgeable salespeople with no hassles.
>
> Our customers have a right to expect strong technical support on the back end.
>
> Our customers have a right to expect us to do it right the first time, every time.
>
> Signed,
> The Employees of XYZ Company

Unique Selling Proposition

The fourth customer messaging tool is the unique selling proposition (USP). The history of the USP goes back to World War II America. An advertising agency in New York City coined the expression. The USP also has been referred to as the *Big Idea*. It is the one thing that you can lay claim to that no one else in the market or industry can say. The USP is your bragging rights. What is different about your customer experience from the rest of the market? It is the outstanding difference that makes you stand out in your market. This difference must be unique, specific, compelling, and defendable by you. The clearer your USP, the easier it is for the buyer to see the difference between you and the competition. Answering these questions will help you to determine your USP:

- We were the first to . . .
- We are the only ones that . . .
- Customers tell us we're unique because . . .

Value Proposition

The fifth customer messaging tool is the value proposition. After conducting a value audit and listing your value added, creating a customer bill of rights, and studying your uniqueness, you are probably developing a sense of pride and clarity of the full impact you have on the customer's world. This impact or downline outcome of your customer experience is your value proposition. It's the long-range impact of your value-added solution on the customer. It is a clear statement of the tangible results customers experience as a consequence of partnering with you. It is the end result of the customer's using all of the value added on your VIP list, enjoying the experience outlined on the customer bill of rights, and appreciating your uniqueness. Getting the value proposition right and communicating it clearly to customers is the number one goal for customer messaging. Our internal research shows that only 46 percent of salespeople understand clearly their value proposition.

Do you know the full impact of your value added on the customer? These are some examples of value propositions. The timeline implicit in each of these demonstrates downline value:

- Helping customers *play bigger* than they are
- Helping customers better serve and satisfy their customers
- Helping customers achieve economic gain (greater profitability)
- Giving customers access to global markets
- Helping customers differentiate themselves in their markets
- Helping customers excel at what they do
- Enhancing their purchasing power
- Adding value to the quality of the customer's product

The first step in constructing your value proposition is to identify the different segments you serve. You cannot be all things to all people. Those suppliers that try end up being nothing special to anyone.

Companies segment customers using different parameters depending on their purposes: demographics, psychographics, geographic location, and even SIC classification. For our purposes in customer messaging, we define a segment as a group of customers with similar needs—either complex or simple. Customers with simple needs expect little more than price and availability from suppliers. Customers with complex needs demand greater value added from their suppliers. Our use of the value proposition even includes different levels of decision makers in an organization. One level of decision maker may define a successful outcome in logistics terms, while another may define success as a product that is easier for salespeople to sell. The tighter your definition of the buyer segment to whom you're selling, the more compelling your value proposition.

Though value propositions identify customer segments, they also describe specific opportunities you pursue. Value propositions are marketing tools that salespeople use tactically. Your value proposition varies by segment, customer, and opportunity. As you will read in Chapters 9 and 27, value propositions vary by level of decision maker. Purchasing may seek a value proposition that reflects logistics concerns. Operations may seek a value proposition that reflects manufacturing ease. Sales and marketing may want a value proposition that makes it easier to take their product to market. Value propositions are as broad as market segments and as specific as individuals.

Once you've clarified your value proposition, prepare a formal statement to use in your customer messaging campaign: sales letters, proposals, social media, sales presentations, and elevator speeches, to name a few.

The One-Sheet

One-sheets are popular in the arts and entertainment world. They are exactly what they sound like—one sheet that describes your offering in enough detail to capture attention and stir interest in the offering. This tool makes sense for salespeople that operate in a world where buyers are inundated with information. One-sheets are clear and concise. They provide a simple format to use many of the tools you have already created.

- The Elevator Speech
  - Who are we?
  - What do we do?
  - To whom do we sell?
- Ten value-added talking points from the value audit:
  - Three company examples of value added

- Three product examples of value added
- Three salesperson examples of value added
- Your unique selling proposition
- Summary statement: value proposition

You can customize the one-sheet for a market segment, a specific account, or even a specific level of decision maker. The value audit list summarizes your value added along the three dimensions while offering an opportunity to reinforce your unique selling proposition. The value proposition, as the summary statement, encapsulates what makes your solution valuable to the customer. Figure 7.1 is an example of a one-sheet that we use in our seminars to illustrate the concept.

LAUNCHING YOUR CUSTOMER MESSAGING CAMPAIGN

The key word in this heading is *campaign*. This ongoing effort seeks to prepare the buyer's mind to choose your value-added solution. This is not a single event or act. Your goal is to surround prospects and customers with the message that your solution is *the* solution they must own. *Campaign, ongoing,* and *surround* sound very much like a continuous wearing down of the walls of resistance salespeople often face. This is more than wearing down or tearing down something; it is building something in the buyer's mind. You are building an image or reputation that induces others to buy.

One more time, you are battling for the customer's mind as well as their business. The enemy is not the customer; the customer is the prize. You are battling competitors and narrow-minded, commodity thinking. The battleground is the customer's mind. Customer messaging is prepping the battlefield for victory. Instead of bombs and missiles, you are firing messages of value.

THE PAIN PROPOSITION

The pain proposition plays a major role as part of your messaging. In Chapter 6, you read about loss aversion and opportunity cost. We made a strong case for pain as a more powerful motivator than gain. People hate to lose. Some hate a loss more than they desire a win.

FIGURE 7.1 **Sample One-Sheet**

BRANDEIS PACKAGING COMPANY
WE VALUE YOUR BUSINESS

Brandeis is a 75 year-old privately owned packaging company that specializes in designing and manufacturing folding cartons and corrugated boxes for the consumer products industry.

Ten Things to Consider When Choosing a Packaging Partner

1. Front-end packaging design and testing

2. Inventory management programs

3. Company-owned truck fleet

4. Depth and breadth of product line

5. Custom-designed packaging solutions

6. Manufacturing quality guarantee

7. Guaranteed accessibility of sales rep

8. Monthly performance reviews by salesperson

9. Inside sales coordinator assigned to account

10. Only packaging company to win the Malcolm Baldrige National Quality Award

Your Value Proposition with Brandeis Packaging Company: When you partner with Brandeis and take advantage of our complete menu of value-added services, you will safeguard the quality and integrity of your products while differentiating your brand in the marketplace.

© 2018 Tom Reilly Training

Salespeople communicate product features and benefits. Then they demonstrate how their product solution leads to a gain in profit, time, or revenue. This is the value proposition, which is the downline, tangible outcome the buyer gains from experiencing your solution. What if the buyer is influenced more by pain than gain? How would that change your message?

Consciously or unconsciously, buyers make decisions to maximize gain and to avoid pain. Your messaging campaign should emphasize what the buyer gains and the pain he avoids. This type of customer messaging is compelling.

Pain and loss trigger different emotions than gain. For buyers to change, they need to stop what they are currently doing and start doing something new. Pain motivates people to stop what they are currently doing. Gain motivates them to start something new.

The pain proposition emphasizes what the buyer stands to lose by not experiencing your value-added solution. In Chapter 6, we called that opportunity cost. Opportunity cost is another way to view the consequences of inertia. There is a cost of doing something and a cost of doing nothing. Making buyers aware of the greater cost encourages them to change. The pain proposition emphasizes the cost of doing nothing, which could mean continuing down a path of destruction.

Everyone fears something more than paying too much for something. In customer messaging, a benign sense of fear makes the buyer aware of what would happen if the buyer chooses another alternative. What pain would she experience? The sense of a lost opportunity. The buyer could lose her competitive edge in the market or miss a valuable opportunity. Challenge yourself with the question, "What does the buyer miss by not partnering with us?" Embed that consequence in your messaging not as a threat but as a matter of fact.

If a buyer must pay 10 percent more for your solution, he may consider that 10 percent differential as a loss. Remember, losses loom larger than gains. What would happen if there was a greater loss of not moving forward with your solution? Loss aversion motivates buyers to tighten their grip on the resources they have. If the buyer is going to loosen his grip, you need to give him something greater to hold onto.

An effective technique for involving a benign sense of pain is asking the buyer questions that call attention to a potential pain point.

For example, your solution might save the buyer on total cost. A question that focuses on her current cost would be a pain proposition. You could ask the buyer, "Do you really know what your current piece of equipment is costing you?" Asking a question that calls attention to a pain point will help the buyer gain perspective.

The pain proposition focuses the message on the buyer's greater concerns. It balances the cost of change with tightening the grip of the status quo. For a buyer to change, there needs to be a combination of pain and gain. Pain is what he will miss, and gain is the outcome of your value. Invoking a sense of pain is not heavy-handed persuasion. It's communicating the implications of doing nothing. You are presenting a fair argument for the buyer to consider.

VALUE-ADDED SELLING REVIEW AND ACTION POINTS

1. Marketing is more than a department; it is every way you communicate with your customers. Customer messaging is the ongoing conversation you have with your customers as part of your marketing campaign. Salespeople execute tactically what marketing designs strategically. Your sales efforts must be consonant with your company's marketing strategy.

2. Conduct a value audit and study your value added. From this exercise, you can create a VIP list—a listing of all your value added. This is your first customer messaging tool. Other customer messaging tools you can create are an elevator speech, the customer bill of rights, which describes your customer experience; your USP, which is the stand-out difference that makes you outstanding in your market; and the value proposition, which is the outcome of the customer's experiencing your value added and uniqueness.

3. The one-sheet is a summary of the messaging tools we presented in this chapter. It answers the most important questions about the value of your solution.

4. With your collaterals in hand and messages clear, your next task is to launch a campaign to surround the target market with your messages.

5. The pain proposition makes the buyer aware of the opportunity cost of not going with your solution. You are not inventing the pain of loss; you are pointing it out.

VALUE–ADDED SELLING STRATEGIES

Part II explains the strategic side of Value-Added Selling. Strategy is a coherent response to a challenge, in this case, penetrating and dominating accounts. Strategy answers the question, "What should I do to sell value added?" Your Value-Added Selling strategy is your master plan to direct your selling efforts. It's the link between your dreams and reality. The methods you use to implement this plan are the 11 Value-Added Selling strategies listed in this part. These 11 strategies fit into four categories—two groups of offensive selling strategies and two groups of defensive selling strategies.

The first group of offensive selling strategies is *focusing*. Focusing is becoming more effective. It means working on the right things. This includes high-value target (HVT) account selection—chasing the right business; target account penetration—talking to all the right people; and customer-izing—learning to think the right way, as customers think.

The second group of offensive selling strategies is *persuading*. Persuading is a process, not an event. It means surrounding customers with the right message. This involves positioning—crafting an image for your solution; differentiating—standing out from the crowd; and presenting—delivering a compelling argument for why the customer should buy your solution.

The first group of defensive strategies is *supporting*. Supporting makes it more painless and seamless for the customer to do business with you. This involves process support—logistics; and people support—building and strengthening relationships with your customers.

The second group of defensive strategies is *after-marketing*. After-marketing is the sale-after-the-sale. This involves tinkering—value re-creation; value reinforcement—getting credit for the value your company delivers; and leveraging—growing your business organically.

Here are some key points about these Value-Added Selling strategies:

- Even though these strategies appear sequentially, many of them occur simultaneously and out of the order in which we present them.
- These strategies involve both face-to-face and behind-the-scenes activities.
- Before determining which Value-Added Selling strategy to use, you must consider where the customer is in the buying process.
- Failing to execute these strategies or skipping a strategy can lead to a stalled sale or a longer and more frustrating sales cycle.

Fundamentally, value-added salespeople chase the right business, penetrate accounts thoroughly, think as customers think, position their solution as the value-added solution, differentiate themselves from the competition, present a compelling reason for the customer to buy, support the customer, build strong relationships with customers, seek ways to re-create additional value, reinforce their efforts in the customer's mind, and leverage their sales opportunities.

CHAPTER 8

High-Value Target Account Selection

Your first Value-Added Selling strategy answers this question: "Am I chasing the right business?"

One of the great challenges in sales training is helping salespeople who chase the wrong business. Many attend seminars because they have a marketing problem, not a sales problem. They are pursuing business in segments where they are noncompetitive. Their companies have one value proposition and attempt to apply it broadly across their customer base, and salespeople take the fall for it. You cannot pursue every customer with the same message; that is seller-focused thinking.

Other salespeople suffer from the Mount Everest effect—they chase the business because it's there. No one has taught them that not all business is good business. These salespeople are issued marching orders to "Get the business," and so they begin kicking over every rock to see what's there. They lack strategic focus.

This chapter is about identifying and chasing the right business and building your future on this foundation; maximizing the return on your sales time investment; and learning how to think and approach your territory strategically.

At the end of this chapter, you will be able to:

- Explain the power of discernment and how it helps you make better decisions about using your sales time
- Select viable target accounts
- Identify profit piranhas that chew away at your bottom line
- Design an account strategy, including a small-wins approach, for your high-value target accounts

THE POWER OF DISCERNMENT

Do you want every order, or do you want every opportunity? When we pose this question in seminars, some attendees respond quickly with, "Every order." They jump at the chance of getting an order. Others in the group respond more prudently: "I want every opportunity. There's some business I don't want, but I at least want the opportunity to turn it down." This is how value-added salespeople think—strategically.

There is some business that you would like the competition to have—some of that low-margin, high-aggravation-factor, slow-pay, no-pay business. In fact, you want your competitors to get as much of that as they can handle. Yet, you want the opportunity to turn it down.

To paraphrase from George Orwell's *Animal Farm*, all customers are equal—some are just a little more equal than others. All customers deserve the courtesy and respect of the value-added attitude, but not everyone wants, needs, or deserves the intensity of the value-added sales effort.

Peter Drucker has written magnificently on managerial effectiveness. In his book *The Effective Executive*, he points out that being effective is more than knowing what to do; it's also knowing what *not* to do. This is the power of discernment.

For salespeople, we can say that the mark of a good salesperson is knowing which business to pursue, but the mark of a great salesperson is knowing which business *not* to pursue. When you develop this power of discernment, you acquire a sixth business sense that gives you a nose for good business and bad business.

If you are confused about the type of business your company wants you to pursue, discuss it with your boss. Seek clarity regarding the business the company wants you to pursue as well as the business it wants you to avoid.

PARETO PRINCIPLE

At the end of the nineteenth century, an Italian economist, Vilfredo Pareto, was studying the wealth patterns of western Europe and observed a fundamental imbalance—most of the wealth was owned by a small number of people. Pareto, an avid gardener, observed this same imbalance in his garden. Most of the peas he harvested came from a small number of pods. These insights gave birth to a theory that has been variably called the Pareto law, Pareto rule, Pareto principle, 80-20 law, and 80-20 principle. Fundamentally, this principle states that a lot comes from a little—80 percent from 20 percent. Is it always 80-20? No. Sometimes, it is 70-30, 90-10, 85-15, and as you will read later in this chapter—sometimes it is 16-84. The principle describes leveraged outcomes. This can be widely applied across life. For example:

- Eighty percent of your results come from 20 percent of your efforts.
- Eighty percent of your growth comes from 20 percent of your investments.
- Eighty percent of the calories you consume come from 20 percent of the foods you eat.
- Eighty percent of what you wear comes from 20 percent of your wardrobe.
- Eighty percent of the complaints you hear come from 20 percent of your customers.

During the World War II era, a quality guru, Joseph Juran, similarly observed that most product quality problems came from just a few products. He called this the phenomenon of the "vital few and trivial many." This was a rediscovery of what Pareto observed—a fundamental imbalance in life that a lot comes from a little. Neither invented the phenomenon; they simply observed what was already there.

Salespeople can extrapolate from this information and use it in many ways. The specific application for this chapter is identifying viable customers. Following Pareto's observation, 80 percent of the value you extract from your market comes from 20 percent of your customers. We call these high-value targets (HVTs). Conversely, 80 percent of the loss you suffer comes from 20 percent of your customers. We call these profit piranhas (PPs). We call the remaining 60 percent chunk of customers equity customers; these are the ones from whom you get as good as you give.

The daily reality of running a business is cash flow. For salespeople, time is money. How you manage your time determines how your cash flows. This reality coupled with the Pareto principle gives you the unique opportunity to invest your sales time for maximum return.

STRATEGIC FOCUS: DEVELOPING MARKET SAVVY

What type of business (not specific accounts) do you want to pursue? What type of business do you want to avoid? What do you know about your industry? How many different segments of the market does your company serve? Which is the most profitable segment? What is good business for your company considering its long-range plans? On what type of foundation must you build the business? Where can you have the greatest impact with your solution? Your knowledge about your industry, market, competitors, and customers is your market savvy. Answering the foregoing questions helps you effectively direct your sales efforts.

Our research fine-tunes the Pareto principle for value-added sales-people. Most industries have three segments represented by a bell curve. (See Figure 8.1.) The segment on the left side of the curve is the HVT segment. These value-added proponents are innovators in their industries—those willing to take risks and to experiment with new ideas. They embrace advances and are always in the vanguard of change. They perceive value added as a competitive advantage. These buyers are sophisticated, well informed, and involved throughout the life cycle of your product or service. They take a long-term view, perceive relationships as partnerships, and seek a total solution to their needs. They are truly value-added buyers. Price is less of an issue in these accounts. This segment represents about one-sixth of the market. Note that we are using 16 percent versus the 20 percent from the Pareto principle, though it remains that a lot comes from a little.

The segment to the extreme right are price shoppers—the 16 percent called profit piranhas. These are the true price shoppers discussed earlier. You're wasting your time selling value added to them. They rarely pay for value added. This segment also represents one-sixth of the market. If you allow this segment to become more than 50 percent of your business, you have positioned yourself as a discount house. Another problem with targeting this price-only segment is that once you begin to do business here, you adopt some of these customers'

FIGURE 8.1 **Market Segments**

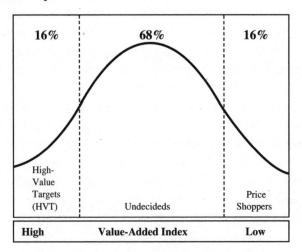

characteristics as you adapt to their thinking. Birds of a feather flock together. This segment takes a short-term view, prefers a transactional relationship with sellers, and seeks to buy a core-commodity, naked product solution.

There is a key distinction here that we need to make. For the HVT segment, the conversation you will have is about money. For the PP segment, the conversation you will have is about price. Money is a better conversation to have than price. There are many ways that you can help customers drive more money to their bottom lines. Selling the buyer on the notion that money is a better conversation is a conceptual sale. When you achieve that small win, you are on the path to a value-added sale.

The two-thirds segment in the middle—equity customers—is up for grabs, and these people could go either way. They are undecided as to what is more important to them—price or value. This segment holds promise for you as a value-added salesperson. In this middle, you can at least make your argument.

Your immediate focus is the one-in-six HVT segment. Your success in Value-Added Selling correlates to your ability to identify and pursue this segment. To identify this segment, you must study their viability. Viability criteria will help.

Do you know what is good business for your company? Our research shows that only one-in-five salespeople have a profile for their ideal prospect. This means 80 percent of salespeople are clueless. That is a profoundly shocking number. Beyond that, only 18 percent of salespeople believe that they focus their time and energy on pursuing ideal prospects. Where are the rest wasting their time and energy?

Viability criteria define this HVT segment and answer the question, "What is fundamentally good business for our company?" You must come up with your own list, but this sample list is a starting point for you to identify your HVT segment: innovative thinkers, profitability of the sale, longevity of contracts, leveragability of the business, ease of doing business, equitable return on your investment, and cultural consonance. Cultural consonance means that the buyer's company culture looks a lot like your company's culture. This includes the notion that the buyer's company sells value-added solutions to its customers, and at a gut level, the buyer understands the importance of value-added solutions.

This viability criteria exercise helps you build market savvy. What is good business for your company? If you don't know, ask your boss. Don't be surprised if you draw a blank look from your manager. Our research shows that only 35 percent of sales managers have clearly defined good business for their companies. We have even heard managers say in seminars that they want all the business that is out there. This exercise concerns the *type* of customer that is good business, not specific customers. That comes next.

TACTICAL FOCUS: TARGETING SPECIFIC ACCOUNTS

Now that you're equipped with an understanding of your market, you can follow the lead of 84 percent of top-achieving salespeople who have a systematic way to classify their accounts into some type of A-B-C ranking. Use your strategic understanding of your market to select specific accounts that fit different profiles: HVTs, equity customers, and PPs. You already have a strategic sense of these three groups of customers from the previous section. In Figure 8.1, HVTs fall to the left, PPs to the right, and equity customers in the middle. Let's drill down on each of these three.

HVTs

Again, the HVT account is that one-in-six that is a disciple of your value added. To find other HVTs, begin by identifying specific customers who meet your list of HVT viability criteria.

Another way to target HVTs is to profile your best customers. First, list your six best accounts. *Best* can mean anything: volume, profit, product mix that you sell to them, or any other consideration you deem important. Next, identify three common denominators of these best accounts. It could be their size, revenue, number of employees, Standard Industrial Classification (SIC) code, location, or a host of other industry-specific variables. The more of these search criteria you can pinpoint, the better the results. With this data in hand, refer to your list of prospects and select six accounts that match the common denominators of your best customers. The acid test for prospecting is that, on paper, your best prospects resemble your best customers.

Once you have selected your six HVTs, you're ready to move to the next step in targeting: studying a specific account. Fewer than one-in-four salespeople have a detailed plan of attack for their number one account; yet, our BSP research found that 42 percent of top achievers have a detailed plan of attack for their top customer, which means there is still room for growth among the best. The following groups of questions will help you develop an in-depth understanding of this customer's business and identify opportunity areas where you can make a real difference with your solution.

Situation Analysis

- Is this account a leader or a follower in its industry?
- Is this account a product-innovative company or a low-cost provider?
- Where is this prospect headed (long and short-term goals)?
- What are the most important trends affecting this prospect's industry?
- What outside forces are applying pressure to that industry?
- Who are this prospect's customers, and what do they want from your prospect?
- Who are this prospect's competitors?
- What are this prospect's competitive strengths and weaknesses?

Summary of Buyer Needs

- What is this prospect looking for in a product, a supplier, and a salesperson?
- What does this prospect want more of and less of?
- How does this prospect define value?
- What pressure points affect this buyer?

Key Player Profile

- What is this prospect's power base distribution?
- Who are the decision makers, and what is their decision process?
- What are their priorities and concerns?
- What motivates these decision makers?
- What are their fears?
- Who are the influencers in this account?
- What are the group dynamics?
- What silo issues are there?

Competitive Information: Describe Your Competition

- How does the prospect meet current needs?
- What does the prospect like about this solution?
- What problems does the prospect experience with this solution?
- How do these problems affect the prospect?
- How is your competitor vulnerable in this account?

Opportunity Areas: Dream for Your Customers

- What does this prospect want to be able to do tomorrow that can't be done today?
- What is the prospect's biggest headache?
- What does the prospect hate to do that we can do instead?
- What are this prospect's profit and resource piranhas?
- What does this prospect need in order to become more competitive in the market?
- What opportunities does this prospect miss but would like to pursue?
- What type of solution would the prospect ideally like to have that no one seems to offer now?

- What would cause this prospect to pay more to do business with us?

Goals
- What are my short-term goals for this account?
- What are my long-term goals for this account?
- What small wins will help me achieve these goals?

Strategy
- What is our best solution for this account?
- What can we do to bring more value to this relationship?
- What resources can I use to sell this concept to the prospect?
- What is my selling strategy to achieve these account goals?

When we ask salespeople to review these questions for their top customer, most of them tell me they cannot answer all of these questions. This exercise makes them painfully aware that they need to learn more about their customers.

Ask and answer these questions for three of your HVTs. If you attempt to perform this analysis for all of your accounts, you won't finish the exercise because it will seem overwhelming. You can do it for a handful of your HVTs. Once you do, you'll find that the strategic thinking ability that you develop from this activity will also help you with those other accounts: You will automatically process information about other accounts using this questioning format.

Profit Piranhas
Profit piranhas chew away at your profitability. They return goods more often, complain more, demand special treatment for which they do not want to pay, expect lower prices, want extended terms, and would like to enjoy your value added without paying for it.

The first step is to identify why you are losing money in these accounts. Is it for the above reasons, or is it for something as simple as the customer's ordering patterns? Next, you want to have a frank conversation with these customers and explain you cannot continue to sell under these conditions. If some corrective action fails to achieve your goal, you must consider other alternatives. For example, you could begin to charge for value-added services like delivery, raise prices, increase minimum orders, enforce payment terms, switch the customer to inside sales, or guide the customer to online ordering, to name a few. Your objective is to stop losing money on this group of customers, and if that is not possible, then tactfully guide them to the competition.

Use the questions above to identify your three HVTs and your PPs. Leveraging your HVTs and stopping the bleeding from PPs are two things you can immediately initiate. For your equity customers, the planning process may take longer as you ask many of the same questions you would ask and answer for your HVTs.

VALUE-ADDED SELLING REVIEW AND ACTION POINTS

1. The power of discernment is knowing which business to pursue and which business to avoid. You must invest your selling time as if it were money, because it is. You extract the most value from the top 16 percent of your customers and the most loss from the bottom 16 percent. This is a variation of the Pareto principle.

2. There are three segments in most industries: HVTs, PPs, and equity customers.

3. Money is a better conversation to have with buyers than price because there are many ways that you can help drive more money to their bottom lines. Price is only one way to affect profitability for buyers, and it is not always the positive impact that they believe.

4. Understand the type of business that you want to pursue including the viability criteria that define good business for your company. These two questions guide your account selection: What is fundamentally good business for our company? Can we create or capture value in this account?

5. Once you have identified three HVTs and the PPs, study these accounts using the questions provided in this chapter to formulate your strategy.

CHAPTER 9

Target Account Penetration

Your second Value-Added Selling strategy answers this question: "Am I talking to all the right people?"

While targeting value-added accounts is one part of focusing, target penetration is another part. Many salespeople enter the decision process late and limit their penetration to lower-level influencers. They fail to take advantage of a simple Value-Added Selling principle: few things are as powerful as the right idea, at the right time, in the right place, and for the right person.

This chapter is about timing and buying criteria, generating support for your ideas throughout the buyer's organization, and making sure that you're dealing with people who can say yes to your solution.

At the end of this chapter, you will be able to:

- Name the three rules for account penetration
- Describe the three levels of decision makers
- Explain what is important to each level of decision maker
- Discuss how your value proposition must appeal to each level of decision maker

THE THREE RULES OF ACCOUNT PENETRATION

There are three rules for account penetration. You must penetrate the account early, deep, and high. If you were to revisit every significant opportunity you have pursued to no avail, you would discover that you violated one or more of these three rules. Let's examine them in depth.

Penetrate the Decision Process Early

According to an article by *Google Marketing*, B2B corporate buyers are already 57 percent of the way down the path before they reach out to potential suppliers for information.[1] This means they conduct online due diligence before meeting with suppliers. Most salespeople then are late to the game. Biases are set. Early cuts have been made. What is left are those that have been prescreened by the buyer. Further, 71 percent of those B2B searches are for generic queries, not branded searches. When the search is for generic solutions, commodity price resistance follows. Generic searches lead to generic prices. Early exclusions and a predisposed commodity search should haunt salespeople. These two numbers present a compelling argument for the early bird getting the worm.

If you enter the decision process early, you have an opportunity to sell the uniqueness of your solution in a way that overshadows the competition. When you enter the decision process late, the buyer places a greater emphasis on price, as you find yourself selling against a competitor's product versus meeting the buyer's needs.

In Chapter 4, you learned the importance of understanding the buyer's Critical Buying Path. By penetrating the decision process early, you can help the buyer understand his or her needs along the CBP. Buyers make purchasing decisions based on their interpretation of their needs, wants, and constraints. Entering the decision process early means you can help buyers develop a more in-depth understanding of their needs and shape their perceptions of how your solution uniquely addresses their primary concerns. You may even have a chance to help write the specifications.

Early penetration in the budgeting phase also gives you the chance to shape buyer expectations about what they can get for their money. If they have underestimated their budget, now is the time to help them adjust it. This is an easier task to assess early versus later in the decision process.

We were sharing these thoughts one day in a client seminar when the president of the company stood and said to the group, "Ladies and gentlemen, every significant piece of business that we lost this year to price resulted from our entering the decision process too late. We were constantly selling from a defensive posture versus an offensive position. We never had a chance to shape the buyer's criteria in a way that would call attention to our unique strengths."

Entering the decision process early positions you as a team member. You're there from the start, which means the buyer sees you as a partner—someone with an insider's view and an in-depth understanding of his or her situation. As you establish trust early in the process and build a solid relationship with the buyer, you make it more difficult for the competition to gain a foothold in the account.

Penetrate the Account Deep

When you purchase a new home or automobile, how many people do you involve in that decision process? For most people, it normally involves input from spouses or significant others, trusted advisors like real estate agents or bankers, and oftentimes, family members. Your customers are no different. How many people are involved to one degree or another in the buying decision: purchasing, operations, sales and marketing, finance, administration, or more?

Your objective is to penetrate the account thoroughly. Surround the account. Become a professional mole and burrow your way deeply into the account. The more contacts you make within the account, the more supporters you have singing your praises. These are your internal champions.

Every successful sales and marketing campaign has both *push* and *pull* dynamics working in its favor. *Push* is the business you pursue, and *pull* is the business you attract. For salespeople, *push* means the direct selling activities in which you engage to drive the sales. *Pull* is the support you generate for your ideas inside the buyer's organization. This support takes the form of internal champions who promote your solution from within the buyer's company.

Our research shows that there are at least five people involved in B2B buying decisions, more for capital expenditures, and fewer for MRO purchases. MRO stands for maintenance, repair, and operation. These purchases are often viewed as reordering commodity-type, consumable items. It makes sense that for consumables, fewer people would be involved once a product is approved for use.

In Chapter 4, you read about the silo effect in organizations. Nowhere is it more felt than when it comes to purchasing something.

Your challenge is to bridge the chasm that exists when various departments in the buyer's organization do not communicate. It could be benign neglect or active sabotaging. It matters not. When the influences in your accounts fail to communicate, it hurts you as much as it does their organizations. Full account penetration is your remedy. Value-added salespeople help break down silos in their HVTs.

Penetrate the Account at the Highest Levels

The single greatest Value-Added Selling opportunity area for you is to call higher in your customer's organization. Few salespeople feel comfortable with high-level calling. Fewer than 10 percent of salespeople call at this level, for one reason or another. They may not know how to penetrate at this level or how to talk to high-level decision makers. They may fear offending a lower-level contact. They may embrace the defeatist attitude that the high-level decision maker will not meet with them. Or simply, they may be intimidated by the thought of a high-level meeting. If you avoid these attitudes and penetrate at this level, you will find yourself in the minority of successful salespeople who penetrate from the shop floor to the top floor. We have found that top-achieving salespeople call on high-level (Level III) decision makers twice as often as the average salesperson calls at that level.

How high should you penetrate the account? You must call high enough that the person with whom you're meeting can approve the funds for your ideas. Many people in a company can say no to an idea, but few can say yes. A great rule of thumb is to never accept a final no from someone who cannot give you an absolute yes. Why would you allow a lower-level decision maker to control your efforts or limit your sales destiny? If the buyer does not have budget authority, you're not calling high enough in the account.

High-level decision makers (HLDMs) have the authority to create money for an idea they like. If you're not calling on an HLDM, you're not calling high enough, period. Ninety percent of your peers fail to do this. They get stuck at lower levels. Consider the wonderful opportunity that exists for you since most salespeople do not call on the HLDM. The noise level for calling on the HLDM is incredibly low. Value-added salespeople make it a habit to do what others can't or won't do.

Here's an example. One day, we met with a vice president of sales along with his boss, who was the vice president of marketing, and the president of the company. We were proposing a training solution for 500 salespeople. Our fee is based on time and materials. While no one objected to the seminar fee, the vice president of sales and the vice president of marketing both challenged the materials cost because it exceeded their budget constraints. The president of the company countered, "The heck with the budget. I like the program. Find the money." That's high-level, Value-Added Selling. Had we met with only the two vice presidents, we would have fought a significant price battle. If you're not calling on the HLDM—the one person able to give your price a nod—you're not calling high enough.

LEVEL I–II–III DECISION MAKERS

The Level I-II-III concept is a simple way to explain the different levels of decision-making authority in a company. Assuming you penetrate the decision process early, you can use this Level I-II-III concept to plan your sales strategy. A decision maker in a given level perceives his or her situation differently from members of the other two levels. Each wants level-appropriate solutions. Your challenge is to frame your ideas within the context and content of the person's level-specific perceptions, needs, wants, and concerns.

Level–I Decision Makers: Logistics Buyers

Level-I decision makers are logistics buyers. They concern themselves with the supply side of products and services. They may be purchasing agents, buyers, materials managers, storeroom clerks, office managers, or anyone else involved in the acquisition of products or services. Their common denominator is what they need in a solution. Level-I buyers focus on logistics: price, delivery, lead time, packaging, freight issues, credits, returns, payment terms, and so forth. They are the most price sensitive of the three levels, and salespeople ironically spend the most time with them.

These lower-level buyers have varying degrees of authority, depending on the organization. Level-I buyers may be able to shift business around depending on supplier relationships, but they rarely have the authority to create money for ideas they like. They process orders that someone else generates. They fill requests; they are responsive by their job description and function. They are the procurement arms for most organizations. Their time horizon is short term and transactional.

Even though Level-I's have limited authority to buy on their own, you must establish a relationship with them. They are critical to your success. Level-I's can make your company look bad if they don't like you. Conversely, they can give you the benefit of the doubt when you need it. Can they create pull for your solution? The most underappreciated people in companies are Level-I buyers. They hear from their internal customers when their internal customers don't have what they need when they need it. Your Level-I's greatest fear is the phone call at 2 a.m. with the caller wanting to know where the inventory is.

Integrated supply, outsourcing, on-site vending machines, and online purchasing are presenting challenges for Level-I buyers, and many feel threatened by these trends. They are anxious about their futures. Help them look like heroes, and you have supporters for life. They *need* logistics support, but they *want* security, genuine appreciation, and a safe purchasing alternative.

Level-II Decision Makers: Influencers

Level-II decision makers are user influencers. These mid-level decision makers include maintenance people, safety officers, equipment operators, users of the product, technical influencers, resellers of your product (if you sell through distributors), and operations managers. These are the people who are most affected by change, and any time they buy something, it's a change. The priority of Level-II influencers is usage: ease of operation, maintenance, efficiency, conformity to specifications, technical support, product performance, safety, and user-friendliness.

Level-II influencers have user-type concerns: quality, function, deployment, and operation. They use the product, operate it, maintain it, supervise others who work with it, must have it as a part of something they create, or resell it to their customers.

Level-II's have influence over the sale because they can specify a product, a brand, or a supplier. They generate requests that the

Level-I's process. Level-II's also create pull for your solution. Conversely, their rejection of a product on technical or functional grounds can be the kiss of death for a salesperson. The time horizon of Level-II's is longer than that of the Level-I buyers. Unlike the Level-I buyer, Level-II's think beyond the acquisition point to how the product or service will make their lives better as they use it. While the Level-I thinks *acquisition*, the Level-II buyer thinks *utility*. Their mindset is more operational and transformational than logistical and transactional—the mindset of the Level-I buyer.

With the Level-II on your side, you have an internal champion to sell for you when you're not there to do the job yourself. The Level-II can be a sounding board for new ideas that you want to present to upper-level management. This person can be your guide through the organizational maze of decision making. Their power and value is that they can endorse your product.

Level-II decision makers may need a quality solution, but they want you to make their lives better, safer, and easier.

Level-III Decision Makers, the HLDMs

Level-III decision makers represent upper management. These HLDMs are company executives, high-level managers, business owners, and directors. Level-III's think differently from Level-I's and Level-II's. Level-III's focus on profitability and loss, cash flow, competitive posture, employee issues, customer satisfaction, industry trends, and shareholder value.

Level-III's have the authority to use money any way they see fit to achieve organizational objectives. This is what determines a Level-III buyer—the authority to create funds for an idea. However, many will defer to a lower-level influencer for input. If a Level-III likes your idea, it's a safe bet that you will get the business. That's why you must penetrate the account at this level.

The time horizon for Level-III's is long term. They think in years. They think, plan, and execute strategically. Fundamentally, they want to know how your solution fits into their long-range growth plans. Beware. They do not buy products. They form strategic partnerships.

HOW TO TALK LIKE A LEVEL I-II-III DECISION MAKER

Each level of decision maker speaks a different language. You can see that in Figure 9.1. Level-I buyers are logistics people and focus on short-term, transactional issues during acquisition. Level-II buyers are users, operators, mid-level managers, and resellers whose time horizon is more operational and transformational. Level-III buyers, the HLDMs, speak the language of money. Their long-term, strategic view offers a broader definition of money than simply acquisition price. Thus, the conversation with HLDMs is about partnerships, not products. It is a business-to-business conversation. The HLDM wants to know that you are first and foremost a good businessperson. Logistics and product discussions happen at Levels I and II respectively.

Your value proposition is different for each level of decision maker. The outcome of your value for Level-I buyers reflects their logistics concerns—price, delivery, availability, and so on. The outcome of your value for Level-II influencers reflects a technical solution. It may help them operate more efficiently, move product, or transform your ideas into value for their company. The outcome of your value for Level-III decision makers is money oriented in some fashion. Here are some sample value propositions by level of decision maker:

Level-I: The downline advantage of the purchasing power we offer you is complete access to a global supply network that can expedite shipments and stabilize materials cost.

Level-II: The result of your implementing our production solution will be increased product quality and greater manufacturing flexibility.

Level-III: The outcome of our partnership is opening up new global markets to your company.

Keep in mind that each one of these value propositions may refer to the same core product. The difference is how each level of decision maker views the outcome of this customer experience with your solution—your value proposition. You can combine the value proposition, level of decision maker, and the CBP. See Figure 9.2.

You'll notice that Level-I decision makers focus on the front end of the CBP. This is because many of the front-end activities are

FIGURE 9.1 **Levels I–II–II Needs Hierarchy**

	Needs	Wants	Fears
Level III	Industry trends	Control	Loss of control
	Company direction	Freedom	More to do
	Competitive challenges	Practical	Complexity
	Outside pressures (government)	Simple	Having to answer
		Mainstream	Too much exposure
	Profit piranhas	Consensus	Looking bad
	Underutilized resources	Career protection	Not politically expedient
	Serve customers better	Widely accepted	Not fitting in
	Reduced cycle time	Results-oriented solutions	
	Employee issues		
	Lower cost of doing business		
	Increased efficiency & effectiveness		
	Maximize shareholder value		
Level II	Quality standards	Technically proven	Surprises
	Service & support issues	No guesswork/surprises: CYA	No backups
	Creature comforts		More to do
	Productivity issues	Data to make decision	Unproven ideas
	Maintenance & design issues	Eliminate the human factor	Complexity
	Training needs	Easier to operate/maintain	Guesswork
	Compliance issues	Safe to use	Unpredictable variables
	Safety concerns	Make my job simple	
	Performance standards	Stability	
		Painless	
Level I	Time	Appreciation	Crises
	Special handling	Security	Too much challenge
	Packaging	Respect	Mistakes
	Lead time	Little techno-talk	Techno-talk
	Budget	Safe purchase	No substitutes
	Ordering concerns	No ripples	No loopholes
	Delivery issues		The call at 2 a.m.
	Availability		

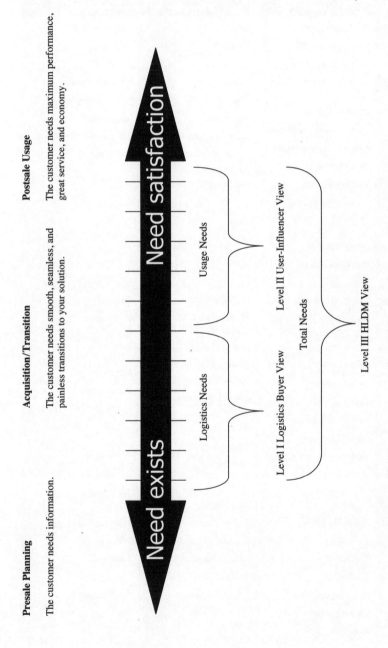

FIGURE 9.2 The Critical Buying Path and Decision–Maker Value Proposition

transactional and logistical. The Level-II decision maker focuses more on the second half of the CBP because that's where usage and/or transformation takes place, after the commitment to buy has been made. The Level-III decision maker takes a full-range view of the CBP and must consider the outcome of the entire path over the long haul. This view of the value proposition along the path simplifies your understanding of the outcome the buyer desires.

VALUE-ADDED SELLING REVIEW AND ACTION POINTS

1. The three rules for account penetration are to get in there early, deep, and high. Penetrate your accounts *early* to help buyers understand their needs and write specs, *deep* to create pull for your ideas, and *high* to generate funding for your solution.

2. You will call on three levels of decision makers to thoroughly penetrate your HVTs. Each level of decision maker has different priorities—needs, wants, and fears. Study their priorities and present your solution as it satisfies the level at which you're calling.

3. Your value proposition (the outcome of your solution) will vary by level of decision maker. Level-I buyers want a logistics outcome. Level-II buyers want a utility-based outcome. Level-III buyers look for a money-based outcome. Customize the presentation of your value proposition by the level of decision maker with whom you are meeting.

CHAPTER 10

Customer-izing

Your third Value-Added Selling strategy answers this question: "Do I understand my customer's needs, wants, and fears?"

A fundamental principle of Value-Added Selling is that buyers, not sellers, define value. It follows that if you define value in customer terms, customers pay for it with a higher selling price. If you define value in your (seller) terms, you pay for it with a bigger discount.

Some sales executives encourage their salespeople to create a need for what they sell versus understanding the buyer's need and then creating a solution. More U.S. sales training dollars are spent on teaching product knowledge than selling skills. Salespeople interpret this training phenomenon as a benchmark for how they should spend time with buyers—talking versus listening. This practice translates into firehouse, feature-benefit presentations in which the salesperson dominates the conversation—a monologue, not a dialogue.

Multiple studies demonstrate that buyers expect salespeople to be subject-matter experts and to know about the buyer's business. A CEB survey found that customer-focused sellers performed 36 percent better over time than seller-focused companies.[1] Earlier you read that buyers are 57 percent down the path to buying by the time they reach out to suppliers. Salespeople are dealing with knowledgeable buyers today. Are you working as hard for information as your customers are?

Coupled with HVT selection and target penetration, Customer-izing completes the overall focusing strategy that value-added salespeople use. This chapter is about the face-to-face and behind-the-scenes activities you engage in to acquire an in-depth understanding of the customer.

At the end of this chapter, you will be able to:

- Define and discuss customer-izing
- Differentiate between needs, wants, and fears
- Describe and identify buyer pressure points that take priority over price

CUSTOMER-IZING AS A PROCESS

Customer-izing is a process of immersion and assimilation. You immerse yourself fully into the buyer's world. You assimilate into the culture. You develop a firsthand understanding and insight that enables you to think as buyers think.

It's important for you to understand the customer's buying process and listen to the buyer's needs, wants, and fears. It's not enough to know the buyer's needs—you must understand these needs. Customer-izing helps you to develop an in-depth understanding of the buyer's needs *and* the driving forces behind these needs—the *what* and *why* of the needs. It's seeing life from the buyer's unique point of view, drilling down on the buyer's definition of value. This deep-dive exploration and understanding of the buyer's needs, wants, fears, and pressure points allow you to experience firsthand your value added as value received.

Thich Nhat Hanh, a Vietnamese Buddhist monk, wrote in his book *Peace Is Every Step* about this type of understanding: "When we want to understand something, we cannot just stand outside and observe it. We have to enter deeply into it and be one with it in order to really understand. If we want to understand a person, we have to feel his feelings, suffer his sufferings, and enjoy his joy." How deeply have you entered into understanding your buyers?

While you're developing this in-depth understanding, you help buyers understand all their needs more thoroughly. Buyers who understand the complexity of their needs are more open to value-added solutions. Designing a customer-oriented solution positions you as a trusted partner and confidant. The buyer perceives you as an important resource. You're vital to his or her success.

There is another advantage to this type of understanding. It helps you to live the Value-Added Selling philosophy. This level of understanding empowers you to do more of that which adds value and less of that which adds little or no value. Remember, the things you do that add cost without value diminish your position in the market.

Customer-izing, like other Value-Added Selling strategies, can be conducted face-to-face and behind the scenes. It means touring customer facilities, talking to all decision makers and influencers, studying the customer's website, visiting with the customer's customer, taking a start-to-finish walk-through of the buyer's project, studying the company's marketing messages, and spending a day in the life of your buyer. These insights will help you shape your value proposition to the level of the decision maker and to the depths of his or her needs, wants, fears, and pressure points.

Organizational Needs

Buyers have a complex set of needs that include both organizational and individual influences. The analogy of the iceberg in Figure 10.1 illustrates this point. The tip of the iceberg represents the obvious, visible organizational needs. Organizational needs are different from personal wants. The buyer uses the objective buying criteria of organizational needs to evaluate competitive alternatives. Organizational needs include compliance with specifications, quality, delivery, terms, price, product performance, ordering convenience, and other fundamental buying criteria. The buyer attempts to satisfy this set of needs when making a buying decision. To understand the buyer's organizational needs and objective buying criteria, follow these suggestions:

1. What are your buyer's *total* organizational needs for a solution? Are there different departmental matters to consider? What are the driving forces behind these needs? Do you know the buyer's objectives and overall mission?
2. What is your buyer's decision process? This includes the timetable, people involved, and steps buyers must go through. It also includes how buyers will make the decision. What is the buyer's decision paradigm: will he maximize or satisfice?
3. How is power distributed throughout the buyer's organization? What is the relative input of the Levels I-II-III decision makers, as discussed in Chapter 9? Will one department have veto power over another? What political considerations are there?

FIGURE 10.1 Needs and Wants Iceberg

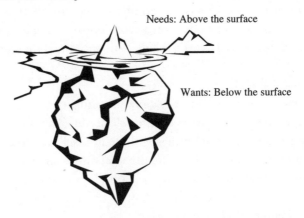

Needs: Above the surface

Wants: Below the surface

Is an internal power battle going on? When one department battles another, you may end up being a casualty of that war. Understand your buyer's battleground. In Chapter 22, "The Needs-Analysis Stage," we offer you a tactical approach to discovering these needs during a sales call.

4. What opportunity areas exist? These include areas of pain or gain that are sufficient to motivate change. These opportunity areas provide the emotional catalyst for change. People change when the pain is greater than the gain. When buyers are dissatisfied with the status quo, they will change. If there is an area where customers perceive an opportunity to improve, they will often act on this desire to achieve a gain. Your job is to snoop around to identify these opportunity areas.

5. What are your buyer's critical issues for this purchase? What is most vital to this buyer's achieving her goals? This area includes mission-critical activities, the success factors vital to the buyer's success. When you identify the absolutes that must happen for the buyer to achieve success, you shift the focus from price. Critical issues may include timeliness of delivery or scheduling, absolute quality standards, technical support during transition, and even the ability of your solution to integrate into the buyer's current procedures.

Collectively, these various needs compose your customer's organizational profile. This is the tip of the iceberg. These are highly visible issues that any curious salesperson who is willing to invest the time should discover. The less-visible issues are the individual's wants.

Personal Wants

Whereas *needs* refer to the organization, *wants* refer to the individual. We make this distinction for clarity in this book. One of the great opportunity areas in business-to-business selling is the emotional component of the buying decision. Business-to-business salespeople tend to underestimate the role that emotion plays in the sale. Emotion drives buying decisions. This statement is true even for the most technical sale. People still buy from people.

Human beings are emotional creatures. They make emotional decisions and often use reason to justify them. Current research from neuroscience confirms that most decisions are made at the emotional level. If humans made purely rational decisions, no one would smoke, eat or drink to excess, or engage in high-risk hobbies. People listen to and respond to their emotions. When the emotional beast screams, people feed it.

Personal wants, desires, and fears often lie beneath the surface in the iceberg analogy, as these issues are not always visible. Some buyers may even attempt to hide these wants and fears, feeling it may leave them too exposed in a negotiation. These beneath-the-surface issues represent a personal win or loss for the buyer. They are emotional buying motives that drive the sale. On a personal level for the buyer, he or she answers the question, "What's in it for me?" Here is an important Value-Added Selling principle: Buyers prefer to buy what they *need* from salespeople who understand what they *want* to *achieve* and what they want to *avoid*.

Again, buyers make emotional decisions based on what they want to achieve and what they want to avoid—gains and pains. Personal gains include things people want more of: control, image, power, security, stability, ego gratification, greed, and other gains.

Fears include what they want less of: risk, more work to do, too much exposure on something, a call at 2 a.m. asking where the supplies are, loss of control, damage to their image, being politically vulnerable, making a mistake, and other pain areas.

Selling on both levels—organizational needs and personal wants and fears—gives you a powerful advantage. You create solutions that help buyers achieve their organizational objectives while satisfying their personal goals. Figure 10.2 offers you a view of needs, wants, and fears against the backdrop of Level I-II-III decision makers. Customer-izing is studying this complex set of needs, wants, and fears, which allows you to customize a solution.

Buyer Pressure Points

This area deserves special attention because of its impact on your negotiation with the customer. Buyer pressure points mitigate price. The more pressure points operating in the sale, the less important price is. Pressure points offer you a window into the buyer's nonprice motivation to buy. Your objective is to identify as many of these pressure points as you can and use them to draw the emphasis away from price.

Here is a rundown of these pressure points:

- Timing and a sense of urgency—the buyer needs it ASAP
- Uniqueness of the problem the buyer is experiencing
- Brand preference for what you sell
- Supplier preference for your company (being the incumbent supplier)
- Critical impact of this decision on the buyer's business
- Availability of supply
- Uniqueness of the solution
- Multiple barriers to direct product comparison
- Other customers competing for your time
- A bad experience with your competition
- Few perceived substitutes for your product
- A painless transition to your solution
- Budget availability—the buyer has the money
- Budget deadline—spend it or lose it
- Healthy state of the buyer's business
- Compliance requirements
- Favorable location of your company
- Negative impact of "cheap" on the buyer's image
- Questionable credit status—the buyer has problems

FIGURE 10.2 **Positional Needs, Wants, and Fears of Level I–II–III Decision Makers**

Level of Decision Maker	Organizational Needs	Personal Wants	Personal Fears	Your Strategy
Level-I Logistics Buyer	Supply-and-demand conversations that focus on logistics and transaction issues: price, on-time performance and delivery, packaging, broad selection of ordering options, lead time, terms, shipping, availability, budget, specification compliance, special handling, supply alternatives, etc.	Safe and secure decisions, nontechnical explanations, easy-to-understand options, avoid problems and mistakes, genuine appreciation, and respect	Crises, complexity, no backups or alternatives, mistakes, and the call at 2 a.m. looking for products	This is a logistics discussion. Present nontechnical, low-risk solutions that make it easy to justify the expense. The buyer wants to look good in the eyes of his management and internal customers.
Level-II User/ Influencer	Technical conversations about features and benefits: quality, service and support, training, productivity and performance, maintenance, compliance, safety, innovation, guarantees, operational issues, utility, etc. Better yet proven mousetraps, backup systems, and application tips or suggestions	Safe, easy-to-use and maintain products with plenty of support, training and service, proven, field-tested ideas, data, reliability, smooth transitions, etc. Creative freedom to invest, yet standard operating procedures and state-of-the-art technology	Exposure and risk, unsafe or difficult to use, surprises, unproven, too much effort, too complex or theoretical for practical use, more to do, and intangibles, etc.	This is a technical discussion. Present technically sound, low-maintenance, easy-to-use and implement solutions that are fully supported with training and customer service. This buyer wants proven solutions with no surprises.
Level-III HLDM	Partnership conversations about higher level needs: market conditions, competitive issues, outside pressures, deployment of resources, ROI, bottom-line results, leverage, profit, cash flow profit piranhas, total cost of doing business, shareholder value, employee issues, etc.	Business owner: control, freedom, winning, compliance to their agenda, practical and simple solutions Corporate: mainstream ideas that build consensus and avoid too much exposure, nothing to defend, and will share the glory if they can share the risk and blame	Too much to do, loss of control, inefficiency, complexity, taxing resources, demands on time, etc. Exposure, not politically correct, looking bad, too much left to chance, too much accountability, etc.	This is a high-level conversation about partnerships, not products. Present your assets (value added) as something the HLDM can leverage with her resources. HLDMs want easy-to-implement and widely accepted ideas that will improve their bottom line.

Notice that timing is number one on the list. When buyers are in a hurry to purchase something, price is less compelling. Likewise, in the face of a brand or supplier preference, price is secondary. If there's a limited-supply situation, again, buyers do not shop price. Do you see a pattern here? The more of these pressure points that exist, the stronger your negotiating position. Your understanding and usage of this knowledge is not permission to take advantage of the buyer. What it does do is help you make prudent seller decisions. Why give away the store?

Look for these pressure points on your sales calls. Turn on your sales radar. Ask questions to unearth this information. Send a follow-up letter to buyers after the sales call, recapping some of the relevant pressure points, and use them to rebut price objections. Before succumbing to a request for a discount, review how many pressure points the buyer is experiencing. A negotiating principle is at work here: Whoever feels the most pressure makes the most concessions. A solid understanding of this dynamic will make you a better negotiator.

One of our clients told Tom how a new salesperson on his team used the pressure points concept to negotiate a higher selling price for his company's engineered solution. The salesperson was working on the biggest sale this company had seen in a while. The customer asked for a 20 percent discount. When the salesperson presented the deal to her company, the consensus among the company elders was that the deal was good, even at the 20 percent discount.

The young salesperson said, "I don't believe we need to discount. The buyer is feeling too much pressure to not do business with us. Let's use the pressure point concept and see what happens." The group was nervous about losing this order, but the vice president of sales deferred to the salesperson's instincts.

The salesperson wrote the buyer a letter recapping the pressure points in a positive way and built a presentation around how her company would help the buyer satisfy his needs while relieving the pressure points. The company got the order without cutting the price. The 20 percent amounted to a $180,000 difference! Not bad for a simple concept, is it?

This strategy of demonstrating positively what the buyer could lose by making a price-only decision is powerful. It saves the buyer headaches down the road when the luster of a cheap price wears off and problems with a cheaper alternative arise. How more customer oriented can you be than helping your buyer make better long-term buying decisions? This is Value-Added Selling at its best—looking out for the customer's welfare while protecting your margins!

VALUE-ADDED SELLING REVIEW AND ACTION POINTS

1. Customer-izing is learning to think as your customers think—viewing your solution as value received, not just value added. Study your value added from the buyer's perspective to sharpen your customer value focus.

2. Completing a profile of the buyer's needs, wants, and fears means that you must study the buyer's organizational needs as well as personal wants and fears.

3. Needs are objective buying criteria, and wants are more personal and emotional buying criteria. Looking out for both brings you closer to the buyer.

4. You can improve your negotiating position by looking for buyer pressure points. These conditions shift the accent from price to other relevant buying criteria. The more aware you are of these pressure points, the more effectively you can sell your value added and avoid price objections.

CHAPTER 11

Positioning

Your fourth Value-Added Selling strategy answers this question: "Am I projecting the image of a value-added supplier?"

Chapter 10 completed the first group of Value-Added Selling strategies—focusing. Chapter 11 begins persuasion, the second major group of strategies that value-added salespeople use. Persuasion positions your solution as the value-added solution, differentiates you from the competition, and presents a compelling argument for the buyer to choose your solution.

Persuasion often gets a bad rap. People hear the word and think of manipulation and mind control. Here's a reality check: persuasion has existed from the time Eve induced Adam to take a bite from the forbidden fruit. It's around us in everyday conversations. Parents persuade children to make the right decisions. Spouses persuade their partners to accept their point of view. Teachers persuade students to learn. Bosses persuade employees to do the job. Doctors persuade patients to accept treatments. Lawyers persuade judges and juries. And salespeople persuade buyers to purchase. Persuasion is part of life.

Persuasion is more than a conversation—it's a process of influencing others. It's every way you communicate your message to the receiver of that message. In persuasion, the messenger is as important as the message. Your credibility and sincerity influence the buyer's decision making.

This chapter is about positioning, the first of three persuasion strategies. Positioning is necessarily the first of our persuasion strategies because it predisposes buyers to receive your other messages—differentiation and presenting. Another way to view positioning is that it is your effort to soften the beachhead of your buyer's mind before you launch your other communications. Understanding and using this concept means you create expectations in a buyer's mind about your solution. Buyers use these high expectations to judge every other competitor. Your image thus becomes the standard by which the customer measures everyone else.

At the end of this chapter, you will be able to:

- Name five key points about positioning
- Discuss your company's image
- Offer some ideas on how to communicate this image
- Describe how social media plays an important role in positioning
- Explain personal branding

POSITIONING IS IMAGE BUILDING

You have been positioning since you were a young child and understood the value of having a good reputation. In the old days you called it your *rep*, short for *reputation*. Positioning is a marketing strategy that salespeople execute tactically. It's crafting an image in the customer's mind; it's building a reputation; it's shaping how you want others to perceive you and influencing expectations. Positioning does all of these things. Salespeople use positioning as part of their customer messaging campaign to persuade others that their solution is *the* value-added solution.

Here are five key points you should know about positioning:

1. The battleground is the customer's mind. Advertising gurus Al Ries and Jack Trout wrote in their book *Positioning: The Battle for Your Mind*, "But positioning is not what you do to a product. Positioning is what you do to the mind of the prospect." The battle you fight is never with the customer; the battle is with the way the customer thinks.
2. Positioning is a campaign, not an event. This ongoing process completely surrounds the customer with the message you want to send. This is a well-planned and coordinated sales and marketing effort.

3. Positioning happens face-to-face and behind the scenes. For example, your sending an article about your company to the buyer is part of your image-building campaign. How you conduct your face-to-face sales call communicates something about your professionalism. Both are positioning.

4. Every company owns a position in the customer's mind. What image comes to mind when you hear the company name Volvo? Safety? What image comes to mind when you hear the company name Apple? Innovation? What image comes to mind when you hear the company name BMW? Engineering? These companies have worked hard over the years to craft this image in their customers' minds. What image comes to mind when you hear your company name? How clear is this image to your customers? Right or wrong, the position you own in the customers' mind is based on their perception of who you are. When we ask groups of salespeople this question, "What image does your company own in the market?" we find little consensus with the answers. They vary based on the size of the group. The larger the group, the more diffused the company's image.

5. Everything you do affects this perceived position, one way or the other. Your company can spend millions of dollars to promote an image, but the way you present yourself and your solution speaks volumes to the buyer.

YOUR POSITION IN THE BUYER'S MIND

You own a position in the buyer's mind. It is that slice of the industry psyche you occupy; it's the image and impression you have made. It's the industry buzz about your company, your products, and you; it's your status and standing; and more broadly, it's the label others (customers, competitors, and suppliers) attach to you. These questions will help you understand what space and place you occupy in the industry psyche:

1. What do you hear about your company, your products, and you from your customers?

2. What do you hear from competitors in the industry about your company, products, and you?

3. What do you hear from suppliers in the industry about your company, products, and you?
4. What do you hear from others in your company about your company, products, and you?
5. How would you fill in the blank in this statement?
   We are known as the _____ company.

From candid and sometimes painful responses to these questions, you can begin to understand your real position in the industry. This is a place to start. Then, you turn your attention to the position you want to own. What image do you want to project in each of these three areas?

- **Product.** You might include quality, durability, state-of-the-art technical superiority, and user-friendliness.
- **Company.** You might include ease of doing business, support, commitment to innovation, management flexibility, and stability.
- **People.** You might include helpful, concerned, informed, and customer oriented.

To position your solution effectively, you must have a clear understanding of the image you want to communicate. What theme do you want to permeate your customer messaging? Since marketing is every way you communicate, what message do you want embedded in every customer touch point?

Once you are crystal clear on the message you want to communicate and the image you want to build, you can use a variety of means to help communicate this effectively. Send favorable articles to the buyer about your company or your products. Tell the buyer about awards your company wins; some companies make copies of these for their salespeople to use on sales calls. Dedicate sections of your customer newsletter to promote your image. Use advertising to shape this image. Infuse your sales vocabulary with terminology that supports your position of value: "One of our value-added services is . . ." Highlight sections in your literature that reflect the image you want to project. Leave a message on your voice mail that reminds the customer that you are the value-added supplier. Your strategy is to surround the buyer with your message or position.

In Chapter 7, you read about social media and messaging. Two separate studies have shown how important this tool is in helping you shape your image in the buyer's mind. B2B buyers are embracing technology to do a more effective job. More than half of B2B buyers use social media in their search, and that number is higher for younger buyers.[1] *Forbes* magazine featured a study in which researchers found 78 percent of salespeople use social media to sell.[2] If you are not using social media as part of your positioning campaign, you are missing one of the most effective ways to shape your image in the buyer's mind. In fact, not using social media crafts a negative image in the buyer's mind as you become conspicuous by your absence.

PERSONAL POSITIONING

Personal positioning refers to how the buyer perceives you as a salesperson. Others perceive what you choose to project. Every salesperson projects an image to the buyer. Does the buyer perceive you as a deal guy who is interested only in the transaction, or as someone who is interested in making a difference? Does the buyer view you as an expert in your field? Are you a valuable resource on whom the buyer can rely? Buyers perceive you as either part of the solution or part of the problem.

Buyers have an imaginary collage of faces on their office walls. In this collage are the faces of all the salespeople they know. Either your face stands out in three-dimensional fashion because you've positioned yourself as the value-added salesperson, or you blend in with the rest of the crowd. Standing out in three-dimensional fashion is a great opportunity area. Your behavior will differentiate you from the rest of the pack.

These factors affect your personal position with the buyer:

- **Your knowledge.** Most value added is knowledge based. Your knowledge can position you as an expert—an important part of the team. Do your buyers perceive you as a viable source of information?

- **Your appearance.** Do you look like a success? Value-added salespeople dress to the top of their market. Do you dress for success? Perceived value includes personal packaging in addition to product packaging.
- **Your use of time.** Buyers value their time. They also watch how others use time. Successful people use time effectively. Your effective and efficient use of time communicates the image that you respect this valuable resource. Others will respect your time if you respect it.
- **Your personal organization.** Do you have it together? Are you organized or agonized? When you make the time to organize your presentation, it shows. When you fail to make the time to organize, it also shows. If you can't keep yourself together, why should buyers think you could pull it together for them?
- **Your communications.** How well do you communicate your thoughts? Do they make sense to the buyer? Are you easy to follow, or do you ramble incessantly about subjects that bore your buyer?
- **Your presentations.** Are your sales presentations impressive? Are they convincing? Do you present a compelling reason for the buyer to choose your alternative? How much time do you invest in planning for the sales presentation?
- **Your passion.** Aristotle recognized that passion sells and enthusiasm is contagious.[3] If you're not excited about what you offer, how can you expect the buyer to get excited?
- **Your sincerity.** Buyers want to trust sellers. Sincerity builds this trust. The fundamental question that your buyer asks is, "Can I trust you?"
- **Your success.** Do you have a record of success? Nothing sells like success. Buyers like to do business with others who know how to create success. Brag positively. Selective name-dropping works well.

In our BSP research, we discovered that buyers brand salespeople. They have a name for the salespeople that call on them. This surfaced when one buyer responded to our request for information on the top-achieving salesperson we were studying: "You mean our go-to guy?

That's what we all call him." What a great moniker. What is your personal brand? How do your buyers label you? How do you want them to label you? And how will you communicate this brand to the customer to form the image you want to come to mind when the buyer thinks of you?

Personal Positioning Using Social Media

Social media is a new frontier in sales messaging. An Aberdeen Group Study found that users of social selling outperformed their nonuser counterparts. In this study, social selling users attained quota more often and had higher customer retention rates.[4] Another study, conducted by Jim Keenan and Social Centered Selling, found that 72.6 percent of salespeople using social media outperformed nonusers of social media.[5] Yet our internal research shows that only 43 percent of salespeople are utilizing social media. Who has a better social presence, you or your competition?

Some salespeople falsely believe that social selling can be a substitute for face-to-face selling. You can't tweet your way to a quota. It's a complementary tool that provides additional touch points to position you as a salesperson.

Every company and every salesperson owns an image in the customer's mind. Every face-to-face meeting, e-mail, and social media posting impacts the buyer's perception of you. You are what you share on social media. Are you building that image up or breaking it down?

Traditional marketers focus their positioning effort toward products. The sales process has become more transparent. In a matter of minutes, prospective buyers can research companies and products. Products and companies look the same, feel the same, and blend in. It's not enough to just position products; you must position yourself.

Today's buyers utilize multiple channels to research products, companies, and salespeople. Demand Gen's *2016 B2B Buyer's Survey Report* found that 53 percent of buyers utilize social media to research vendors.[6] Given the popularity of social media, terms like *social selling* have emerged. But social selling is a misnomer. *Social positioning* is a more accurate description. Social positioning is utilizing social media to shape the buyer's image of you, the salesperson. Use these tips to help you build and promote the right image.

Identifying Your Social Image

How do you want to be known? Identifying your personal image is similar to identifying your company's image. Ask yourself the following questions to identify how you are personally positioned:

- What do customers say about me as their salesperson?
- What type of business do I attract?
- What do these customers say about me to my colleagues or managers?
- If all my customers gave me a testimonial, would they say the same thing? If so, what are the overlapping descriptors/ characteristics?
- How would you fill in this blank?
  I am known as the _____ salesperson. Would you be the "go-to guy" we talked about in the last section?

In seminars, salespeople have trouble answering these questions. They are not sure how they are positioned. Some salespeople will candidly say, "Nothing really stands out when I look at these questions." If nothing stands out, then it's hard to convince a buyer that you are outstanding.

Personal positioning is perception and reality. A strong personal positioning campaign is not about building a perception, it is about being what you claim you are.

If you want to be known as the knowledgeable expert, build your expertise and *then* promote that image. If you want to be known as the problem solver, focus on solving problems and *then* promote that image. Your personal image is built by actually *doing* those things that reinforce the image you want to project and *then* promoting that image.

It's not enough to build a perception in the buyer's mind, you actually have to be what you claim you are. Social media cannot build your image, it only provides the platform to promote and support your image. Social media is the new medium to share relevant content that adds value and builds your image. Once you build your image, it's time to occupy the buyer's mind.

Building Your Social Network

Imagine you have prepared a great sales presentation and you are in the prospect's office by yourself. Would you still present your solution? Probably not. Trying to promote your image without a network of people is fundamentally the same as making a sales presentation to an empty room. The next step of social positioning is to build a social network of business colleagues, prospects, and customers.

Your social network is your account list on steroids. Building your social network creates a web of relationships. Whether meeting people at trade shows, networking events, or at the gym, salespeople make face-to-face connections every single day. All you need to do is transfer your existing social network to a digital social network. Building this digital social network ensures that you have an audience to promote your image, too.

Consider this example. You are a heavy equipment salesperson attending a conference. You meet a potential prospect. The new acquaintance has no immediate need, but you connect with her on a social networking site. Over the next several months, you share relevant content that positions you as a problem solver in the equipment industry. One day, that individual contacts you. Since you have positioned yourself as a problem solver, the prospect reaches out to you first. These serendipitous opportunities are a result of personal positioning and building a network. Each opportunity begins with a connection.

Building Your Social Image

You are what you share. A social media post never dies. It never goes away. Remember that before you hit the "share" button. Social media is the megaphone that enables you to promote your image, or destroy it. Demonstrating your personal value builds a positive image in the buyer's mind. It can take years to build a positive image through social media, and seconds to destroy it.

Consistently sharing image-promoting content shapes the buyer's perception of you. In a commoditized market a better-positioned salesperson is more likely to win the business. According to LinkedIn, there's a 50 percent chance that the buyer will use social media as part of the buying process.[7] Based on your social presence, who is better positioned to win the business, you or the competition?

Consider the following scenario. Two similar vendors are competing for a piece of business. The buyer expects the salesperson to be reliable and a problem solver. What if your competitor is doing a better job of positioning himself as the reliable problem solver? Your competitor has shared several case studies demonstrating his company's capabilities, posted several testimonials demonstrating his problem-solving abilities, and created content that details how to solve common industry-related problems. This salesperson is well positioned. The salesperson represents 25 percent of the value, and in a commoditized industry, the salesperson's positioning could be the difference maker.

The greater the overlap between shared content and customer relevancy, the greater your perceived value. When you are positioned as a value creator, price becomes less of an issue. When buyers perceive you as a value creator, they call you before the competition. A strong social presence provides the opportunity to build your personal image in the mind of the buyer.

If you struggle to find great content to share, create it. Work with your marketing team to create meaningful and relevant content. Content marketing is not directly selling or promoting your solution. Content marketing is creating and communicating information (videos, articles, studies, etc.) that adds value to your network. Make your content valuable enough for your target audience to share with their network. Share-worthy content can exponentially grow your network and build your image. What if your personal value added went viral?

A well-positioned salesperson has a significant advantage over his or her competitor. This salesperson delivers more value to customers and extracts more value from customers. A well-positioned salesperson generates more momentum early in the selling process. A well-positioned salesperson is also a magnet for good business. When you are positioned a certain way, you will begin attracting prospects that believe you can help them. Your network feels more comfortable referring you and recommending you. Imagine being so well positioned that prospects would wait in line just to work with you. That's the power of personal positioning.

VALUE-ADDED SELLING REVIEW AND ACTION POINTS

1. Persuasion is every way you communicate with your buyer—it's a process, not an event. What do you communicate to your buyer about your company's value-added solution? What image does your company own in the buyer's mind? This is your position.

2. Effective positioning is surrounding the buyer with this image. How will you continue to support this image and surround the buyer with it? Social media offers salespeople the opportunity to completely surround the customer with messages of value.

3. Buyers perceive what you choose to project. When the buyer thinks of you as a salesperson, what image comes to mind? What brand do you personally want to own in the customer's mind? And how will you shore up that image in the customer's mind?

4. Social media offers salespeople an incredible opportunity to position themselves as knowledgeable problem solvers. Your social media strategy must become part of your overall Value-Added Selling strategy.

CHAPTER 12

Differentiating

Your fifth Value-Added Selling strategy answers this question: "Have I differentiated our status as a value-added supplier?"

In 1934, a Russian biologist named G. F. Gause published a book titled *The Struggle for Existence*. He wrote about the competitive exclusion principle, "Two species competing for the same resources cannot stably exist." One will always have a slight advantage and outcompete the other. The second species will have two choices: go extinct or change the way it competes so as to not directly compete for limited resources. Though Gause was studying bacteria growing on yeast cultures, he could have been describing the state of business today.

There is a pandemic identity crisis today in business. Merger and acquisition activity is high, which means most companies are like blended families—a little of this and a little of that. The commoditization of products and convergence of services has created a frustrating assortment of look-alike supply alternatives. A solid majority of sales and marketing executives say the biggest threat to growth is an inability to differentiate. Over half the people that attend our seminars cannot answer the opening question to this chapter.

Neuroscience has helped us understand the human brain better. Humans are hardwired for simplicity. We like things simple and are programmed for contrast. It's a survival mechanism that keeps us safe. We like things to stand out—especially that snake slithering across the path in front of us. It makes little sense that businesses create look-alike products and services when humans are wired for contrast. Humans like differentiation. It simplifies the buying decision.

Like positioning, differentiating makes it easier for the buyer to choose your solution over the competitor's. Buyers are inundated daily with hundreds of marketing exposures: billboards, radio and TV ads, print media ads, direct-mail pieces, e-mail advertising, social media posts, and phone solicitations. Differentiating makes you jump out from the crowd, establishing degrees of separation between you and your competitor.

At the end of this chapter, you will be able to:

- Define differentiation and explain its vital role in Value-Added Selling
- Discuss the rules for differentiating your solution
- Identify what makes your solution different
- Create barriers that defy direct comparisons
- Discuss ways to sell your differentiated solution

THE POWER OF DIFFERENTIATION

Roberto Goizueta, the late CEO of Coca-Cola, said, "In real estate, it's location, location, location. In business, it's differentiate, differentiate, differentiate."[1] You are outstanding; now, you must stand out. You have a genetic mandate to be different. It is your DNA. People spend so much time trying to fit in that they forget it is their God-given right to be different. When buyers fail to perceive a difference among their supply alternatives, they reduce the buying decision to the core-commodity, naked product, which means the cheapest price. How would you compete if price were not a decision variable? You would have to compete on everything you do for the customer and how you stand out from the crowd. That is the essence of differentiation.

RULES OF DIFFERENTIATION

These simple rules of differentiation can help you stand out. First, it's OK to be different. In fact, it's more than OK; it's necessary. When a customer says to a distributor, "I can buy the same thing down the street cheaper," it is not a price objection. It is a failure-to-differentiate objection. The same thing applies to online purchases. If customers tell you that they can buy it online cheaper, they are saying that they perceive no difference in your offering. This is a failure to differentiate.

Second, be more curious about your potential than concerned about the competition. Too many salespeople are more focused on beating a given competitor versus chasing their own potential. If your focus is beating a competitor, you may create something that is only good enough to beat a given competitor. You have failed to create something that looks more like your potential. Go to market in a way that is so uniquely yours that others compete with you, but you do not compete with them.

Third, innovate, not imitate. A primary cause for lack of differentiation is a lack of imagination or initiative. This means that many companies fail to put forth the effort to stand out. Instead, they wait for someone else to step out from the pack and then imitate their ideas. Me-too is the opposite of differentiation. If you decide to offer an inventory management program, twice-a-day deliveries, and training because the competition does these things, you are commoditizing value added. Besides, imitating another supplier positions your company as a me-too supplier.

The reality is that no one can really copy the competition and claim ownership of a uniqueness. Norman Myers wrote in his book *The Long African Day*, "Anyone who thinks a leopard skin looks as good on another creature's back as it does on a leopard hasn't seen a leopard. It is so much at one with itself that you cannot own part of the leopard."

Fourth, solve unique problems, or solve common problems in unique ways. What problems do other distributors or manufacturers shy away from? Everyone goes for the low-hanging fruit—the easy problems. Tackle the tough ones. What challenges have customers given up on because they think no one can handle the challenge? What is the one thing that keeps your customer awake at night? What makes her rise early in the morning? How can you help her?

Fifth, study your differences along the three dimensions of value. What features and benefits make your products stand out? What is there about your company that separates you from the pack? How do your people stand out from others in the market? Identify the standout differences that make you outstanding in the market.

Sixth, differentiate by your customer base. Be selective in the customers that you pursue. Not all business is good business. Imagine the industry buzz as you develop the reputation of only working with the most progressive, innovative, and leading customers in your market. For customers, it almost feels prestigious to work with you. You are known by the company that you keep. If you associate only with the price shoppers and bottom-feeders of your industry, others assume guilt by association. When you are selective in how you invest your resources, you can be selective in your customer experience as you customize your value proposition for each customer.

Once you have decided how you will stand out, you have a ready-made answer for the next time the customer says, "You and so-and-so are all in the same business." You will respond by saying, "We are in the same industry but not the same business, and here's why."

YOUR DEFINABLE AND DEFENDABLE DIFFERENCES

Only 41 percent of salespeople believe they offer a meaningfully different solution. How about you? What are your definable and defendable differences? Most salespeople struggle to answer this differentiating question.

Imagine you're in a room with 50 of your peers, and you have 15 minutes to discuss the primary differences between you and your two largest competitors. Would you need all 15 minutes? At this point, you blush, your heart rate increases, and you feel a knot in your gut. This is the reaction most salespeople would have if they were presented with that challenge.

The best way to determine the most significant differences between you and the competition is to return to the three dimensions of value: product, company, and people. The Differentiation Matrix in Figure 12.1 illustrates a spreadsheet comparison of three competitors, using 36 variables. We use this matrix in our seminars to lead a discussion of competitive differences. This is a generic matrix that you can use for many industries. You may want to tailor this form to your company and your competitors. Add value to the exercise by including some industry-specific variables.

Having reviewed this matrix, how would you answer the question, "What are the definable and defendable differences between you and the competition?" Most salespeople need some time to work on it.

FIGURE 12.1 **Differentiation Matrix**

	Our Company	Competitor A	Competitor B
Product Attributes			
Availability			
Packaging			
Warranty			
Acquisition price			
Quality			
Usage cost			
Durability			
Performance			
Brand name			
Efficiency			
Safety			
User-friendliness			
Company Attributes			
Ease of doing business			
Service guarantees			
Reputation			
Technical support			
Terms			
Return policy			
Inventory levels			
Service policy			
Ordering options			
Management flexibility			
Industry leader			
Postsale support			
Presale assistance			
People Attributes			
Knowledgeable			
Follow-through			
Understand needs			
Problem solving			
Empathy			
Accessible			
Integrity			
Straightforward			
Innovative			
Good listener			
Eager			
Organized			
Gets things done			

Go ahead and study the differences. Seek input and information from other people. Share your competitive knowledge. Be prepared for the buyer's inevitable question: "Why should I buy from your company versus another?" If you can't answer it before the sales call, you won't be able to answer it on the streets.

CREATE BARRIERS

Oscar Wilde wrote, "Be yourself; everyone else is already taken." Creating barriers helps demonstrate your uniqueness. Creating barriers between you and the competition makes it difficult for the buyer to simplify the decision process and choose a supplier based solely on price. Barriers defy direct comparisons. The best way to create barriers and to distance your solution from the competition is to think in terms of what the buyer needs versus what the competition is selling. Differentiate your solution by projecting yourself into the buyer's situation.

Value-added salespeople sell to the customer's needs, not against the competition's package. Putting the emphasis on the customer instead of the competition automatically differentiates you from the rest of the pack. Your competitors devote more attention to their competition's product than to the buyer's needs.

Create barriers by using a timeline to present your solution. Lay out your solution along the CBP. This format gives you a model to present your chronology of value. In doing so, you stretch the buyer's time horizon calling attention to your downline value. Stretching the timeline moves the focal point away from acquisition price and onto your total solution. The long-range outcome of your solution is your value proposition.

Create barriers by making it easier for buyers to do business with your company than with a competitor. This idea surfaces often and in many ways in buyer surveys. Make it easy to place orders, get technical support, and reach customer service. Customers want to do business with companies that demonstrate they want to do business with buyers. Flexibility wins a lot of business for companies. Identify those areas where the competition is difficult to do business with; those areas stick like thorns in the buyer's side. Demonstrate how your way of doing business avoids those inconveniences.

Create barriers by providing direct access to people who can make things happen. Technology has allowed companies to avoid direct personal contact with customers. Elaborate phone systems that promise increased efficiency via submenus epitomize technology's impersonal touch. Buyers say that they hate these systems. If it takes buyers five submenus to get to a real person, they become irritated and agitated. How do you feel when you must run through a series of submenus and then are put on hold? Because buyers get frustrated with these automated phone systems, they pursue suppliers who give personalized attention. Wouldn't you?

A sales rep told us about a new account he got because the competition put the buyer on hold for an average of 22 minutes every time he called. The buyer got mad and decided he would get even by transferring his business to a competitor who did not put him on hold for 22 minutes. This buyer managed one of the largest fleets of heavy equipment in the country. Imagine losing business because your company put a large account on hold too long. Consider the irony of losing business as a result of employing the technology that promises to help you deliver better service.

Create barriers by packaging your products and services in a unique bundle and choosing a different pricing model. Why would suppliers package and price their goods and services exactly the same as everyone else in the industry? They make it painless for buyers to choose the cheapest alternative. Creating a unique packaging barrier makes it difficult for the buyer to choose solely on price. Why set yourself up for commodity comparisons? It's not just OK to be different—it's necessary to be different. That's the essence of differentiation. If the buyer complains, explain that the uniqueness of your packaging is only the tip of the iceberg; you're unique in many ways. Why would the buyer pay more to buy from you if you look just like the competition?

Create barriers by offering options at different price levels. The subtle message you're sending is that if price is a major consideration, the buyer must look at a different package. Printers are notorious for this. Printers always demonstrate the cost-effectiveness of buying in larger quantities. They up-sell. Buyers who will eventually need and use the higher quantity can take advantage of the cheaper, higher-quantity prices. This higher-quantity pricing strategy also preempts price objections. It signals buyers that they can get overall cheaper prices by increasing the size of their initial order.

Create barriers by using your creativity—there's no commodity in creativity. When you view the buyer's needs, wants, and fears from his or her point of view, it gives you a unique vantage point that will stir your creativity. Think outside of the box when designing your solution. Look for unconventional solutions. That's the essence of differentiation—doing things uniquely.

Ask "What if" questions to direct your efforts: "What if we could do this for the customer?" "What if we could change this?" "What if we could improve this feature?" Stretch to the edge of your imagination. Buyers will pay for creative and fresh approaches to old problems.

YOUR UNIQUE SELLING PROPOSITION

Every company must have a stand-out difference, the one thing that only your company can claim as its own. Some call this the Big Idea or the unique selling proposition (USP) that you read about in Chapter 7. Your USP must be unique, compelling, defendable, and simple. To determine your USP, complete these sentences:

- We were the first to . . .
- We are the only ones that . . .
- Customers tell us we stand out because of . . .

Once you are clear on your USP, it is time to broadcast it loud and clear. This uniqueness theme must run throughout your customer messaging campaign. You want to surround your customer with this obvious difference that you stand out from the crowd.

TIPS FOR SELLING YOUR DIFFERENCES

You understand the uniqueness of your buyer's needs and the differences between your solution and the rest of the pack. Now you're ready to stand out from the crowd. How do you sell these differences?

1. **Never discount a differentiator.** Your difference is what makes you stand out. If you discount it, you are telling the customer that it wasn't that special to begin with. How can you give away something you wanted to charge for but conceded in a price discussion? Where's the value? If it's worth nothing to you, how can you expect the buyer to assign worth to it?

2. **Keep things positive.** Always take the high ground. Avoid negative selling—bad-mouthing the competition. It's possible, and even desirable, to discuss your unique advantages that happen to be weaknesses for the competition. Put the spotlight on what you do well versus what the competition fails to do. Smart buyers know what you're doing and respect the fact that you are not taking an easy shot at a weak opponent. This is especially important when the buyer has purchased from this weak competitor in the past. He or she may feel the need to defend a previous buying decision or take pity on the underdog. Either way, you lose.

   If the buyer attempts to draw you into a direct comparison, remain focused on your strengths: "We're in the same industry, but we're definitely not in the same business. I'd like to discuss what makes our company special and unique in the way we solve your problems." Resist the bait. Maintain the high ground. You'll feel better about your approach and gain the buyer's respect in the process.

3. **Use comparison tools to spotlight your differences.** A product comparison matrix offers you a format to highlight your advantages. It's similar to the differentiation matrix in Figure 12.1. In the left column, list the primary comparison variables. Across the top row, list three or four competitors. In each cell of the matrix, place a symbol to indicate which supplier offers a specific product feature. In addition, you may be able to rank each supplier.

   Another comparison tool is a spreadsheet financial analysis that compares your solution vis-à-vis the competition. You may include acquisition price, energy costs, operating costs, maintenance costs, disposal costs, residual value, and other life-cycle costs. This is a financial justification of your product over its lifetime versus alternatives.

4. **Get others to sell for you.** Use testimonial letters to call attention to your advantages over the competition. Encourage buyers to talk to your existing customers who have used other suppliers in the past. Use quotes from third-party endorsers of your product or company. If an outside testing service rates your product favorably, use its analysis.

5. **Acknowledge the generic similarities between you and the competitor.** Use acknowledged similarities as a springboard to launch into your value-added presentation. You might say, "Granted, there are a few similarities between the competition and us, but I would really like to focus on the value added that makes us different." At this point, detail your value added that is, coincidentally, a weak spot for the competition.

6. **Create barriers with a *ten-things-to-consider list*.** Select 10 of your value-added extras. List them as statements on a page and label the list *Ten Things to Consider Before Purchasing*. You are calling attention to your value added and encouraging the buyer to use these 10 points as decision criteria. You may also design this list in question format: *Ten Questions to Ask Yourself before Buying*. Your value-added extras are now questions for the buyer to ask and answer before making the buying decision. Asked and answered, your questions should favor your solution. These 10 degrees of separation make it easier for the buyer to justify the difference in your pricing. Common sense dictates that if there are 10 ways you are different, of course there will be a difference in price.

VALUE-ADDED SELLING REVIEW AND ACTION POINTS

1. Consolidation, mergers, and acquisitions have presented buyers with a confusing array of look-alike products and services. Compounding this problem is that most salespeople fail to differentiate their solution from the competition. To make it easier for the buyer to choose your alternative, you must be able to answer this question: "What are the definable and defendable differences between you and the competition?"

2. These differentiation rules will help you stand out. It's OK to be different, be more curious about your potential than concerned about the competition, innovate, solve unique problems, study your differences along the three dimensions of value, and differentiate by your customer base.

3. There is something so special about your company or products that it has earned the label of the unique selling proposition. The USP is your definitive argument for the difference in your value. You will make this part of your customer messaging campaign.

4. Create barriers that defy direct comparison between you and the competition. You can differentiate along the buyer's CBP in addition to the three dimensions of value: product, company, and salesperson.

5. When selling your differences, maintain the high ground. It's tempting, even momentarily, to disparage the competition. When selling these differences, point out how your solution is better, which is generally the competition's weaknesses. The buyer will respect your approach. Create sales tools like the ten-things-to-consider list or a spreadsheet that financially justifies your solution.

CHAPTER 13

Presenting

Your sixth Value-Added Selling strategy answers this question: "How compelling is my argument for our solution?"

Our internal study found that only 34 percent of salespeople offer a solution that is compelling enough for the buyer to change. For buyers to pay premium prices for a solution, they must feel a solution is worth more to them than their money. They want to feel that the solution is special and equitable. They want to be excited about where their money is going and what they are getting in return. Here's where presenting comes in.

Presenting is your third essential persuasion strategy in Value-Added Selling. It is the most prescriptive of the three persuasion strategies. Buyers want to purchase from salespeople who can present a compelling argument. This especially applies when the buyer is purchasing something for the first time. McKinsey and Co. found that 76 percent of customers prefer to deal with a salesperson directly when purchasing a new product or service.[1] That number drops to a low of 15 percent on repeat sales of commodity-type items. These buyers recognize that salespeople are a valuable resource when they need information. This presents a compelling argument for why salespeople should maintain contact even and especially when the buyer slips into a reorder mode with commodity-type items.

Whereas positioning and differentiating have a strategic marketing tone, presenting sounds much more like tactical selling. Presenting is your face-to-face communication with the buyer. It is one part content and one part context. It includes your substance and your style. Your effectiveness in organizing, customizing, and delivering this message influences the buyer's willingness to choose your alternative.

This chapter is about a four-part model for presenting your value: your message must reflect the buyer's personal definition of value, you must take advantage of your perceived value, you must demonstrate the performance value of your solution, and you must offer proof.

At the end of this chapter, you will be able to:

- Personalize your message to the buyer's needs, wants and fears
- Communicate your perceived value
- Demonstrate your substance
- Discuss proof sources to shore up your argument

PERSONALIZE YOUR MESSAGE

Does your message reflect the buyer's definition of value? Are you acting from the buyer's point of view? Buyers want to feel that you understand their definition of value and have designed a solution that reflects their priorities. This is customer-oriented selling at its best. Consider this: It's their problem, it's their money, and it's a solution with which they must live. Your solution should reflect their definition of value.

There is a fundamental communication truth that is especially relevant for salespeople. The most powerful word to use when talking to customers is "you." It draws them deeper into the conversation. It shines the spotlight on them. It compels you to frame your sales messages in a way that resonates with the buyer. Consider these two examples of presenting the same benefit:

"We use only the best materials in manufacturing our product, which increases the quality of what we sell to our customers."

"You receive world-class quality when you purchase our products. We begin our manufacturing with the best raw materials in the market to deliver to you the best solution in the market."

Both statements are claims and require elaboration and proof. Which would appeal more directly to the customer? The second one directs the benefits to the customer.

As you review the following suggestions, remember, the sale is more about the customer than the seller.

Use Analogies

The analogy is a powerful presentation tool because adults act on precedent. Previous decisions influence current decisions. Show consonance. Buyers process information quickly and effectively when new messages reflect what they already know. By using an analogy, you ask buyers to make decisions similar to ones they have already made. Their new decisions are consistent with what they've done in the past. Identify the broader concept you're selling. Demonstrate how the buyer has already embraced this concept. Show the conceptual linkage to your idea.

For example, if you sell office interior furnishings, be aware of the image the buyer's company promotes in its advertising. The inside of this company's office should reflect the image it promotes in the market. This image is all the more important when the company's customers visit its offices. You're selling continuity and consistency, so the analogy makes it easy for the buyer to understand the benefits of your solution.

You're asking the buyer to use the same logic when deciding about your solution. For example, you say to your buyer, "You've invested heavily in creating and promoting a special image for your company in all areas of your marketing. Doesn't it make sense to invest in office furnishings that support the image you've created in your advertising?"

Look for some other area in the company in which the buyer has made a buying decision similar to what you're proposing. Use that previous behavior as justification for the buyer's acting on your suggestion. It greases the skids for moving forward with your idea.

Choose Buyer Buzzwords of Value

Every buyer has a unique way to describe what he or she wants and needs. Listen carefully to the exact wording your buyer uses, and incorporate this wording in your presentation. Infuse your sales vocabulary with the buyer's terminology. This approach reduces the psychological distance between you and the buyer because you're speaking the same language.

For example, your buyer may use words such as *revenue growth* versus *increased sales*, *productivity* versus *performance*, and *contribution dollars* versus *profitability*. Mirroring specific buzzwords sends a message that you have listened and understood priorities, and you have a solution that sounds a lot like what the buyer wants. Speak your buyer's language.

Sell to the Buyer's Total Needs

This includes different departments and different levels of decision makers—Levels I-II-III. The reality of selling to organizations is that multiple decision makers may be involved in the decision process. Cover yourself on all bases. Sell to the logistics buyers, the users and influencers, and the high-level decision makers (see Chapters 9 and 27). Present your solution in a way that all departments can see the potential benefit of working with you—that your total solution (the three dimensions of value) meets their total needs.

Your ease in moving from one level to another and from one department to another affects your success. You must develop this flexibility in order to reach your full potential in sales. The versatility of value-added salespeople is one of their great strengths. To develop this skill, meet with everyone involved in or affected by the buying decision. Remember, Level-II users are most affected by change. Seek input at all levels to develop a composite understanding of their total organizational needs and personal wants.

Customize

Study the buyer's promotional literature and visit the company's website. Identify common themes and then fill your presentation with these messages. Following your buyer's communications path is a strong message of parallel thinking. It says that your company operates much the same way as the buyer's company. Companies with similar philosophies should do business with each other, shouldn't they? Birds of a feather flock together. How can the buyer reject your offer when it mirrors his or her thinking and promotional themes? To charge value-added prices or fees, you must customize. Buyers will not pay higher prices for generic solutions.

Give Permission to Buy

Sometimes, people must be nudged. They need to know it's OK to spend more than they anticipated. Whether it's the number that scares them or the notion of extravagance, you must reassure buyers they deserve the best. They have worked hard to achieve their status and owe it to themselves to own the best. Luxury goods manufacturers discovered this long ago. That's why you will see advertising themes advocating, "When you deserve the best . . ."

Demonstrate Consonance

For the same reason that managers hire people like themselves, buyers like to do business with sellers who do business the way the customer wants to do business. Demonstrating the consonance of your company's values with the buyer's company values is one way to do this. If the buyer's company embraces integrity, transparency, and innovation, be prepared to discuss your company's business practices, openness, and commitment to innovation. Who better to trust with their needs and money than someone who thinks as they think?

MAXIMIZE YOUR PERCEIVED VALUE

Is it sexy? Does it sizzle? Does it have flash? These are questions to ask yourself about how your stuff looks—your style. Perceived value is the *context* of your message. It influences the buyer's expectations. It gives buyers a warm and fuzzy feeling about your solution. In order to generate this feeling, every steak must sizzle. Maximizing your perceived value is a quick way to make a positive impact on your presentation. Perceived value is how something looks, feels, and sounds to the buyer. Does it pop? Does it have splash? Does it make the buyer's blood race?

Dress It Up

Put your best foot forward. How do your materials look? Do they have instant visual impact? How well do you use color and graphics to communicate your message? The quality of what you present to buyers must parallel the quality of your product. Humans are visual processors. Seventy percent of the information that humans process comes through visual input. Technology and color printers make it possible for any salesperson to add sizzle to presentation materials and proposals. Buyers judge books by their covers.

If you present a message that your company is the value-added supplier, your materials must reflect that image. If they fail to mirror that image, you create cognitive dissonance; as a result, the buyer rejects your offer because it doesn't feel right.

Use the Value-Added Sales Jargon

When buyers hear something often enough, they start to believe it. Form an association between your company's name and the words *value added*. Use these words in your presentations, casual conversations, and correspondence.

Discuss your value-added services, describe your value-added benefits, and make a list of your value-added extras. Surround the customer with your value added. Make it a word association exercise. What two words should pop into the buyer's mind when he or she hears your company name? *Value added*, of course.

Choose Positive Focus Words

There are many ways to frame a sales message. Some are positive, and some are negative. Choose positive expressions. Do your buyers want more uptime or less downtime? Do they want greater compliance with specs or fewer rejects? Do they want quicker availability or less waiting time for the product? Do they want to cut costs or earn greater profit?

You always have a choice in how you frame your message. A young salesperson lost an order because of the way he presented a benefit. He told the buyer that his product ran so quietly that it was "almost dangerous." The buyer perceived this as a disadvantage and purchased another alternative. From these words, the buyer could think only of the likelihood of an industrial accident. How would you like to lose an order to a benefit—especially one that is supposed to be a differentiating factor?

Present Your Price Carefully

There is only one way to present your price. Use these three words: "the price is." Anything other than that creates doubt in the buyer's mind. "Your price" sounds as if everyone gets a different deal. "List price" signals that there are many pricing levels. Look the buyer in the eye and say, "The price is . . ." The time to exude complete confidence is when you're asking people for money. A buyer who perceives any wavering or lack of confidence on your part will not purchase.

Present Long-Term Solutions Along the CBP

Stretch your buyer's time horizon by presenting your solution along a timeline that describes how they will decide, buy, and use your product. Most of the value added that companies deliver occurs during ownership and usage. Unless your buyer is thinking long term, he or she will not perceive your value added.

Present your chronology of value to the buyer by saying, "We support you from start to finish, and here's how it happens." At this point, lay out your solution procedurally to emphasize the long-term benefits you offer. Many buyers find it easier to visualize your total solution as you lay it out sequentially and over the long term.

Clean up Your Proposals

Creating proposals is an area where most salespeople admit they can improve immediately. Begin with a summary of the buyer's needs to spotlight all the reasons why he or she is pursuing a value-added solution. Use your value proposition as an executive preview of what is to follow. Include a summary of your value added—your VIP list, as explained in Chapter 7. Offer proof and data to reassure the buyer. Stress that you guarantee complete satisfaction. Insert your customer bill of rights. Top it off with a personal commitment letter from you to the buyer detailing the personal value added that you as a salesperson will deliver.

If possible, deliver your proposals in person. Because days get chaotic and you're busy, it's tempting to e-mail your proposal to the customer. After all, the customer has told you to do it. Consider this: Your proposal looks only as good as the buyer's printer prints it. Remember, every steak must sizzle!

DEMONSTRATE PERFORMANCE VALUE

Performance value is your profit impact on the customer's business. It's the steak behind the sizzle—the quantitative behind the qualitative. While perceived value defines your style, performance value demonstrates your substance. This is the content of your message. Our research found that only half of salespeople can demonstrate how their solution has a positive impact on the customer's organization. Use these suggestions to establish your performance value.

Demonstrate Opportunity Value and Opportunity Cost

What do you give the buyer the opportunity to do tomorrow that he or she cannot do today? This is the most overlooked value that companies bring to the table. What problems can the buyer fix because of your solution? What markets can the buyer now pursue because of the relationship with your company? Your ability to empower buyers to go beyond where they are now is real value added—opportunity value, a real gain. This is as far from commodity selling as you can get. You bring hope and possibilities to the table. Your answers to these questions encourage buyers to dream again about possibilities.

A missed opportunity is a thorn in the buyer's side. This is the opportunity cost of not pursuing your idea. What if you could turn back the hands of time and recapture a missed sales opportunity? Hindsight is always 20/20. Selling opportunity value is selling hope. Selling opportunity cost is making the buyer painfully aware of what he or she misses by not going with your idea.

Discuss Synergy

You add value to the buyer's solution through your collective solution. It's the "Intel inside" concept. You can have the least-known, no-brand-name computer, but when you put a sticker on the front that says "Intel inside," the buyer perceives it to be a quality system. The Intel component adds value to the computer. How does your solution add value to the buyer's solution? Do you add to the company's product quality, customer response time, or end-user acceptance?

Sell Your Investment Value

Words matter. Certain words trigger defensive reactions in buyers. The word "expense" is a trigger word. Buyers perceive your product or service as either an investment or an expense. When buyers perceive it as an expense, they're thinking about all the money leaving the company. This triggers a negative reaction. When they perceive it as an investment, they're thinking about the money returning to the company. This triggers a more positive response from buyers. How does your solution represent an investment to each customer?

Is your solution an investment in product quality, customer satisfaction, or competitive advantage? As an investment, your product or service becomes a value-added solution. As an expense, your product or service becomes a commodity purchase, which brings price sensitivity into the picture. Sell your investment value instead.

Sell All Three Dimensions of Value

This includes product features and benefits, company value-added services, and your commitment to serve. For each buyer need, you offer three levels of benefits: the product, the company, and you. Figure 13.1 displays a planning matrix that you can use to build a three-dimensional solution. It encourages you to ask how the product, the company, and you satisfy each buyer need. Three needs multiplied by three dimensions of value equals nine categories of benefits for the customer. The same product from the same company from two different salespeople represents two separate solutions.

FIGURE 13.1 **Presentation Planner Matrix**

3-D Solution

Need	Company	Product	Sales Rep

Use a Value-Added Worksheet

This sales tool quantifies your value added. Figure 13.2 presents an example. On the worksheet, list your value-added services and their value to the buyer. Compute the total value for the whole package. This is proof positive that your value-added solution has a real profit impact on the buyer's situation. You have "tangible-ized" your value added.

FIGURE 13.2 **Value-Added Worksheet**

Item	Calculated Value	Extended Value
EDI	Customer usage: 121 times/year @ $35.00 savings/use 121 × $35 = $4,235	$4,235.00
Safety training	Two seminars for customer's employees 2 × $1,500 = $3,000	$3,000.00
Profit enhancement program	Annual audit of purchasing habits. Two percent efficiency savings on $120,000 purchases: 0.02 × $120,000 = $2,400	$2,400.00
Equipment extension of life cycle	Six pumps at 12% life cycle extension: 6 pumps @ $15,000 = $90,000 $90,000 × 0.12 = $10,800	$10,800.00
TOTAL VALUE ADDED DELIVERED		$20,435.00

Present Your Value Added in a Spreadsheet

The spreadsheet—a value analysis—compares your product or service to a competitor's by using input variables important to the buyer. This direct-comparison selling includes acquisition price, installation, energy consumption, maintenance costs, training costs, disposal costs, and other costs. As Figure 13.3 demonstrates, your acquisition price may be higher, but your operating costs lower, and the residual value is greater. Thus, your product or service is a better long-term decision for the buyer. Buyers who are involved throughout the life cycle of a product understand these comparisons. Buyers call this a value analysis.

FIGURE 13.3 **Economic Value Analysis**

	System A	System B
Acquisition cost	$18,795.00	$13,770.00
Annual energy costs	$675.00	$1,405.00
Product life cycle	15 years	10 years
Trade-in value	25%	0
Annual cost to own over product life cycle	$1,928.00	$2,782.00
Trade-in value	$4,698.75	0

OFFER PROOF

Doug Hall, a pioneer in the innovation field, found that proof increases the likelihood of sales success by 42 percent.[2] Add meaningful uniqueness to that proof source, and it increases the likelihood of success by 53 percent.

Buyers love proof. They have an aversion to loss. How can you mitigate risk for your buyer? Offering proof reassures buyers. It provides them with the peace of mind that they are making a good buying decision. There are multiple ways you can offer proof.

Social proof demonstrates how others have implemented your ideas or purchased your solution. Humans are social creatures. Most buyers like to know that others have made the same decision and benefitted by it. A UPS study of industrial buyers found that 60 percent of the buyers used word of mouth as a proof source. It's important when you use social proof that the proof source has great credibility. When possible, keep your proof source level-specific. For Level-I buyers, offer logistics proof. For Level-II technical people, offer technical proof. For Level-III decision makers, offer proof from other business owners or high-level executives. Customer satisfaction surveys, data, third-party endorsements, and case studies add credibility to your presentation. Customer testimonials are especially powerful. Ask the customer to comment on all three dimensions of your value—the product, company, and you.

Another important way to mitigate risk is warranties or guarantees. This is a tricky one. For most people, these are remedies. The buyer has a problem, and you promise to fix or replace it. It protects the buyer and makes him or her feel better about purchasing. But there is a more positive application of guarantees with Value-Added Selling. Stress the positive impact of your guarantee: "Ms. Buyer, the thing that makes our guarantee special is that we guarantee your satisfaction. We will work with you until you are completely satisfied with our solution." If you were the buyer, which would you prefer, the salesperson who tells you that she will replace something if you're not happy, or the salesperson who guarantees your satisfaction?

VALUE-ADDED SELLING REVIEW AND ACTION POINTS

1. Reducing the distance between the sender and the receiver of a message makes communication more effective and persuasive. When you personalize your message to reflect the buyer's needs, wants, and fears, you make it easier for the buyer to say yes to your solution.

2. Perceived value influences your buyer's expectations. It is the *context* in which you present your message. When you maximize your perceived value, you put your best foot forward.

3. Performance value demonstrates the profit impact you have on the buyer's business. It is the *content* of your message. While perceived value defines your style, performance value defines your substance. There are several tools you can use to demonstrate your performance value.

4. Offering proof increases your probability of success while reassuring the buyer that he or she is making a sound buying decision. Social proof, data, third-party endorsements, testimonials, and guarantees are a few of the things you can offer.

CHAPTER 14

Supporting

Your seventh Value-Added Selling strategy answers this question: "How painless have we made it for the customer to implement our solution?"

Dwight D. Eisenhower, thirty-fourth president of the United States, was the Supreme Allied Commander in World War II. He said this about logistics: "You will not find it difficult to prove that battles, campaigns, and even wars have been won or lost primarily because of logistics."[1]

When you are a consumer and ready to pay, which checkout lane do you normally choose? The longest? The shortest? The one where the person in front of you has the fewest items in the basket? How do you pay? Cash, check, debit card, credit card, gift card, or smartphone? Do you buy things that are assembled or those that require some assembly? If the item you purchase is bulky, do you arrange to have it delivered? If this is a complicated electronics item, do you pay extra for installation? If you have questions after the sale, do you prefer an automated phone attendant or a real person you can understand? If you're like most people, you choose speed, ease, and simplicity—the shortest line, the easiest way to pay, and the simplest way to get up and running with your new purchase.

Most people opt for convenience. According to Pew Research, 8-of-10 people shop online.[2] A 2017 KPMG study lists convenience, not price, as the number one reason people shop online.[3] Price is important to online shoppers, but 24/7 ordering convenience is more important. This peek into the consumer's mind provides an interesting backdrop for B2B buying behavior. B2B buyers want ease, speed, efficiency, and support.

So far, you've learned about focusing and persuading—two of the four groups of Value-Added Selling strategies. The third group of strategies is supporting, which includes process and people support.

As you begin this supporting phase of the Value-Added Selling process, you have reached the shift point from offensive to defensive selling. This transition is a point of differentiation for Value-Added Selling from all other forms of selling, as we emphasize the importance of defensive selling. In offensive selling, you're pursuing new business opportunities; your focus is the acquisition of new customers. In defensive selling, you're protecting existing business; your focus is the retention and growth of existing business. In the offensive mode, you diagnose a problem and prescribe a solution. In the defensive selling mode, you support the customer and grow the business. It's the difference between promising and delivering.

At this shift point in the sale, the customer's greatest need is for a smooth, seamless, and painless transition to your solution. This chapter is about the support that you provide your customers.

At the end of this chapter, you will be able to:

- Describe the logistics support you offer to ease the transition
- Discuss ways to support the people who are most affected by this change

PROCESS SUPPORT

Now, you're wearing your logistics support hat. You've transitioned from sales to service. Your primary job function is facilitator, expediter, implementer, change agent, catalyst, supply chain manager, and coordinator. Your focus is the transition from whatever the buyer did yesterday to what you sold him or her to use tomorrow. Like most of the CBP your activities parallel the customer's needs and activities. Here is a sampling of these activities and how you add value:

- Verifying order status
- Expediting orders and chasing back orders
- Providing substitute shipments

- Helping things run smoothly
- Following the supply chain
- Processing credits and returns
- Preparing facilities
- Receiving and warehousing products
- Redistributing goods

To provide the level of support that customers require, you must use your internal selling skills. These are the skills you use to make things happen inside your own company. Working with the credit department to help better serve the customer is internal selling. Convincing the shipping department that packaging flexibility is important to this buyer is internal selling. Selling your manager on the concept of a customer appreciation golf outing is internal selling. And you thought your job was only to sell to external customers. Internal selling is encouraging and leading your internal team members down the path of complete customer satisfaction. It's helping them understand how they contribute to the value your company creates for the customer.

Our research found that buyers' number one concern when switching suppliers is whether or not the new supplier can and will deliver on its promises. In the process-support mode, you follow the order from receipt to delivery to assure timeliness and accuracy. Likewise, your customers want seamless and painless transitions to your solution. Your job is to make the path smooth.

In our seminar, we met a heavy-duty truck salesperson who is a master of defensive selling. He begins his support by confirming the order to ensure that it is correct. He monitors the progress of the order and provides his customer with periodic updates. When the truck is being prepared for delivery, he conducts a predelivery inspection to ensure that the specifications match the order. When the truck is ready for delivery, he performs a walk-around demonstration to ensure that the buyer understands the truck's operating features. If the buyer has any questions about the documentation or registration, the salesperson clarifies that information also. This salesperson takes great pride in taking care of his customers. He treats each sale as if it were his first sale with this customer. You can bet it's not his last.

PEOPLE SUPPORT

Now, you are wearing your people-support hat. You're serving people, not just the process. You're a supporter, champion, mediator, ally, partner, trainer, and cheerleader. Your focus is those people most affected by the transition. You're an advocate for the customer and a liaison for your company. You are the customer's safety net, hand-holder, and therapist all rolled up into one. Your defensive selling activities parallel the customer's needs at this point. You provide value as you serve in the following ways:

- Introducing cross-functional teams to each other
- Training as needed
- Offering technical support
- Fielding inquiries and questions
- Following up on requests
- Providing backup as needed
- Helping to lighten the load

Some people call this the softer support you offer. To the customer, this is as real as it gets. The TLC, hand-holding, and information you provide reassure customers that they made the correct decision in selecting your alternative. This personalized service after the sale is what continues to position you and your company as the value-added solution in the industry. You allay fears and confirm the customer's decision to buy. This eliminates buyer's remorse.

Customer satisfaction is a function of your performance vis-à-vis the customers' expectations. Meeting their expectations results in customer satisfaction. Exceeding their expectations results in customer delight. To meet and exceed their expectations, you must first be aware of what they expect. Clarify expectations throughout the buying process.

Another salesperson who attended our seminars is a great people supporter. She realizes that during the transition phase some people at the customer's company may resist the change to a new supplier. She makes it a point to meet those affected by the change and to listen patiently to their concerns. If they require training, she offers her assistance there. She will contact her internal trainers and explain the situation. Her concern for people makes her buyer look good and the transition go more smoothly. The heads-up support she provides to her trainers makes her look good internally, also.

You must embed in your sales messaging your company's ease of doing business. Buyers want it. Though the term "ease of doing business" may sound vague or a given, buyers want everything that goes with it—transparency, simplicity, responsiveness, and flexibility. Ease of doing business is unique in that it is qualitative value added, and it can be measured quantitatively. It is a feeling and a fact. It begins as a feeling that buyers can then measure factually.

VALUE-ADDED SELLING REVIEW AND ACTION POINTS

1. Supporting marks the shift from offensive to defensive selling. The buyer has studied his or her needs and made a purchasing decision from among several alternatives. You demonstrate your commitment to serving by providing logistics and people support to facilitate this transition and ratify the buyer's choice for your solution.

2. In supporting the transition process, you wear two hats. The first is a logistics hat. This hat has you playing several roles: expediter, facilitator, and supply-chain manager. Direct your attention to attending to the demand-and-supply process.

3. The second hat you wear has you supporting people affected by this transition. You are a trainer, hand-holder, and team leader. As you attend to people issues, you reassure all people involved of your full commitment to their complete satisfaction.

CHAPTER 15

Relationship Building

Your eighth Value-Added Selling strategy answers this question: "How is my personal and professional relationship with the customer?"

Relationships are the cornerstone of Value-Added Selling. When buyers make a value-added buying decision, they commit to something bigger than a product; they commit to the relationship with the seller.

There were two striking findings in our BSP research. The first was the power of relationships. We asked top-achieving salespeople what percentage of their success they attributed to their relationship with customers. They admitted that an astounding 79 percent of their success came from customer relationships. In a recent follow-up study, purchasing agents admitted that 59 percent of their success is attributable to the relationship they have established with supplier salespeople.

Gallup conducted a global in-depth study into customer centricity and discovered a startling fact. They found that 71 percent of your business is at risk because these customers are not fully engaged with their suppliers.[1] Let that number sink in. Seventy-one percent of your customers are ready to pack their bags and move on to another supplier. The impact of this reality is crippling for businesses. It results in lower sales revenue, decreased profitability, smaller wallet share, and higher customer attrition. This does not mean your customer relationships are doomed. It points to an opportunity area for increasing customer engagement.

In a high-tech age, people fear they will get lost in the shuffle. Not according to our research. Selling is relationship management. This chapter is about nurturing long-term, mutually rewarding business relationships.

At the end of this chapter, you will be able to:

- Discuss six principles of relationship building
- Describe how to build a personal and professional relationship with customers

PRINCIPLES OF RELATIONSHIP BUILDING

There are a number of principles that define solid relationship building with customers.

Trust is the currency of all great relationships. When two people like each other, trust each other, and want to do business with each other, they will work out the details. And price is a detail. We asked sales managers in our BSP research how salespeople built relationships with customers and heard a unanimous chorus of, "They earn it by following up and doing what they say they will do." Customers know they can depend on these salespeople.

The sale is always about the customer. It's the customers' problem, their money, and a solution with which they must live. The sale should be more about the customer. What is the focus of your relationship with your customer? Is it about you or the customer?

Empathy is your internal monitor. You can be as aggressive as you want in pursuing an opportunity if you balance it with an equally strong measure of empathy. In this context, empathy is perceiving your solution as value received, not just as value added. It requires that you first put the spotlight on your customer. The behavioral side of empathy is asking questions and listening to customers. You must be empathic to understand fully the customer's needs.

Reality is in the eye of the beholder. The only reality that matters in selling is in the customers' minds. Their perception is your reality. You and your peers may believe that your company delivers great service, and it's important that you believe this. But it's imperative that your customers believe this. Your service is great only when your customers say it's great. Customer satisfaction is a function of how your solution measures up to the customers' expectations. If you meet customer expectations, you satisfy your customers. If you exceed their expectations, you delight them.

Success is a two-way street. Your success depends on your ability to help other people succeed. This is the boomerang effect. You get back what you throw out. Helping customers achieve whatever they want to achieve is the first step in your achieving what you want to achieve. This evolves into the reality that you will enjoy as much success as you can handle if you help enough other people achieve the success they desire.

People long to belong. Everyone needs to belong to something bigger than himself or herself. This is a simple human relations reality. We all must fit in somewhere. Humans are social creatures. One of our primal needs is to socialize—assimilate into our culture. This is why there are motorcycle gangs, country clubs, and everything in between. Do your customers feel like they are a vital part of your organization? Do they feel like they matter to you? Are they part of the family? Your tapping into this fundamental human need can make the difference between a transaction or a relationship with the customer. Our studies found that two-thirds of customers will abandon a supplier if they feel they are being treated as a number.

BUILDING PERSONAL AND PROFESSIONAL RELATIONSHIPS

Building personal and professional relationships with customers is a full-time job. You want to earn their loyalty and respect. This comes from a customer-first attitude of gratitude for their business. Marketers design sophisticated strategies to create brand loyalty. In reality, they must settle for brand preference because loyalty is something people reserve for other people. Imagine the impact on your sales when the customer prefers your product and has an abiding personal loyalty to you. That is an unbeatable combination. You must earn that loyalty.

Listen More Than You Talk

God gave you two ears and one mouth. He was telling you something. You demonstrate empathy more with your ears than your mouth. Listen to this: listening is the fundamental selling and interpersonal skill for value-added salespeople. In our BSP research, top-achieving salespeople reported that they spend 60 percent of their sales call time listening to customers. Researchers studied the power of listening on influence and found that people rated peers as more influential if they were good listeners. They viewed listening more positively than talking. You can become more persuasive by using your ears more than your mouth.

Carl Rogers, the father of client-centered therapy, wrote that people fail to listen because of the huge risk they incur in attempting to understand other people.[2] When salespeople listen their way into the customer's world, they risk challenging what they themselves believe, in an attempt to understand fully what the customer is saying. What if the customer is right? It's risky to hear this. However, it's even riskier not to hear this. Denial rarely works. The customer knows how he or she feels. Aren't you curious about those feelings? Listening is an honest-to-goodness way to increase your influence with buyers. It builds trust and provides you with the information you need to make better recommendations to customers.

Entertainment Is a Great Way to Get to Know Your Customer

Seventy-one percent of our BSP top achievers use entertainment to get closer to customers. Everyone is in a hurry today. Customers are pushed for time also, yet they value this time with sellers. A director of purchasing told us that he likes to use entertainment as a form of getting to know his key suppliers. "I get to see another side of these people. I watch how they treat servers in restaurants and beer vendors at a ball game. You don't see that in a negotiation. How they treat others outside of my office shows the real person I'm buying from."

Companies are always looking for ways to cut expenses and trim budgets. Reducing the number of social contacts that salespeople have with customers is not the place to save money. Managers, leave the entertainment budgets alone! For every dollar you cut, there is a competitor champing at the bit for the opportunity to spend that time with customers. Cut somewhere else, but leave your hands off entertainment.

Demonstrate Genuine Interest in Your Customer

People know when you're a phony. When you hand over the spotlight to the customers, make it real. Be truly interested in their welfare. Ask about their families and listen. Find out what's going on in their lives. Plan to spend time with them on and off the job. Avoid giving them the bum's rush on a sales call. Let them know that you care about them beyond the order sitting on their desk. Be sincere.

Perform Acts of Consideration for Your Customers

Send birthday cards. When the name of a customer's child appears in the newspaper as a result of an accomplishment, send the article and a congratulatory note to your customer. Let your customers know that you care about them above and beyond the order.

Make Your Buyer a Hero

When Tom was a chemical salesman, one of his customers told him that his job was to make the customer a hero 24 hours a day, 365 days a year. He said, "Reilly, there's only one reason the Almighty put you on the face of this earth—to make me a hero. You make me a hero, and I'll make you a hero. When the production people call me to ask how I'm able to find this material during a shortage, I'll say, 'Don't worry. I've got you covered.' When accounting asks how I get you to jump through hoops for them, I'll say, 'I'm on it.' Do you get the point, Reilly? Make me look good."

What a gift! Whatever Tom did, his job was always to make the customer look good. It was a crystal-clear mission. The customer was a straight shooter. Sometime down the road, the distributor through whom Tom served this account gave him the help he needed to open his first business.

As a construction industry salesperson, Paul had multiple opportunities to make the customer a hero. In one situation, Paul was entertaining his biggest customer and the customer's eight-year-old son at a St. Louis Cardinals baseball game. Paul arranged for the customer and his son to get passes to be on the field for batting practice before the game. They were able to meet and talk with future Hall-of-Fame players. Though Paul made this happen, the real hero that day was the customer—in the eyes of his son.

Involve customers in your business. Make each of your customers feel like an important member of the family. Ask for their input. Create customer advisory councils. When customers feel as if they are an important part of your business and that you value their opinions, it strengthens the ties that bind you.

Immerse Yourself in Their Business

We've met salespeople who volunteer to work at a customer's business during inventory or during seasonal promotions when the customer needs the extra help. These salespeople send a strong message to customers—being part of their business is a priority to them.

Our training center is located in a floodplain in Chesterfield, Missouri. During the Great Flood of 1993, we saw firsthand how supplier salespeople valued their customers' business. When you see a supplier salesperson on weekends, dressed in jeans and boots, or shorts and a T-shirt, helping fill sandbags or helping clean up after the flood, you'll never forget it. Businesses cannot buy that kind of personal loyalty. Would you fill a sandbag for your customers?

Design Customer Loyalty Programs

Loyalty programs encourage customers to return. Frequent-buyer programs, special training seminars, rebates, and bonus-purchase options are just a few examples. One industrial distributor offers his customer an annual 3 percent rebate based on the quantity of purchases during the year. The customer then uses these rebate credits to purchase additional products from this distributor.

Deliver Proactive Service

Keep customers ahead of the curve. Take the initiative to nip problems in the bud. Keep your customers out of trouble. A sales rep told us that every Monday morning, she checks her back-order reports for her top customers. She gets updated shipping information on back-ordered items and relays it to customers. She explained, "When I call them, it's service. When they call me, it's a complaint." She said, "The best part of being proactive with my service is never having to say I'm sorry."

Help Grow Your Customers' Businesses

One of the more positive ways to have an impact on your customers' world is to look for ways to help them grow their businesses. This demonstrates your genuine concern for their continued success. This is especially true for small businesses that generally operate with limited resources. Offer growth suggestions. Give them leads. Introduce them to other businesses with which they may develop a supplier relationship. When you help them grow their businesses, you're solidifying your future with them. You've become part of their marketing effort.

Increase Access

Be available to customers 24 hours a day, seven days a week. In our BSP study, buyers told us that access to the sales rep was one way to describe top salespeople. There are few things more frustrating than needing help and being unable to reach your lifeline. Customers want you to be their safety net as they cross the high wire. How would you feel if your safety net was not there?

One final thought on personal and professional relationships with customers. You want to get close to customers, but you want to maintain enough professional distance to make the tough decisions that sometimes come along in business, especially when it comes to price. Make it personal but keep it professional.

VALUE-ADDED SELLING REVIEW AND ACTION POINTS

1. Selling is relationship management. Your customers may prefer brands, but they reserve loyalty for people. You can earn the buyer's trust, the currency of good relationships, by delivering on your promises.

2. Your personal relationships with customers grow as you invest time with them. Listen and demonstrate genuine concern for their welfare. This is most obvious in your customer-first attitude of gratitude for their business.

3. Building strong relationships with your customers also means seeking ways to help build their businesses. Immerse yourself in your customers' businesses, and pursue ways to help them grow their businesses and run them more efficiently. This helps you to become a valuable resource to customers.

CHAPTER 16

Tinkering

Your ninth Value-Added Selling strategy answers this question: "Are we working as hard to keep the business as we did to secure it?"

The following quote is attributed to Charles Darwin: "It is not the strongest nor the most intelligent of the species that survives. It is the one that is the most adaptable to change." Whether or not he penned these exact words, he certainly implied it in his writings on evolution. Organizations, like organisms, evolve over time—some into extinction and some into excellence.

Chapter 16 begins after-marketing—the fourth and final group of Value-Added Selling strategies. After-marketing is the sale-after-the-sale. It's nailing shut your back door so that you don't lose business from the back door as fast as you bring it in your front door. There are three after-marketing strategies: tinkering—seeking ways to re-create meaningful value; value reinforcement—getting credit for the impact of your value added on the customer's world; and leveraging—growing your business organically by focusing on existing customers.

Markets mature. Products develop similar properties. Strategies and services converge. Competitors constantly seek ways to close the performance gaps between themselves and the rest of the market. Those who evolve as others stagnate enjoy a leadership position in their industries.

Fundamental to Value-Added Selling is the pursuit of excellence. This carries with it a productive discomfort with the status quo. For some, this is a burden; for others, it's a blessing. This chapter is about chasing potential and tinkering with the status quo.

At the end of this chapter, you will be able to:

- Define tinkering and explain why it is a viable and valuable part of professional selling
- Name the barriers that interfere with business excellence
- Describe how to tinker to re-create meaningful value for the customer

WHAT IS TINKERING

The tinkers were a nomadic group in Europe centuries ago. They would travel from town to town, eking out a living by repairing tin pots and pans. We believe this is the origin of the word *tinker*—to mend or repair or experiment with machine parts. Some even hold a negative view of tinkers as clumsy or bungling. Our view is different.

We define tinkering as growing, evolving, and emerging. Tinkering is about renewal, innovation, growth, streamlining, and kaizen—the Japanese word that describes an attitude of continuous improvement. Tinkering is blasting out of comfort zones. It's the itch you cannot scratch. It's seeking ways to re-create meaningful value for the customer by pursuing one's potential. Conversely, not tinkering is the height of arrogance, believing that what you do is good enough and you need not improve.

Fundamental to Value-Added Selling is the pursuit of excellence. This carries with it a productive discomfort with the status quo. Tinkers reach beyond the status quo. They are restlessly and desperately curious about their potential. Tinkers discover that there is no commodity in creativity and no traffic jam on the extra mile. Contrast this to those who are stuck where they are. They delude themselves into believing they are in a groove and wake up too late to the realization that they are in a rut.

Tinkering is working as hard to keep the business as you did to get the business. Tinkering is treating your customers as if they were prospects, because they are . . . for the competition. When you tinker, you're doing what a good, quality competitor does to earn the business. Customers want to partner with suppliers who drive the industry versus go along for the ride. They want to buy from sellers who are innovative and who put it all together and then push the change curve. What a wonderful opportunity for tinkers.

If you are sales manager reading this and a salesperson requests a lower price for an existing customer, ask that salesperson, "How much tinkering have you done in this account?" Delighted, or even satisfied, customers who believe you are working hard to re-create value seldom complain about price. They complain about price when you get complacent about service. Many salespeople protest this question: "That's not fair. You know how it is in our business. I get busy. I fight a lot of fires. I grease a lot of skids. There's no time to tinker." If there is no time to tinker, how is there time to find new business to compensate for the business you lose?

Andy Grove, founder of Intel, said this about complacency, "Success breeds complacency, and complacency breeds failure. Only the paranoid survive."[1] We call this a constructive sense of insecurity about your current levels of success. The element of doubt can be a powerful motivator to keep you at the top of your game.

Value-added salespeople treat their customers well. How would you respond to a customer who asks, "Am I better off being your prospect or your customer?" Sadly, too many salespeople treat their prospects better than they treat their customers. They work harder to get the business than they do to keep the business.

HOW TO TINKER

Tinkering is acting on your productive discomfort with the status quo. It is the behavioral response to your insecurity of *owning* the business. It is the quest that follows the query. Do you see the common theme running through here? Action. Tinkering is an action word. This verb moves. Therefore, you must move to tinker. These tinkering rules will help guide your efforts.

Challenge Everything

Go after sacred cows. A sacred cow is any established rule or procedure that defines your routine. It is the boss's idea. It is the philosophy upon which your company was founded. It is standard operating procedure. Habit makes it neither right nor wrong. St. Augustine wrote, "Habit, if not resisted, soon becomes necessity." Those people who are so heavily invested in the status quo will fight the hardest to preserve it. Ask these questions to challenge everything: Does this policy, process, or procedure add value or cost? Does this paperwork add value? Things that no longer contribute value should be challenged.

Perform a failure analysis and ask the five whys. This analytical method was vital to Toyota's success in production and quality. This means you ask *why* five times to continue to drill down on the root cause of problems you are dealing with. For example,

> *Question:* "Why did we lose that last piece of business on price?"
> *Answer:* "Because our costs were too high."
>
> *Question:* "Why were our costs too high?"
> *Answer:* "Because of our purchasing arrangements."
>
> *Question:* "Why do we have those arrangements?"
> *Answer:* "Because at the time we established those relationships that was all that was available."
>
> *Question:* "Why have we not pursued other relationships?"
> *Answer:* "Because we have standardized on their materials."
>
> *Question:* "Why have we not upgraded our process?"
> *Answer:* "Because we didn't know the importance of tinkering."

Encourage unbridled dreaming and positive action, not necessarily perfection. Some things need not be perfect to bring value. Perfection can be the enemy of action if you wait endlessly for that final improvement to take place. Oftentimes, new product launches invite evolution and continuous development. The critical component is that you get busy dreaming and doing. How many successful products ever go to market in their finished and complete state? Few if any. Most marketers send their new ideas to the market as soon as feasible knowing they will continue to evolve and improve.

Barrier Analysis

Identifying and eliminating barriers that prevent your company from delivering world-class service are important in tinkering. What gets in the way of your delivering this type of service? We've asked this question of hundreds of employees in a variety of companies, and here's what they've told us:

- **Negative attitudes.** These include the attitude that says, in effect, "This would be a great place to work if it weren't for the customers." When employees view serving as a privilege, not a pain, they naturally behave in ways to better serve customers. When employees view serving as a hassle, customers know it because it's obvious in the way these employees interface with customers.
- **Communication breakdowns.** Included here are incomplete instructions or a failure to communicate with other employees or with customers. Salespeople may fail to provide inside staff members with the full instructions they need to process specific customer requests.
- **Mistakes.** Consider the irony. There is not enough time to do something right the first time, but there is always time to do it over again. Careless mistakes in one's job suggest someone who feels no ownership or pride in his or her work. How do you think customers view these mistakes?
- **Time constraints.** In a world that is moving at breakneck speed, lack of time is perhaps the most understandable barrier to providing top-notch service. There is always too much to do and too little time to do it. As with mistakes, there's not enough time to do something right to begin with, but there is always time to do it again.
- **Lack of resources.** Salespeople may face shortages of people, money, and equipment. Again, there is too much to do and too few resources to do it. It's difficult to do your job if you don't have all the tools required. Most companies today are working lean, the legacy of downsizing and reorganization. That's one reason why value-added organizations see good employees as assets and treat them as if they were gold.
- **Unrealistic expectations.** These are primarily the customer's expectations. Someone influenced the customer, a salesperson no doubt, to expect more than what is possible to deliver. Recall our earlier definitions of customer satisfaction and

customer delight: customer satisfaction results from meeting your customer's expectations; customer delight is the pleasant surprise of your exceeding their expectations. A prescription for success in any business is, "Promise a lot and deliver more." Create realistic expectations with your customers, and meet or exceed these expectations.

- **Lack of authority.** Along with insufficient resources and time, a lack of authority means that employees feel powerless to create the results the customer wants. Part of the problem is management's delegating tasks without delegating the responsibility for the outcome of the work. Another part is a lack of initiative by employees. They do not take ownership.

  One company has a simple yet effective problem-ownership policy. If a customer calls you with a problem, it is your problem until your company solves it. You may not have the resources to solve the problem yourself, but you are responsible for seeing that it is resolved. This practice keeps you in the loop and builds accountability. Everyone in this company feels responsible for creating satisfied customers.

- **Inflexible procedures.** When employees view policies and procedures as something more than guidelines and rigidly adhere to them, customers hear responses such as, "I'm sorry, sir, that's the way it is. That's our policy." Customers perceive inflexibility. This barrier is generally the result of management's not informing employees that policies and procedures are performance guidelines, not gospel.

  A useful tinkering activity is to ask this question inside and outside your organization: "What gets in the way of our delivering the kind of value-added service that we know we can deliver?" Ask employees. Ask customers. Both may know better than you about these barriers. Asking that question, discovering various barriers, and eliminating them is one way to release your brakes and deliver value-added service.

Build a Better Mousetrap

Tinkering is at the heart of differentiation. Emerson is attributed with saying, "If a man can write a better book, preach a better sermon, or make a better mousetrap than his neighbor, though he builds his house in the woods the world will make a beaten path to his door." Seeking to build a better mousetrap is living the "What if" question. "What if we could do it this way?" "What if we could make our product do this?" Every great product innovation is the evolution of another great idea.

Customers want to feel that you're keeping them ahead of the curve with your innovation. Tinkers think forward and visualize endless possibilities, stretching their imaginations to their outer reaches.

You can ask the "What if" question throughout your company and with your customers. "What would you like to see from suppliers that is not currently available?" and "What would you like to have that you cannot get now?" You may work for one of the oldest companies in the industry, but these questions make you one of the more progressive competitors in the industry. You sound like an innovator.

Make It Easier to Do Business with Your Company

Earlier we asked this question: "How easy is your company to do business with?" Do customers use words such as *inflexible, single-minded, arrogant, indifferent,* and *seller focused* to describe your policies and procedures? Or, do they use words such as *flexible, considerate, patient, customer-focused,* and *easy to do business with*?

In our BSP research, buyers told us they wanted to work with sellers who made it easy for them to do business. Customer service ranked number two, behind quality products. Standing behind what they sell and ease of doing business rounded out the top three company attributes buyers want from sellers. What can you do to make it easier for your customers to order? How does your credit department perceive its role: Does it build bridges to draw people in or build walls to keep the bums out? Are there more convenient ways for your customers to pay for your goods and services? Would special packaging options make it easier for your customers to redistribute your goods and services internally? Can you bundle different product groups more efficiently to reflect special buyer needs?

Create a customer feedback system to collect information on how well you perform. Discover what you do right and areas where you can improve. Many companies have suggestion boxes, seeking customer feedback, but the tone is generally a complaint box. Why not seek feedback where you are excelling for customers? You may discover that simple things you do are viewed as incredibly special by the customers. In that case, you want to continue doing them.

One organization we trained created an e-mail suggestion box with a special address: suggestions@companyname.com. Any customer or employee at any time could offer suggestions for improvement. Management reviewed the suggestions regularly and implemented several of the customers' and employees' ideas. That is a great example of a customer-value focus and tinkering.

At the heart of this strategy is an attitude that says, "We can and should look for ways to make it easier to buy and use our products." *Painless*, *seamless*, and *customer-centric* are words that describe the results of your efforts when you tinker to make the customer's life easier.

Even more fundamental is the belief that people continue to grow and develop if they are open to change and humble enough to admit that they aren't finished yet. Value-added organizations are proud of what they have accomplished, but they balance their pride with an equally strong measure of humility that says, "We're not finished yet. We still have some distance to travel."

VALUE-ADDED SELLING REVIEW AND ACTION POINTS

1. After-marketing is your fourth group of Value-Added Selling strategies. It is the sale-after-the-sale. Are you working as hard to keep the customer's business as you did to get the business originally? You must continue to look for ways to re-create value for your customers. This is tinkering. When you tinker, you treat your customers as if they were prospects, because they are . . . for the competition.

2. You tinker as you challenge the viability of the status quo. Habit is a poor excuse for continuing a practice or sustaining a procedure. You tinker as you identify and eliminate barriers to better service. Ask this question inside your organization and of your customers: "What gets in the way of our delivering the type of world-class service we would like to deliver?" The answers to this question will help you direct your attention to areas where you can improve. You tinker as you innovate and take Emerson's advice about building a better mousetrap.

3. You tinker when you ask your customers these questions often to better serve them: "What would you like us to do differently tomorrow from what we are doing today?" "What are we currently doing that you would like us to continue to bring you value?" The answers to these questions will provide you with direction for improving your solution.

CHAPTER 17

Value Reinforcement

Your tenth Value-Added Selling strategy answers this question: "Are we getting credit for all of our value added?"

When we ask this question in seminars, fewer than 5 percent of the attendees claim they get the credit they deserve. Let's be clear at this point: no one gets the credit they deserve; they only get the credit they ask for. We didn't invent that concept. It's a simple reality in all walks of life. Many people are uncomfortable with this notion, and we get it. Bragging sounds gauche. In your job, do you get credit from your management for all the wonderful and selfless things you do? Probably not. It is no different for your company and customers.

Most companies deliver superior value but rarely get credit for everything they do. In most cases, their customers are uninformed about the extent of this value added. As most people are unaware of the air they breathe, most customers are unaware of the value they receive. How can you fault buyers taking for granted your added value when they don't know the value of your total solution? The solution is simple—tell them. When customers grow accustomed to receiving value-added services, especially those for which they do not pay directly, they take these services for granted. They expect free services all the time. Today's value added becomes tomorrow's expectations.

Buyers are under tremendous pressure to justify their purchasing behavior. This is especially true for incumbent suppliers. Buyers, like sellers, must explain why they continue to purchase from a given supplier. In a previous chapter, we introduced you to a Gallup study that found 71 percent of your business is at risk because of a lack of customer engagement. The combination of client churn and salesforce turnover leaves existing customers wondering if they will renew with current suppliers at the end of the contract. Treating all business (that you want to retain) as at-risk business is a prudent strategy. Value reinforcement is a powerful way to increase retention.

Like tinkering, value reinforcement is an after-marketing strategy. Value reinforcement means getting credit for what you do. It's simple—tell them. The best defense is a great offense. Value reinforcement is defensive selling at its best. This chapter is about getting credit for what you do.

At the end of this chapter, you will be able to:

- Discuss the three rules for value reinforcement
- Define and explain the power of value reinforcement
- Document your value added
- Value remind through positive bragging
- Conduct value audits to reinforce your value

THREE RULES OF VALUE REINFORCEMENT

As the incumbent, you are in a strong position. There are psychological forces that work in your favor. Because of cognitive dissonance, people often seek ways to justify the decisions they make. This means buyers often overlook minor problems and overestimate services delivered. It makes them feel smarter about their decisions. Humans also have a status-quo bias. They want things to run smoothly and predictably. Behavioral economists like to talk about the endowment effect—people confer more value on things they own or use. The bottom line is that incumbents have a unique advantage if they exploit it fully.

These three rules will help you in your value reinforcement campaign. Notice the word *campaign*. This implies continuity. Value reinforcement is an ongoing effort for as long as you want to remain the incumbent.

First, value reinforcement must take place at all levels. This means Levels-I-II-III. Your logistics successes, which appeal to Level-I, have value to Level-II and Level-III as well. Let them know about it. The pressure to control costs comes top-down in most organizations. Insulate yourself from this by maintaining high-level contact and sharing your messages of value. Executive turnover is high these days;

one-in-five top managers turn over annually. Companies move leaders in and out depending on the financial performance of the organization. When a new leader arrives, you want to be the first to welcome the leader and share your commitment to his or her complete satisfaction.

Second, this campaign must be regular and ongoing. Make this part of your defensive selling strategy. Handled properly, customers will value this input because it gives them the justification they need to maintain the relationship with your company.

Third, use a mix of quantitative and qualitative tools. Quantitative value reinforcement includes analytics that provide tangible or numeric feedback. This includes on-time performance, cost savings, increased productivity as an outcome of your solution, and so on. Qualitative value reinforcement deals more with how the customer feels and reacts to your solution. Asking questions about delivery performance or product usage that elicit positive responses tells you how buyers perceive your solution and its performance. How buyers feel is at least as important as how well your solution performs. The buyer's feeling contributes to his or her engagement with suppliers. You want buyers to feel connected by your value.

THE POWER OF VALUE REINFORCEMENT

In their book *Angel Customers and Demon Customers*, authors Larry Selden and Geoffrey Colvin write, "No value proposition will succeed in delivering exceptional economic profit to a company unless the target-customer segment *perceives* the offer as meeting its needs best. So it's not enough to create the best experience and execute it well; it must also be communicated superbly." How effectively do you remind customers of your value? In our BSP research, we discovered that 82 percent of top-achieving salespeople review their value added with customers. That is a strong benchmark.

Value reinforcement is more than simply bragging. It is a vital component in your customer messaging campaign. Value reinforcement, by whatever means you choose, spotlights the impact of your value added on the customer's world. So, it's not just, "Look what we did for you today," it's more of, "Look at the impact of this on your business." Customers are less concerned with what you've done than they are with the effect it has had on them. If you are one of those sales-people who are uncomfortable with bragging about your service, this distinction is critical. You are bragging about the improvements that the customer has made because of the impact of your solution. This places the focus correctly on the customer. You benefit by the association, but the real focal point is the customer's gain . . . because of his or her work with you.

Since the effect of your value added is your value proposition, you are reinforcing in the customers' minds the value in your proposition and validating their decision to embrace your decision. This is important because buyers want to feel they made a good buying decision. Let them know how good a decision they made. There are at least three groups of strategies to do this.

Documentation

Ernst and Young found that 81 percent of buyers expect their suppliers to financially quantify their value added.[1] Are you able to attach a dollar value to the services you offer? Can you calculate the profit impact on the customer's business? How much are you really worth to your customers? The answers to these questions provide the backdrop for the financial justification of your solution. This is quantitative value reinforcement.

Documenting your value-added services is one of the most proactive ways to manage price resistance. One sales rep showed us how he used *no-charge invoices* as a way to inform customers of the dollar value of his services. For example, his company once sent two technical people into the field to resolve a problem. After they finished this assignment, the sales rep calculated the expense his company incurred, including travel and field time. He sent the customer a no-charge invoice for $4,400. On the bottom of the invoice, in bold print, he typed, "No charge—part of our value-added service." This was his way of quantifying and reinforcing his company's value added.

Another client uses a *project savings report*. When the company completes a technical assignment, it sends a recap of the work and its impact on the customer. This report documents the benefits offered by this supplier. It quantifies the impact so that the customer can appreciate the real dollar difference that results.

Warranty reports detail the value of work performed under warranty. Many times, customers misunderstand the cost burden of warranty work. As far as they're concerned, it's free. Tom experienced firsthand the benefit of documenting value added when he had a problem with the brakes on his car. The dealer spent two days repairing the problem. The factory reimbursed the dealer for only 1.8 hours. Tom paid nothing. The service manager showed him the warranty documentation and said, "Just keep us in mind when you need an oil change." This type of communication is especially important for service plans and extended warranties.

Be aware that the service department in many companies plays a vital role in the sale-after-the-sale. The salesperson may sell the first item—a piece of equipment—but the customer's total experience with the company sells the next product or service. That's why Value-Added Selling is a team sport. Everyone is involved.

Customer service action reports, another useful tool, list the situation, the action taken, and the outcome for the customer. One of our clients combines a customer satisfaction survey with an impact statement. After the customer completes side one—the satisfaction survey—the customer estimates the impact of the service on side two. The two-part survey links performance with satisfaction and a positive outcome for the customer, thus reinforcing the company's value to the customer.

Other examples include on-time and *delivery performance reports*, written user *testimonials* that you can share with purchasing, *service level reviews* that spell out the savings enjoyed as a result of implementing your solution, *thank you notes* recapping your value added, *cost-savings* and *profit-impact reports*, and the list continues to the edge of your imagination.

One very creative salesperson sends a *birthday card* on the anniversary of the customer's purchasing his product, stressing the savings that the customer has enjoyed since taking receipt of goods and implementing the solution.

Two other tools are useful to sell buyers on a new idea and reinforce existing customers' decisions to partner with you. The first is the *ROI*—return on investment. This allows your customer to estimate the financial impact of your solution. If customers invest $100,000 in facilities upgrades and leverage those upgrades for a $50,000 gain in a given year, that's a 50 percent ROI. How many places can they achieve a 50 percent ROI in a year? This is a compelling argument if you can quantify your impact vis-à-vis the investment. The other tool is the *cost-benefit analysis (CBA)*.

The CBA may be easier to ascertain in that it allows for some qualitative value of the decision to act. For example, if the customer invests $100,000 and gets a blend of quantitative and qualitative benefits, the aggregate gain may be great enough to act on. The quantitative gain may be a $20,000 return, while the qualitative gain may include a safer, more convenient way to do something, which is more difficult to quantify. Both tools, ROI and CBA, are effective analyses that empower you to make a compelling argument for your solution. To get the most value from this exercise, involve other team members in this exercise and ask the customers to validate your metrics.

Documentation is one way to make tangible your value added for the customer. It makes it easy for the customer to perceive the dollar value of your relationship. It is easier for you to justify your higher prices against a backdrop of documented value-added services. For this reason, a 90-day documentation campaign prior to price increases sets a positive tone for your discussions. It provides the proof that customers need to ratify their original decision to go with you.

Value Reminding

Value reminding is *positive* bragging. It's looking for ways to remind customers of everything you do for them and the impact on their business. For example, when a customer calls you for technical support and you must pass this request along to someone else, you should follow up with the customer to ensure satisfaction. This action demonstrates your concern while reminding the customer of your service.

A manufacturer's sales representative prepares a weekly recap of her joint calling activity with the distributor's reps detailing the business they uncovered on their joint calls on end users. After several days of these joint calls, she sends this report to her distributor sales manager to remind him that she is adding value with her sales efforts. Attaching a dollar value to this discovered business quantifies the impact of her efforts and gives her something to follow up with the reps.

If you help a customer secure a piece of business, follow up to see how it benefited the customer. Doing so reinforces that you're working for the customer. Imagine the impact when the customer tells you that your lead resulted in a large sale. You've proved that you're a viable resource. You're part of the customer's sales team.

Testimonial letters also provide a unique way to reinforce your value added. When a customer writes you a testimonial letter, it's to tell you about the great job you've done. More important, the customer is actively remembering the great job you've done. If you want to do something that requires chutzpah, in your next proposal to this customer, include a copy of his or her own testimonial letter to you. Who better to remind the customer of your value added than this very same customer? Testimonials are also a nice fit in your company newsletters. Be sure to ask for testimonials that reflect all three dimensions of value—the product, company, and you.

When you ask a customer for a testimonial quote, print that quote on a page with several other quotes gathered from other customers. Send each customer on the list a copy so that each can see how you've used his or her words. All of these quotes on one page have great visual impact, and this page serves as a value reminder to each customer who reads it.

Value reminding is an activity for everyone in the company. Service technicians can value remind as they work on equipment in the customer's office. Customer service reps value remind when they proactively deliver service and let the customer know they did it. Credit department employees can value remind when they help customers qualify for special terms. The list is endless. Value reminding reflects an attitude that everyone is responsible for reminding the customer of your value added.

Value Audit

The value audit—either formal or informal—is a way to check on your performance with the customer. Formally, it's a customer satisfaction survey. It could be as detailed as the surveys that auto manufacturers use to measure your buying and owning experience. In the customer satisfaction survey, you measure performance and how it produces buyer satisfaction or dissatisfaction.

A supplier performance appraisal recaps your performance using the list of the value-added services you promised. Use your VIP list as a report card for grading your postsale value added. As you check on yourself, you're reinforcing the value added you provide. It's also a value-reminding exercise.

A value audit could be as informal as asking questions in follow-up visits. "Mr. Customer, I wanted to meet with you today to check on ourselves, to ensure that you're getting all the value on the back end that we promised you on the front end. How are we performing for you? How can we improve? What would you like us to do for you tomorrow that we didn't do for you yesterday?"

Remember, the best defense is a great offense. By checking on yourself, you're doing what a quality competitor should do when pursuing new business. It's better, however, for you to know your strengths and weaknesses before the competition discovers them. Customers will give this feedback to someone—you, the competition, or even other customers. You want to get ahead of this feedback and correct issues before they become complaints. Use these corrections as an opportunity to walk the talk on service.

One of our clients used the value audit concept as a monthly service check. The audit contained a list of questions designed to get in-depth feedback about the company's performance while calling attention to its value-added services, thus combining value reminding with value audits. Not only does this check on the company's impact, it gives the salespeople valid reasons for their follow-up visits. Imagine the impact of promising you will follow up to check on yourself, actually following up, and then reporting on it. You earn credibility and credit for your efforts. Your follow-up becomes the benchmark against which all other competitors are measured.

Like many defensive selling strategies, value reinforcement is working as hard to keep the business as you did to get the business. It's treating your customers as if they were prospects, because they are . . . for your competitors. You cannot hear this message too often.

VALUE-ADDED SELLING REVIEW AND ACTION POINTS

1. No one gets the credit he or she deserves. People only get the credit that they ask for. For the same reason, most companies deliver significant value added for which they never get credit. Are you getting credit from your customers for all of the value added that your company delivers? Begin today by adopting the value reinforcement paradigm.

2. There are three rules for value reinforcement. Take your value reinforcement campaign to all three levels of decision makers and influencers. Make this an ongoing and regular part of your defensive selling strategy. Use quantitative and qualitative reinforcement. Data is convincing, but how the buyer feels about the data is compelling.

3. Value reinforcement is an essential part of your customer messaging campaign. Seek ways to get credit for your value added by documenting its impact on the customer, positively bragging every chance you get, and checking on yourself with value audits.

CHAPTER 18

Leveraging

Your eleventh Value-Added Selling strategy answers this question: "Are we maximizing our value?"

There are several advantages to growing your existing accounts. The average company could increase its sales in a given year, even if it didn't bring on board one new customer, by simply doing a better job of selling to existing customers. Organic growth, growing existing customers, is a cost-effective and time-efficient way to expand sales. Expanding your business organically versus growth-by-acquisition is a more stable way to grow. It means you are going deeper with your installed base of business. It takes an average of seven calls to close a prospect on a new idea, compared with three calls to close an existing customer on a new idea. The transaction costs of selling to existing customers are significantly lower than selling to new customers because your company gets better at servicing these accounts.

So, why do salespeople persist in chasing new customers while walking past business in their existing accounts? It could be that the grass looks greener in other pastures. Salespeople could be facing pressure by management to fill the pipeline with new business opportunities. Managers get restless when salespeople fail to land new accounts, so they design compensation systems to reinforce this behavior. Some companies suffer from a market-share mania philosophy. This means chasing new customers while ignoring the opportunities they have with existing customers. They are obsessed with new customers. This chapter is about leveraging, the third after-marketing strategy that allows you to maximize your potential with your existing base of customers.

At the end of this chapter, you will be able to:

- Define leveraging and discuss its importance to salespeople
- Describe how companies expand sales to existing customers with vertical and horizontal account penetration
- Elaborate on how to capture the natural spin-off business opportunities that exist in all forms of selling
- Explain the concept of cross-serving as a way to create value for your customer and your company

THE POWER OF LEVERAGE

Leveraging is concentrated and focused energy. It's an effectiveness strategy that helps you maximize, optimize, and multiply your efforts—doing more with less. It's achieving a high ratio of outcome to input, achieving a 150 percent return on 100 percent effort. It's selling deeper and broader into your accounts, expanding your base of existing business organically. In our BSP research, we discovered that top-achieving salespeople spend 80 percent of their time working with existing customers, fully leveraging those relationships. A 2014 Manta-Dell study of 3,025 small business owners found that the business owners valued repeat customers as 3.6 times more important than making the first sale with a new customer.[1] These owners are close to the action and understand the value of building strong, long-term relationships.

Over time and as companies get better at selling to customers, costs go down and service levels improve. The outcome of greater efficiency is more profit. As suppliers continue to prove themselves, the downward pressure on prices relaxes a bit as customers realize the value of this relationship. This, too, results in the supplier enjoying greater profitability. The combination of these two forces results in a marginal difference that is significant for sellers.

W. Edwards Deming wrote of this: "Profit in business comes from repeat customers, customers that boast about your project or service, and that bring friends with them."[2] In his work on customer retention and loyalty and their effects on bottom-line profitability, Fred Reichheld writes,

> Consider the cost of serving a long-standing customer vs. the cost of courting one. Across a wide range of businesses,

customers generate increasing profits each year they stay with a company. . . . Return customers tend to buy more from a company over time. As they do, your operating costs to serve them decline. In addition, return customers refer others to your company. And they'll also often pay a premium to continue to do business with you rather than switch to a competitor with whom they're neither familiar nor comfortable.[3]

A 2016 Gallup study on customer engagement found that engagement depends on suppliers increasing impact: "Impact comes from providing specific recommendations or other valuable products and/or services that enhance the customer's standing and potential in the marketplace."[4]

Selling more to an existing customer is an annuity that pays dividends long after the initial sale. On a practical level, the more ways you connect with customers, the stronger the relationship. For sellers that sell one thing to customers and that is the extent of their relationship, it is tenuous in that one misstep may sever the ties. For another seller that connects at dozens of levels, one misstep rarely jeopardizes the relationship. There are three ways salespeople can leverage their relationships with existing customers.

Vertical Account Penetration

Vertical account penetration means providing more products and services to an existing customer. Some people call this concept *cross-selling*, *up-selling*, or *add-on selling*. "Would you like some fries to go with that burger?" is a popular example of this strategy. Banks, insurance agents, and even online retailers capitalize on the point of sale to increase order size.

Some products and services naturally create regenerative pull for other products and services. One product paves the way for the sale of another product. For example, if you sell equipment, then parts and service work are natural cross-sell items.

McKinsey and Company reported on the power of cross-selling in which one company was able to expand its top line by 25 percent by simply emphasizing with its salespeople the importance of expanding the depth and breadth of products sold to existing customers.[5]

Vertical account penetration expands the mix of your products and services. This benefits the customer as well as the seller. Customers pay more to place orders with multiple suppliers than the same orders with a single source. That's why many customers today seek ways to consolidate their purchases. The transaction costs are higher with multiple suppliers.

On a practical level, customers find it more convenient to buy many items from fewer suppliers. This follows a current trend in purchasing to consolidate purchases. They understand the efficiency of consolidating their purchases and building stronger relationships with sellers.

Customers who buy several items from one source are less likely to bounce that supplier if they have a problem. The more levels at which you connect, the stronger the relationship with the customer. This increases your stickiness with customers, and you want your good relationships to be as sticky as possible. Strong ties with existing customers are like trees with deep roots. They remain steady, even in the most violent storms. Your challenge is to develop rock-deep roots with your existing customers. It's mutually beneficial to consolidate purchases.

Horizontal Account Penetration

Horizontal account penetration is selling additional products and services to other locations and or different people representing the same account. Never assume that you have all the business. Never assume that customers know everything you sell. Ask these questions: "Is there someone else I should be calling on?" and "Are there other locations of your company that I may call on?" Then ask the customer for a referral into these locations.

If you discover additional sources of business within the same account, you may be able to protect all of it with a contract that benefits you and the customer. The more of your products and services your customer buys, the fewer opportunities the competition has to sell into the account. It's both an offensive and a defensive strategy. Leveraging locks in the business and locks out the competition. Vertical and horizontal account penetration means selling deeper and wider into your accounts. It's a win-win situation. Both parties benefit by leveraging transaction costs. Customers enjoy the convenience, and you enjoy the extra business. They leverage their buying power, and you leverage your costs.

Capturing Spin-off Business

Spin-off business is the best way to prospect. It takes the chill out of a cold call. Referral selling is the number one strategy for meeting high-level decision makers. Ask every customer on whom you call, "Is there someone outside your company whom I should meet and get to know?" Take it a step further and ask your customer to help you arrange the meeting. Word-of-mouth testimony from a trusted friend is still the most effective way to promote. A referral from an existing customer is worth 12 cold calls.[6] That's the value of trust.

For the next two weeks, ask your customers this question, and see what happens: "With whom should I be talking?" Leave it that open-ended. Don't limit the leads they give you by adding a qualifying statement such as, "Whom should I call who uses what we sell?" Leave your question completely open-ended. Let the customer brainstorm an answer.

Asking for a referral is one of the most basic concepts in selling. When was the last time you did it? Every satisfied customer is a salesperson for you and your organization. Spin-off business also includes niches. In niches, there are riches. This idea means taking what you have learned and using it in another account. Look at your base of business and determine what you have learned. Have you inadvertently or unwittingly carved out a niche for yourself? Have you learned something about selling to a certain group of customers that you could take to the other customers in that niche? Every salesperson specializes in something but may not know it.

RIGHT WAY AND WRONG WAY TO PLAN YOUR STRATEGY

When laying out your strategy for expanding your business with existing customers, there is a right way and a wrong way to approach this. First, let's examine the wrong way. Do not look at your customer and ask yourself this question: "How can we sell this customer more stuff?" What's wrong with this approach? It's seller focused. It's more about you than the customer. Your focus is on selling more stuff.

Let's examine the right way to do this. Ask this question: "How can we bring more value to the customer?" The difference is your focus. With the first question, you're trying to make a deal. With the second question, you're trying to make a difference. Value-added salespeople are more interested in making a difference than just making a deal. The outcome of this thinking is that you will have all the business you can handle if your focus is on making a difference for the customer. You will sell more stuff as a natural consequence of your making a difference for the customer. Which sale is easier to make—the one where you are in the deal mode or the difference mode?

We asked more than 200 salespeople what they felt was the best way to grow existing customers. Their number one response was to find problems to solve and then create solutions for those problems. This is value creation. When salespeople create value for the customer, they get to share in that value; they, in turn, capture more value for their companies.

Study your list of HVTs (high-value targets) and ask yourself this question: How can we bring more value to these customers? Visit with the customers and ask them the same question: "How can we bring more value to you?" This question, a leverage strategy, is actually a tinkering question because you are seeking ways to get better, and then you will enjoy the benefits of your innovation. As you can see, Value-Added Selling is an integrated set of strategies and tactics.

CROSS-SERVING

What if providing the customer with additional products and services was more of a service function than a selling function? Some salespeople are hesitant to offer additional products and services. They already have a sale and may not want to risk appearing greedy. This can happen if the only prism through which a salesperson views the relationship is the "selling-more-product" prism.

Cross-serving falls under the category of customer service, not sales. Cross-serving goes beyond cross-selling. Cross-serving is about educating the customer and providing the customer with the best overall, end-to-end experience. It's more than adding products or selling up.

Customers don't know what they don't know. They are not experts in your products. They rely on you to educate them on better ways. They use your solution to help them achieve some gain. If you have a better way for them to achieve that goal, you are doing your customers a disservice by not educating them. That's why cross-serving is more of a service function than a selling function.

Imagine the customer's frustration if a salesperson failed to explain an easier, faster way to do something or an accessory that could improve operating performance. Cross-serving is about educating the customer on a better way to do something and giving him or her a choice to buy or not.

Cross-serving is more than offering an additional product or service; it's explaining why you offer it. For example, one equipment dealer trained its salespeople to explain the *why* behind their offer. When a customer came in to purchase replacement hydraulic hoses, the inside salespeople knew to offer hydraulic fluid with the hoses. The salespeople didn't say, "Would you like some fluid to go with your hoses?" They explained why.

Here's how it sounds: "From our experience, most people who buy replacement hoses are replacing broken hoses that are cracked and leaking fluid. You probably need some hydraulic fluid to replace whatever was lost due to the hose failure." Explaining the *why* behind the offer is customer-focused thinking. The takeaway for you is to think *why*, not just *what*.

If there is a better way to satisfy the customer's needs, you are doing a disservice by not recommending it. In the above example, if the counter salesperson failed to offer the hydraulic fluid, it might have cost the customer another trip, costing him or her time and money. Cross-serving is offering additional, relevant products and services that create more value for the customer, which allows you to capture more value for your company.

VALUE-ADDED SELLING REVIEW AND ACTION POINTS

1. In business, there is a dangerous preoccupation with capturing new business. It is market-share mania, and companies often ignore profitable and viable opportunities with their existing customers in the pursuit of new business with different customers. Are you fully leveraging your existing customer relationships?

2. You can increase your penetration with existing customers in one of two ways: vertical and horizontal account penetration. Seek ways to expand the mix of products you sell to a customer's location or expand the mix of your business by selling to other locations of the same account.

3. Referral selling takes the chill out of the cold call. Who better to open the door for you than a completely satisfied existing customer? Expand your business by asking existing customers for the names of other people whom you could serve.

4. There is a right way and a wrong way to approach your account planning for growth. The right way is to ask yourself, "How can we increase our value to this customer?"

5. Cross-serving is an opportunity to educate your customer and create more value with additional products and services while increasing the value of your sale.

PART III

VALUE-ADDED SELLING TACTICS

Welcome to the tactical side of Value-Added Selling. In this part, you will study the application of the Value-Added Selling strategies. In Part II, you learned *what* to do. In Part III, you learn *how* to do what you must do. Here, you learn to execute the value-added philosophy on your sales calls. The tactical side includes cold-calling, getting appointments, precall preparation, the value-added sales call, handling objections, and postcall evaluation.

The value-added sales call model follows the natural path of everyday conversation as well as persuasion theory. Every conversation, phone call, letter, e-mail, in-person visit, casual conversation, speech, television commercial, and direct-mail piece has an opening and a closing. There's nothing magical here, just simple communication. The magic is in the middle, the information exchange—probing and presenting.

While probing is the needs analysis, presenting is how you communicate your message to the customer. Value-added salespeople spend most of their time on the sales call probing and presenting—listening to customers and presenting ideas.

In sales, there's an inverse relationship in how you spend your time on a sales call: the more time you invest on the front end probing and listening to buyers' needs, the less time you must spend on the back end closing and resolving objections. Conversely, the less time you spend on the front end probing and listening, the more time you must spend on the back end trying to resurrect a dead sale.

You will notice that in Part III, the heaviest time investment is on the front half of the information exchange—identifying buyers' needs and presenting customer-focused solutions. This is customer-focused Value-Added Selling.

CHAPTER 19

Filling Your Pipeline

Do you have all of the business you can handle? If you're like most salespeople, your pipeline could be fuller. We've met few salespeople over the years that said they had all of the leads they could handle.

What did salespeople do in the dark ages of selling before the Internet and all of the technology that we take for granted today? Most canvassed areas, carrying pocketsful of coins for pay phones, a briefcase full of literature, and a fistful of business cards. Even though technology enables salespeople to gather large amounts of intelligence in the comfort of an office, there are benefits to physically canvassing an area.

We initiated a research project a couple of years ago in response to a young salesperson who informed us that "cold-calling is dead." Based on decades of training salespeople, we knew this was not true but wanted the data to prove it. So, we surveyed 300 B2B salespeople—distributor salespeople and manufacturing reps—to identify their calling habits. We discovered that the average salesperson makes 11 face-to-face sales calls per week, each one averaging 44 minutes, resulting in eight hours of face time per week with customers. In 1982, salespeople averaged nearly 20 hours of face time weekly with customers. This confirmed something we knew: salespeople are not making as many in-person calls today. Next, we discovered that 80 percent of this group continues to cold-call as a means to fill their pipelines. So much for "cold-calling is dead." Additionally, we found that 43 percent use social media to prospect. That number has grown since our research. And here's a tidbit for those who are more active in their calling. If you make 20 or more calls per week, you are part of the top 20 percent most active salespeople we train.

In Chapter 18, you learned the power of fully leveraging your relationships with existing customers. In this chapter, we explore how to fill your pipeline with new opportunities. At the end of this chapter, you will be able to:

- Benchmark your calling habits to a comparison group of B2B salespeople
- Discuss canvassing and cold-calling as one method to fill your pipeline
- Describe how to get more face-to-face appointments with buyers

BENCHMARK CALLING HABITS

After we surveyed the above group of salespeople to determine their attitudes of cold-calling, we launched another survey of B2B salespeople. The five questions we asked shed light on their calling patterns and attitudes about filling their pipelines.

Which offers you the greatest potential for new business?
- Fifty-seven percent said selling more products and services to existing customers.
- Forty-three percent said finding new customers.

Note: In our BSP study, top achievers said they spend 18 percent of their time looking for new business.

What are the most effective sources for identifying new business? (This is their ranking.)
- Eighty-six percent said referrals from existing customers, friends, or peers.
- Fifty-six percent said networking events.
- Fifty percent said trade shows or professional organizations.
- Twenty-nine percent said cold-calling or canvassing.
- Seventeen percent said Internet search.
- Fourteen percent said business lists.
- Five percent said news/media articles.

What is the most effective way to initiate contact with new prospects?
- Sixty-two percent said in-person visit. (Decision makers concurred in our study of them that in-person meetings was their preferred method of contact for researching new suppliers.)
- Fifty-nine percent said phone call.
- Thirty-six percent said meet at social/business setting.
- Thirty-four percent said introduction call by the person referring you.
- Twenty-seven percent said e-mail. (Forty-eight percent of buyers said this was the best way to initiate contact with them.)
- Ten percent said social media contact.
- Three percent said U.S. mail.

What is your best follow-up strategy?
- Seventy percent said in-person visit.
- Fifty-four percent said phone call.
- Thirty-eight percent said e-mail.
- Two percent said U.S. mail.

What are your greatest challenges in filling your pipeline?
- Forty-eight percent said getting past the gatekeeper.
- Forty-two percent said price resistance.
- Forty-one percent said lack of interest by prospect.
- Forty-one percent said identifying the decision maker.
- Sixteen percent said lack of viable opportunities.

What can we infer from these results? Existing customers and referrals are the two most effective ways to fill your pipeline. In-person visits remain the best contact and follow-up strategies. One way to read these numbers is that while technology offers salespeople many ways to collect and distribute information, personal contact and relationships reign supreme when it comes to filling your pipeline. Sales remains a people business, even in a digital age.

CANVASSING

This is working an area. It is canvassing a business park or office building and calling (without an appointment) on a remote facility. Many companies have open-door policies that require purchasing people to see all visitors. Others require salespeople to have an appointment. Some even hang signs that say, "No soliciting." Unless you are soliciting for a charity, this really doesn't apply to you. How many salespeople do you think this sign discourages? Only the timid ones. Why let a sign reject you when you can get the full treatment from a live person? There is a place for appointments and a place for cold calls.

Let's say you have an appointment with a customer. On arrival, you notice a new business has opened across the street. You have a choice: you can either go back and research it or knock on the door and get the information firsthand. It's a time saver to get the information while there. Additionally, you may be able to collect some collateral pieces on the company. There's an interesting dynamic in new places. Everyone is friendly. They're glad to be there and conscious of the image they project. They receive you warmly.

Some salespeople use canvassing as a way to fill time in between appointment calls. It beats drinking coffee at the local coffeehouse. You may schedule one early-morning and one late-morning appointment and use the time between appointments to canvass an area. One advertising sales rep said he drove a different route each time to appointments to see if another business opened up in his territory.

Canvassing requires you to turn on your sales radar and scan for opportunities. Businesses open and close constantly. Being aware of these changes in your territory can mean a steady flow of new business in your pipeline. You will see things in person that you cannot pick up from a newspaper article or a visit to a website. You want to avail yourself of all the information about a prospect.

Making a planned sales call is not the same as a canned sales call. Canned is rote and lacks spontaneity. That cannot happen when canvassing in person. You must be spontaneous and rehearsed at the same time. That comes with practice. This field-tested, three-step method will get you in the door more often than not.

Step one: Receptionist qualification. Gather as much information as you can get from the receptionist. Be respectful. These gatekeepers are much better at keeping out salespeople than salespeople are at getting in to see decision makers. Identify the decision maker for your type of sale. In case the receptionist is not there, use the company directory or online resources like LinkedIn or the company website.

Step two: Opening statement. When the buyer greets you, use your elevator speech and tell the buyer why you're there.

Step three: Close for time. Once you have delivered the elevator speech and stated your purpose, ask for a meeting. For example:

> "Good morning, Ms. Schaeffer. I'm Frank Harris with Heartland Medical Distributors. We are a local company that helps long-term care facilities deliver cost-effective patient care with our linen programs. The facilities with whom we work tell us that our broad product line and quality service make us stand out in the industry. My reason for calling today is to see if you would be open to spending a few minutes looking at some ideas and deciding if you would like to explore this further. We could make an appointment to do this, or if it's more convenient, we could do it now while I'm here . . . (Pause for response.) . . . Would you mind if I asked a few questions to save some time?" (Now you qualify the prospect.)

With either answer, yes or no, you still want to ask qualifying questions. If the buyer tells you it's a bad time, the questions you ask will help make your follow-up call meaningful. If the buyer agrees to meet now, these questions are an effective way to open your sales call. This is a transition to the Needs-Analysis stage, which you will learn about in Chapter 22.

APPOINTMENTS

Appointment sales calls are different from canvassing calls, though there is a place for canvassing. With appointments, you have a warm prospect versus a cold suspect. Some prequalification has already happened.

Securing an appointment automatically positions you as a professional. When the buyer agrees to meet with you, he tacitly admits that he sees value in your idea. As you never want to be outsold by the competition, you never want to be outprepared by the buyer for a meeting.

Securing an appointment and having the time to research and organize increases your confidence and effectiveness during the meeting.

Decision makers are busy. In sales, you're not only competing with other vendors, you're also competing with everyone else who needs that decision maker's time. Decision makers are unresponsive when there is no perceived need for your solution. If the buyer doesn't believe she needs your solution, she focuses on other, more pressing priorities. There is a limited amount of time between e-mails and meetings when decision makers can tackle other critical priorities. If there is no perceived need, then other priorities take precedent.

To secure an appointment, send a compelling message that builds a perceived need. For decision makers to invest their time, they need to gain something from the meeting. Time is our most precious and fleeting resource. For the buyer to give his up, he needs to gain something more in return.

To get the appointment, GET to the point. GET is an acronym for Grab their attention, Establish the need, Tease the customer with a benefit. Incorporate these three elements into your appointment requests. These three elements work across various channels. The format can be used in e-mails, voice mails, sales letters, or even face-to-face.

Grab Their Attention

Goldfish have an attention span of just nine seconds. Humans have an attention span of only eight seconds. Goldfish have a longer attention span than humans! Your message had better be compelling enough to grab and hold their attention.

Use a compelling statistic. The more shocking, the better. The more relevant, the more interested the buyer will become. Your opening statistic should deliver value, educate, and keep the reader wanting more.

Use a referral. Referrals give you instant credibility. You build trust by association. One study showed that an in-home alarm company experienced a 90 percent sales success rate with referrals when their customers offered a walkthrough to demonstrate their alarm system to their neighbors.[1]

Reference a problem. In our recent buying study, we asked over 50 decision makers, "If a salesperson requested a meeting, which of these statements best describes why you would be willing to meet?" The number one response: "It appears this salesperson can help me with a current business problem or challenge my organization is facing." If the buyer believes you can help her with a problem, she is willing to meet with you. You can't build this perception until you first identify the problems buyers are facing. Talk with your existing customers and colleagues. Identify the common problems your different customer segments experience. Use this information to get the buyer's attention.

Reference a trigger event. A trigger event is any internal or external event that could cause the customer to be more open to your solution. One large wholesaler identified three common trigger events to grab the buyer's attention: ownership transition, change of staff, and inconsistency in bids and projects. If a customer is experiencing these events, he would be more open to meeting with you.

For greater opening impact, combine these techniques. For example, "Jim Doe at XYZ corporation suggested that I reach out to you. Our research shows that 80 percent of manufacturers don't have a backup supplier for their core products. This is one of the greatest supply challenges facing today's manufacturers."

Remember, you have eight seconds to get and hold the buyer's attention. That's roughly 31 words or just a few sentences. If the buyer is engaged, you've bought yourself an additional eight seconds.

Establish the Need

Why should the buyer hear your message? What is the compelling need for your solution? Why is there a need *now*? Answering these questions will help you establish the need for your solution and GET the appointment.

You are attempting to connect the customer's needs to your opening statement. Establish relevance, which keeps the buyer listening to you or reading your content. The stronger the overlap between the buyer's needs and your perceived ability to satisfy these needs, the more likely the customer is to meet with you. These examples expose a need:

> "Jim Doe at XYZ corporation suggested that I reach out to you. Our research shows that 80 percent of manufacturers don't have a backup supplier for their core products. This is one of the greatest supply challenges facing today's manufacturers."

"At ABC Supply we help organizations like XYZ solve this common manufacturing problem. There's never a good time for production to go down."

When you establish the need, you want the reader to keep reading or listening to you. You're not trying to sell them anything, you just want her to keep reading or listening. You grabbed her attention with the attention-getter and established the need by exposing a common problem.

Tease the Buyer

In marketing terms, a teaser is a series of small ad campaigns designed to build up to something greater. You can apply that same teaser concept to attaining appointments. The goal is to tease the customer with a benefit, while hinting at something greater. You are still not trying to sell your solution; you are selling that first appointment. This is a small win. You begin with a limited sales objective—to get the appointment. When you achieve this outcome, you have gained a small win on your path to success with the account.

In this part of the message, emphasize what the buyer gains from your solution. You are providing the customer with a general value proposition. Pain is a stronger motivator than gain. It might make sense to establish a pain proposition as well.

Here is an example of how all three elements come together.

- **Grab their attention:** "Jim Doe at XYZ corporation suggested that I reach out to you. Our research shows that 80 percent of manufacturers don't have a backup supplier for their core products. This is one of the greatest supply challenges facing today's manufacturers."
- **Establish the need:** "At ABC Supply we help organizations like XYZ solve this common manufacturing problem. There's never a good time for production to go down."
- **Tease the buyer:** "When you partner with ABC Supply, we have a detailed process to prevent supply chain failures and increase productivity. Are you available Tuesday afternoon or Wednesday morning for a 20-minute meeting?"

This template is designed to keep the buyer interested in your message. Buyers have short attention spans. Read each sentence and ask yourself, "Have I bought myself an additional eight seconds?" This process is not about selling your solution, you are selling the buyer on the first meeting—your small win. If the buyer agrees to meet with you, that's good news. By giving you his time, he is telling you that he is interested in your offering. Why else would he meet with you?

VALUE-ADDED SELLING REVIEW AND ACTION POINTS

1. Salespeople are making fewer in-person calls today and spending less face time with customers. Existing customers and referrals are the two most effective ways to fill your pipeline. In-person visits remain the best contact and follow-up strategies.

2. Canvassing is one strategy that value-added salespeople use to identify new sources of business. This approach enables you to gain broad coverage of your territory. Use this strategy between appointments or to reconnoiter an area.

3. The elevator speech is a brief introduction to your company. Build this by answering these questions: Who are we? What do we sell? To whom do we sell? What makes us unique?

4. Professionals work from appointments. As you perform your due diligence, you will position yourself as a cut above every other salesperson the buyer encounters. The three-step GET model is an effective way to secure appointments. Personalize your version of this model to increase the number of appointments you get.

CHAPTER 20

Precall Planning

Our research shows that fewer than 1-in-10 salespeople plan regularly for their sales calls. Our internal buyer survey found that only 42 percent of salespeople are well prepared for sales calls. Compare that meager response to the fact that 1,500 salespeople and their sales managers rated planning as the most important skill for long-range success in sales.[1] The tactical side of Value-Added Selling begins with planning the sales call. You cannot achieve your tactical objectives without planning.

Notice that we did not use the word *preparation*. Preparation has a different connotation for salespeople. It elicits different responses from salespeople. "Sure, I prepare. I'm always prepared to make a sales call." Or, "I was a Boy Scout, and we are always prepared." We then ask a follow-up question: "Do you write your plan on paper?" That's when more than 90 percent of salespeople admit that they do not have a plan. *Planning* is a more active verb than *preparing*. Preparing is more about readying yourself; planning is more about detailing a strategy for the sales call.

Planning is creating the future in your mind, on paper, and in the present. Planning is your link between dreams and reality. It's outlining the strategy that will help you achieve your dreams or goals. We use this formula in our seminars: P + P = 2P. Planning and Preparation equals twice the Performance.

The cost of a B2B sales call is high. Our best findings on this indicate that it costs companies approximately $500 USD to make a face-to-face B2B sales call. We have drawn from multiple studies to come up with that number. This includes pay, benefits, travel, and so on. It varies from company to company and sales job to sales job. So, our question for you is, "Are you extracting that much value from your sales calls?" This question casts a different light on sales calls. Whether the cost is $450 or $550, do your efforts result in an equitable return on your time investment?

Imagine that you're sitting on an airplane waiting for the doors to shut. The captain announces over the intercom system, "Thank you, ladies and gentlemen, for flying with us. Momentarily, we will close the doors, push back, and taxi out to the active runway. Once we have climbed to our cruising altitude, we will get back with you and inform you of our destination, how long we think it's going to take to get there, and the flying conditions along the route. We will not know any of this until we get up there." Now, that's a new definition of the term *winging it*, isn't it? How long would it take you to get off that airplane?

Most people laugh off the preceding example because it is so ridiculous. And yet, how many times have you made a sales call with that same lack of preparation? No salesperson plans to fail, but many fail to plan. As a salesperson, are you any less professional than the airline pilot? Of course not, unless you fail to plan.

This chapter is about building your confidence and your competence through better planning.

At the end of this chapter, you will be able to:

- Name six questions to help you prepare
- Complete the call planning guide

HOW TO PREPARE FOR YOUR SALES CALL

Planning is a habit just as not planning is a habit. The more you choose to plan, the more habitual it becomes. The more you neglect planning, the more that neglect becomes your habit. In our BSP research, we found that 95 percent of top achievers plan their sales calls and spend 13 minutes in this preparation. Earlier we told you that fewer than 10 percent of salespeople regularly plan. That 10 percent is the group of top achievers we studied. Call planning for Value-Added Selling involves three steps: reviewing what you know about the account, asking yourself some call planning questions, and completing your call planning guide.

Step 1: Study Your Value-Added Target Account

What do you know about this account already? Review the information in your customer file and bring yourself up to speed with what's happening in the account. The questions from Chapter 8 for your HVTs are a great review. What other sources of information can you tap into in your information quest? How about the customer's website, an online news source, or your company's files and CRM?

You want to seek out opportunity areas with your customers: areas of either pain or desired gain sufficient enough to motivate a change. Study your competitive strengths and weaknesses and how you can make a difference for the customer. Remember, knowledge is empowerment.

Step 2: Ask Yourself Six Questions Before Every Sales Call

These six questions, asked and answered before each sales call, will help you streamline your efforts and achieve your goals.

1. **"What do I want to accomplish on this call?"** Is your objective to gain maximum account penetration, create pull, differentiate your solution, assure customer satisfaction with your solution, reinforce your value-added status, or build a relationship?
2. **"What do I want to ask the buyer?"** When conducting your needs analysis, you may want to discover buyer pressure points, uncover opportunity areas, dislodge your competition with target probing, elicit needs-specific responses, or understand the buyer's personal concerns. List your questions in advance to ensure their compatibility with your call objectives.
3. **"What do I want to tell the buyer?"** Something about your solution? Something to help sell the buyer on the value-added concept? What specifically do you want to tell the buyer about your three-dimensional solution: the product, the company, and you?
4. **"What collateral pieces do I need?"** Do you want to use the VIP list, the customer bill of rights, a ten-things-to-consider list, a differentiation matrix, ROI analysis, CBA, the value-added worksheet, or the economic value analysis? Prepare your collateral support pieces before you make the sales call. Place them in

a presentation folder to build their perceived value. It's embarrassing to fumble through your materials during the meeting with the customer.

5. **"What obstacles do I anticipate?"** Will price be a trouble spot? What about buyer apathy or inertia? Has the buyer had a bad experience with us? You can anticipate an objection without creating one. Be ready for buyer resistance: it's a reality in sales. Here's your benchmark for effectively managing resistance: whoever is better prepared to deal with the resistance—you or the customer—will emerge victorious from the meeting.

6. Your payoff question, the money question: **"What action do I want from the customer at the end of this call?"** Your action objective for this call is how you will close the sales call. You may want the customer to make a follow-up appointment, agree to the next step in the process, commit to purchasing, give you inventory data, or set up a meeting. How you answer this question is how you will close the sales call. It's a quantitative way to measure your success on the call. This action objective is your small win for the sales call.

What do you think would happen if you were to ask yourself the foregoing six questions before each sales call? Most salespeople respond with, "I would increase my sales significantly." "I would be more prepared for the call." "I would feel more in control of the call." Or, "I would be a professional." If that's the case, why not do it?

Step 3: Complete Your Call Planning Guide

The call planning guide, as shown in Figure 20.1, helps you organize your thoughts for making the sales call. Notice that the call planning guide generally follows the call preparation questions: your objectives, probing, presenting, and closing.

One salesperson asked in a seminar, "Do I really need to use the call planning guide before every sales call?"

Our response was, "No, just for those calls where you want to sell something."

We conducted an experiment with a group of salespeople to determine the effectiveness of the call planning guide. We outlined a

FIGURE 20.1 Call Planning Guide

Objectives
Opening
Probing
Presenting
Closing

cold-call scenario and asked group members how they felt about making the call. On a 10-point scale (with 10 indicating a high desire to call, and 1 a low desire), the average score was 4. After only a 10-minute pencil-and-paper planning exercise (without further training), the average score jumped to 7. Their confidence level had almost doubled. What do you think that did to their competence level? The participants felt a deeper sense of control because they planned their efforts.

VALUE-ADDED SELLING REVIEW AND ACTION POINTS

1. The most effective and efficient way to increase the probability of your success is through planning. Planning and preparation equals twice the performance. Fewer than 10 percent of your peers plan their sales calls, while 95 percent of top achievers plan their sales calls. As you plan your sales calls, you automatically position yourself for success.

2. Plan your sales calls by reviewing what you know about the customer, asking yourself the six precall planning questions, and completing the call planning guide.

CHAPTER 21

Opening the Sales Call

Persuasion follows a predictable path. It begins with the receiver's attention. Then, the receiver becomes aware of a compelling need that requires action. Next, the sender of the message attempts to convince the receiver that the seller's solution will satisfy the receiver's need. Lastly, the sender issues a call to action. Every form of persuasive communication follows this path.

Advertisers use color and volume to get the consumer's attention. Then the advertiser helps the consumer become aware of how empty his or her life is without the product the advertiser is selling. Next, the advertiser promises how much better the consumer's life will be with the advertiser's product. Lastly, the advertiser asks the consumer to purchase the product.

A well-crafted political speech follows this path. The speaker says or does something to capture the attention of the voter. Then, the speaker convinces the voter of a compelling societal need. Next, the speaker promises a remedy to the problem. Lastly, the speaker asks for the voter's support.

Need-satisfaction selling follows this same path. The salesperson begins by getting the buyer's attention. Then, the salesperson helps the buyer become aware of a need. Next, the salesperson offers a solution to satisfy the need. Lastly, the salesperson asks for a commitment to buy from the buyer.

You've selected an account to call on and planned your sales call. The next step in this process is to make the call. You will open, probe, present, and close, paralleling the four-step persuasion path we described above.

Opening the sales call is the first step of the value-added sales call and one of the greatest weaknesses of most salespeople. This means a strong opening presents a great opportunity to differentiate you from the rest of the pack. You open with impact to get the buyer's full attention.

The Opening stage is the first step in your face-to-face meeting with the buyer. You're in the buyer's office, on a job site, or in your showroom. The goal of the Opening stage is to get the buyer's attention and set a positive tone for the meeting. Few salespeople do it well. A strong opening is important in all forms of communication.

Newspaper editors always strive for powerful headlines to grab the reader. Book publishers are as interested in a catchy title as they are in a great book. Ad copywriters constantly search for the right hook to snag their target audience. This chapter is about strong openings.

At the end of this chapter, you will be able to:

- Discuss the power of first impressions
- Describe how much socializing you should do at the beginning of the call
- Demonstrate how to open with impact
- Name several things to avoid in the early stages of the sale

THE POWER OF FIRST IMPRESSIONS

First impressions are lasting impressions. There are a couple of explanations for this. The first is the psychological phenomenon of the *primacy effect*. The *primacy effect* means that the first items presented in a series are recalled easier than items presented later in a sequence. There are several explanations for this, but the most common is that there are fewer items competing for the encoding of this information in the brain. People encode data quicker and more permanently when there is little to interfere with this memory process.

A second and related phenomenon is *confirmation bias*. *Confirmation bias* means that a person will search for and interpret information in a way that confirms his or her initial impression of something. People look for and notice information that reaffirms their initial impression. In this case, the initial impression is of a person.

For example, when a salesperson meets a prospect for the first time, the salesperson forms an impression of the buyer, and the buyer forms an impression of the salesperson. If the salesperson is having a bad day and allows that to affect his or her behavior, that could result in a negative first impression of that salesperson. Conversely, if the salesperson is positive, enthusiastic, and professional, that is the impression the buyer encodes. From this point moving forward, the buyer will seek information or cues from the salesperson to confirm his or her impression from the first meeting.

Can this impression be reversed? Yes, but it takes multiple exposures to counterconditioning for this to happen. For salespeople, it makes sense and saves time to create a positive first impression because that is the backdrop against which the salesperson is judged in the future.

GUIDELINES FOR SOCIALIZING

This question surfaces often in our seminars: "How much socializing should I really do with the customer?" A simple rule of thumb is to take your lead from the customer, who will let you know how much socializing is appropriate. A big mistake salespeople make is assuming that the best way to build rapport with buyers is to engage in small talk.

One study found that 72 percent of buyers find unsolicited small talk to be negative.[1] The study concluded that the best way to open the sales call is to tell the buyer why you're there, announce your call objective, and state your intention.

Take your lead from the customer. Some buyers are social, while others are more formal. Social buyers are people oriented, which affects both the context and the content of the sales call. With these buyers, the context of the call is relaxed and social. Getting to know you as a person is a big part of the process for the people-oriented buyer. Similarly, the content of the sales call primarily reflects people issues: training, support, ease of use, safety, morale, and similar concerns. It's important for you to frame your solution within the context that reflects the buyer's priorities—in this case, people.

Other buyers are task oriented. The context of this sales call is formal and businesslike. These buyers generally want to get to business quickly. You demonstrate your competence early by getting down to the task at hand. For content, they prefer to hear about performance, productivity, operational and functional characteristics, profitability, and other quantifiable benefits. If these buyers socialize, it's at the end of the call, after they have completed the task. Then they may relax their guard and give you a peek at the person.

Mirroring your buyer's priority—task orientation or people orientation—is one way to establish credibility. Another way to build credibility and trust is to pace the buyer. Some people move quickly and intuitively. Other people are methodical and analytical. Potential conflict arises when you move at your pace versus the buyer's pace. You can reduce the psychological distance between you and the buyer by mirroring his or her priority and pace. You run into problems when you impose your priority and pace on the buyer.

HOW TO OPEN

Every strong opening has three components. First, if this is your initial meeting with this buyer, introduce yourself and observe the customary amenities. If you already know the person, exchange courtesies.

Second, explain why you're there. State the purpose of your call. In your call objective, include a benefit for the buyer. The more relevant the benefit, the quicker you get the buyer's attention.

You have several ways to tell the buyer why you're there; among them:

- Make a positive reference to your product and how it will benefit the company.
- Ask a thought-provoking rhetorical question, but be careful not to sound self-serving.
- Mention a common acquaintance or friend. This referral opening helps establish quick credibility.
- Make a reference to something about the buyer's company.

The third part of your opening is to ask permission to probe. If it's a repeat call, get permission to review. Why? Because it's polite.

Also, when the buyer gives you permission to ask questions, it implies a commitment to answer these questions.

There's another reason for you to get permission to probe: justification. A sales manager told us that he had difficulty getting his salespeople to ask questions. They felt that they were being intrusive. By teaching them the permission technique, the sales manager alleviated their reluctance; his salespeople said they no longer felt as if they were prying. Learning to ask permission affected their attitudes about probing. They were more open to it.

The following sample openers demonstrate how this technique sounds when you put it all together:

First face-to-face sales call: "Good morning, Mr. Spence. I'm Frank Harris with Modern Research Labs. It's a pleasure to meet you. As I mentioned in our phone conversation earlier this week, the reason I wanted to meet with you today is to discuss the unique bundle of time-saving, value-added services that our company has created specifically for companies that operate in your niche. There are many things I could tell you about us, but I'd like to hear more about your company. May I ask a few questions?"

Repeat call: "Good morning, Jill. It's great to see you again. (At this point, exchange pleasantries.) The last time we met, you told me about a computer glitch that is wreaking havoc in production planning. Is that still an issue? (Pause for response.) What would it mean to you if I told you our engineers have come up with a possible solution? (Pause.) Before getting into that, I need to review a couple of things. Do you mind if I ask a couple of questions?"

Referral call: "Brad, it's a pleasure to meet with you. Our mutual friend, Brendan, gave me your name and suggested we meet. We've worked with his company for the past three years and are responsible for creating his last ad campaign, which took the market by storm. That's why I wanted to meet with you today—to see if we could create the same kind of results for your company. May I lead with some questions?"

In each of those opening statements, the salesperson flirted with a benefit for the buyer: offering a unique bundle of time-saving, value-added services; solving a critical problem; and creating amazing marketing results. The salesperson gave the buyer a reason to listen, it benefited him or her. It made sense for the buyer to listen. And in each case, the salesperson got permission to probe.

THINGS TO AVOID

Over the years, we have collected many opening comments from sales-people, and some read like a list of what not to do on a sales call. Using them demonstrates a lack of confidence in yourself or your product, a feeling that you may be wasting the buyer's time or setting a negative tone for the call. Avoid the following openers:

"I was just in the area visiting another customer and thought I would stop by to see you." You're really saying that this buyer isn't special enough to warrant a separate call. You've made this buyer an after-thought, a time filler between other, more important appointments.

"I know you're busy, and I promise not to take up a lot of your time." You sound like a time waster. This approach automatically relegates you to that status. Buyers feel contempt for people who waste their time. Is that really how you want to position your visit with this customer?

"You probably weren't interested in doing anything today." A salesperson actually walked into our offices, smiled weakly, and said, "You're probably the least-likely candidate today to buy a long-distance service." We answered, "You're right!" He didn't want to sell, and we didn't want to buy. We got along famously. He was bland and obviously unconvinced that his product was worth our time. We agreed with him—it was not worth our time.

"I've heard through the grapevine that your company has had some problems in this area." Now your buyer is suspicious; who's talking about him or her in the marketplace? Suspicion and paranoia are not the emotions you want buyers to feel when you're attempting to build trust and rapport.

"Would you be interested in saving money?" Questions such as this one are too obvious and self-serving. Buyers say in surveys that they reject obvious questions or questionable benefits such as, "We can cut your costs in half."

Planning your opening in advance to grab the buyer's attention and to set a positive tone for your meeting will position you as a professional in a field of salespeople that prefer to wing it.

VALUE-ADDED SELLING REVIEW AND ACTION POINTS

1. First impressions are lasting impressions. You have a choice: prepare for your first meeting in a way that helps you create a positive first impression or spend a considerable amount of time after that first meeting trying to reshape your image in the buyer's mind.

2. A strong opening—the attention getter—is an integral part of communication. All persuasion begins with getting the attention of the receiver of the message. Develop a strong opening statement to begin your value-added sales call.

3. Take your lead from the buyer. Some buyers prefer to socialize; other buyers prefer to get down to business. Your sales approach should mirror the buyer's preferences. You reduce the distance between buyer and seller when you respect the buyer's priorities.

CHAPTER 22

The Needs-Analysis Stage

Imagine that you're in your doctor's office. The doctor is describing a new medication for diabetes patients, extolling the virtues of this revolutionary drug. It is readily available and offers patients an annual savings of 50 percent over standard insulin. Obviously, your doctor is excited about this new product. The doctor writes a prescription for you. You're confused because you're there for a flu shot. Moreover, you don't even have diabetes. The doctor has prescribed without diagnosing your symptoms.

How many times have you done to a buyer what the doctor has done to you? Many salespeople make calls in which they detail their product, assuming that the buyer needs it and is aware of this need. You can't assume that. To sell value added, you must first analyze the buyer's needs thoroughly. This is the essence of the customer value focus.

When reduced to its fundamental dynamic, buying and selling is an information exchange. The buyer gives you information; you process that information; then, you give the buyer information. The degree of overlap between your information and the buyer's information is a measure of the probability that you will do some business. Little overlap means low probability. Higher overlap yields a greater probability.

The needs analysis represents the second stage of the value-added sales call. It is the buyer's opportunity to provide you information about his or her needs. Your questions facilitate this conversation. Top-achieving salespeople report to spending more time in needs analysis than in any other stage of the sales call. This chapter is about developing your probing skills so you can study the buyer's needs.

At the end of this chapter, you will be able to:

- Define the needs analysis
- Discuss the importance of listening to the buyer
- Ask questions effectively
- Demonstrate three questioning areas
- Utilize targeted probing to predispose the buyer to your value added

THE NEEDS ANALYSIS: THE MOST IMPORTANT STAGE OF THE SALES CALL

The needs analysis is a fact-finding mission. It's a deep dive into the buyer's needs, wants, desires, and fears. It's an in-depth examination and assessment of all the variables that may influence the buying decision. You gather data and consider the buyer's perception regarding the identified needs. The needs analysis helps you understand the buyer's definition of value and enables you to determine how and where your solution creates value for the buyer. This is the behavioral side of customer-izing. It is the most important stage of the sale because it enables you to correctly prescribe the solution for the buyer's problem.

By thoroughly analyzing the buyer's needs, you help the buyer objectively understand specific needs. This objective awareness raises the buyer's constructive pain level with the status quo. Your strategic questioning often acts as a catalyst allowing buyers to realize their dissatisfaction with their current ways of attempting to meet their needs. Dissatisfaction drives change.

You're digging for root-canal pain. The premise is that excruciating pain motivates someone to go through a root canal procedure. That pain must be so intense that it hurts too much to do nothing. This is what you're probing for in the needs analysis. Root-canal pain causes buyers to change. People change when the disadvantages of doing nothing exceed the advantages of not having to change—in short, the pain is greater than the gain. When their current situation hurts more than it helps, buyers open up to change. Probe deep. Find the root-canal pain.

Probing for buyer needs unearths the nonprice variables that affect the buying decision. Getting the prospect to elaborate on the importance of these nonprice variables mitigates the role of price in the buying decision. Many times, customers are unaware of these variables until someone asks about them.

Management studies reveal that involvement in the change process builds commitment and lowers resistance to new ideas. Involving the prospect via questioning breaks down resistance to change and builds commitment. When you couple an objective awareness of one's situation with this active involvement, the motivation to change comes from within the individual. The prospect wants to change, and that makes your job easier.

Price-sensitivity studies demonstrate that engaged buyers who learn more about their needs and potential solutions are less price sensitive. Engaged buyers study potential solutions and often recognize benefits that the supplier didn't realize.

Once you get the buyer involved, raise his or her objective awareness level, and create an internal motivation to change, the buyer is more eager to buy than you are to sell. What does that do to your closing ratio? Do you think price plays a major role in the buying decision if the buyer's desire to own your product is greater than your desire to sell? No way. Price instead assumes the position it richly deserves—only one of many buying criteria, rather than the main reason someone buys a product.

Think of this probing technique as icing on the cake. When you probe, you're telegraphing strong messages to your prospect. You're saying, "I care enough to listen—to invest part of my life to hear your problems." This message builds trust and rapport. It also differentiates you from all other salespeople who call on that buyer and deliver canned presentations. You're recording a strong, sincere message on the tape inside the buyer's head.

Probing and listening take advantage of the fundamental human relations principle that people like to talk about themselves. *Scientific American* published a study that people spend 60 percent of their conversation time talking about themselves. With social media, that number jumps to 80 percent.[1]

The prospect thinks, "This person cares enough to listen to my concerns, understand my problems, and commit to a viable solution for them. This salesperson is different from most others who've called on me. I want to do business with this rep because I trust this person."

The premise is simple. If two people want to do business with each other because of trust and rapport, the details (such as price) rarely block the sale. If the buyer trusts you and feels comfortable with you because you genuinely care, price is not on the radar screen. The buyer trusts that your price is fair and reflects equity in what he or she is paying and receiving.

By performing the needs analysis, you communicate, "It's OK to pay more for the value we offer. We understand your problems and share your concerns. We're committed to finding a solution that makes sense for you." The needs analysis enables you to customize your solution for the buyer, and who doesn't want a customized solution?

Not performing a needs analysis leaves you with few options. You regurgitate a canned presentation because you're clueless about what's most important to the buyer. When you fail to ask questions, you miss an opportunity to build trust and rapport.

One point of clarification is necessary at this point. You are not creating a need for your product. You are creating an awareness that the need already exists. Creating a need is a seller-focused mentality that you are manipulating the buyer to purchase. Why would you be calling on a buyer if there is no need for what you sell? Exposing a need means that you are unearthing the conditions that pave the way for you to satisfy that need. This approach is customer-focused selling. If you're struggling with this distinction, let this difference sink in for a minute or two before continuing.

THE IMPORTANCE OF LISTENING

Our Best Practices study indicates that top achievers spend 60 percent of their face-to-face selling time listening to the buyer and more time here (38 percent) than any other step in the sales call. Sixty percent of buyers stop doing business with a company because of a perceived indifference. This shows up in the salesperson's failure to understand the buyer's needs.[2] Too many salespeople are competitive listeners; they listen to respond versus listen to understand.

Asking questions is half of the give-and-take-communications formula. The other half is listening actively to what the other person says. Active listening is not passive hearing. It is more than the awareness of sounds. Active listening is necessary to attach meaning to what the other person is saying. Active listening means inputting what the person says, processing it, and feeding back relevant information. As an active listener, you are busy processing information and adding to the conversational momentum. Top achievers listen more than they talk. This means they put the focus on the buyer, which is customer-oriented selling.

Barriers to Effective Listening

Listening sounds easy, doesn't it? It can be, if you focus. When you submit to distractions—internal or external—listening is difficult. Let's see how many of these barriers you recognize.

- Risk—you fear the information the other person shares.
- Daydreaming—your mind is somewhere else.
- Narrow-mindedness—you believe that you, alone, have all the answers.
- Facts-only listening—the other person's nonverbal messages and conversational nuances escape you.
- Time pressure—you feel rushed.
- Outside noise—you yield to distractions around you.
- Internal noise—you are preoccupied with something else.
- Information overload—you're overwhelmed with too much input from the other person.
- Techno-talk—you're lost (even worse, your customer is lost) in a sea of technical jargon.
- Attending to the technology in front of you—texting, tweeting, etc.

Risk is a major obstacle to effective listening for salespeople. If salespeople actively listen to buyers, they risk agreeing with a buyer's point of view that may differ significantly from the salesperson's call objective.

Carl Rogers said it best: "To be effective at all in active listening, one must have a sincere interest in the speaker. Active listening carries a strong element of personal risk. If we manage to accomplish what we are describing here—to sense deeply the feeling of another person, to understand the meaning his experiences have for him, to see the world as he sees it—we risk being changed ourselves. It is threatening to give up, even momentarily, what we believe and start thinking in someone else's terms. It takes a great deal of inner security and courage to be able to risk one's self in understanding another."[3]

How much risk do you face in actively listening to your buyer? Could the buyer be correct that your product is overkill for her problem or that your price really is too high or that your service levels do, in fact, stink? Honest, objective, active listening is risky business for salespeople. Are you up for the risk?

Irritating Listening Habits

Do you ever find yourself engaged in any of these actions while in conversation?

- Finishing someone else's sentences—putting words in the person's mouth
- Prejudging the speaker because of your bias
- Interrupting the speaker to inject your opinion
- Looking away toward something or someone else—splitting your attention
- Jumping to conclusions before the other person finishes
- Rushing the speaker—verbally or nonverbally dismissing the person
- Stealing the spotlight with one-upmanship
- Using poor posture—slouching or displaying condescending body language
- Playing with your mobile device or other technology

Becoming a Better Listener

When you listen actively to your customer, the focus is exactly where it needs to be: on the speaker, the sender of the message. You're engaged, and so is the other person. When buyers participate in the sale, they buy. The tips presented here will help you do a better job of listening to your buyer.

- **Don't interrupt.** As basic as this sounds, buyers can't talk if you're constantly interrupting. Let others complete their thoughts and their sentences before you respond. It's annoying to have others finish sentences for you. It's also rude to presume you know what someone else would like to say. Aggressive sales types naturally want to move the conversation along. However, you'll discover that listening your way to success is more fun for everyone. Be courteous. Be polite. But mostly, be quiet.

- **Practice silence.** Avoid responding too quickly to the buyer's questions. By the same token, after you ask a question, remain silent and let the other person take time to consider a response. Silence can be intimidating—that's why salespeople have trouble using it effectively. As you practice patience and silent listening, you'll be amazed at what others tell you.

- **Take notes.** When you write down what a buyer says, it directs your attention and also demonstrates that the person's words are important to you. Informing people beforehand that you plan to take notes of your conversation makes them less defensive. Develop your own shorthand for taking notes with customers.

- **Clarify.** When you're unsure about something said to you, clarify. Ask why, or probe to be sure that you fully understand. Clarifying demonstrates that you're paying attention and you care enough to understand fully what you're hearing. Simply ask, "Could you be more specific, please?"

- **Restate.** Periodically restate what the other person says. This demonstrates that you understand and that you're operating on the same level, the same page, as the customer. For example: "So, what you're saying is . . . ."

- **Summarize.** Throughout the conversation, summarize key points to demonstrate that you've heard correctly. Summarizing also serves to refocus a conversation that has meandered: "Let me be sure I understand where we are . . . ."

- **Listen nonverbally.** Watch the customer's nonverbal signals. Are the nonverbal signals open or closed? Do these nonverbal signals move toward you, engaging you? Does your buyer withdraw with his or her nonverbal signals—moving away from you? To demonstrate active listening, lean forward, nod, and use verbal reinforcement to accompany your nonverbal responses, indicating to the buyer that you're actively engaged in the conversation.

- **Use confirmation statements.** You can add momentum with an occasional "Uh-huh," "Mmm," "I hear you," "You bet," or "That's an interesting point." Verbal reinforcement, along with attentive nonverbal responses, will demonstrate the impact that the speaker is having on you.

So, what's the greatest skill a salesperson possesses? It's the ability to communicate with customers—to ask questions that cause buyers to think, and to listen actively to what buyers have to say. You must master this skill to be successful in sales.

MECHANICS OF QUESTIONING

To conduct an effective needs analysis, you must have a thorough understanding of the mechanics of asking questions. You must know how to construct questions that draw the information you desire. When designing your questions, consider these three areas: length of response, intent, and bias.

Open and Closed Questions

Your first consideration in formulating questions is how lengthy a response you want and need. An open-ended question encourages the respondent to elaborate. The question generally requires a lengthy response. The chief advantage of the open-ended question is that the buyer volunteers additional information and explains his or her position more thoroughly. It builds commitment because of customer involvement. A disadvantage of an open-ended question is that the response may be time-consuming and you may lose some conversational control.

Typically, open-ended questions begin with *Why, How, What, Tell me about,* or similar words or phrases designed to gain active participation. A facial expression—raised eyebrows or a look of confusion—is an open-ended question if it encourages the other person to respond freely. Here are some examples of open-ended questions:

- Why do you feel that way?
- What are your main concerns in buying?
- Tell me about your business.
- How do you feel about dealing with more than one supplier?
- Why is price important in your decision process?

Closed-ended questions elicit a short response—generally one or two words. You intentionally limit the response length. Closed-ended questions offer two major advantages: they give you greater conversational control, and they are more time efficient. The primary disadvantage is that the respondent rarely offers unsolicited information. Another disadvantage is that consecutive closed-ended questions sound like an interrogation, not an interview. Don't machine-gun buyers with closed probes because it will shut down the dialogue.

Generally, closed-ended questions begin with words such as *When, Who, Which, Where, How many, How much, Do you, Are you,* or *Will you.* Notice that the following examples of closed-ended questions have one thing in common—they evoke a short response:

- Which of these do you prefer?
- When do you place orders?
- Have you had problems with your current supplier?

You can get the same information by asking your question as either open-ended or closed-ended. For example:

- What role does delivery play in your buying decision? (open)
- Is delivery important in your buying decision? (closed)

Again, the open-ended question encourages a lengthier response. One advantage in the example just cited is that the prospect may tell you *why* delivery is so important. You can dig for information both ways—open or closed. Ideally, you should ask all open-ended questions. Realistically, you may need to ask a few closed-ended questions to regain conversational control or to confirm what you heard from the lengthy response. For example:

- What are your major concerns in purchasing? (open) (Pause for response.)
- Then, price and delivery are your two major concerns? (closed)

Use this rule of thumb to encourage buyers to respond freely: 80 percent of your questions should be open-ended. If the conversation meanders, ask a closed-ended question to regain control quickly.

People often ask in seminars, "How do I get the silent type to open up?" We advise them to examine the nature of the questions they ask their buyers. Asking too many closed-ended questions inhibits buyer participation. Keep your questions open-ended to encourage full buyer involvement.

Direct and Indirect Questions

The second consideration in designing questions is your intent. How obvious do you want to be with your questions? How blunt and straightforward can you afford to be? Can you afford much directness in your questioning?

A direct question is blunt, straightforward, and to-the-point. There is no doubt what you're asking. It's obvious. An advantage of the direct question is that there is no confusion about the information you want. Plus, it may be more time efficient. A strong disadvantage of the direct question is that it can be offensive and threatening. Here are three examples of direct questions:

- Do you have the authority to make this decision?
- Is price important to you?
- Why do you buy from that supplier?

There is a strong element of risk in these questions because they are so blunt. In most cases, it's prudent to soften the delivery and minimize the perceived threat. Do this by using an indirect question instead.

An indirect question veils your intent. It's a roundabout way of getting the same information. Since it's not as threatening as the direct question, the indirect question is easier to answer. Because it is a low-risk question, you're more likely to get a response. In fact, the indirect question encourages the other person to volunteer additional information. A disadvantage is that it may not be as time efficient because what you're asking isn't as obvious. Here are three examples of indirect questions:

- How does your buying process work?
- What things are important when making a buying decision?
- Do you have more than one supplier?

Notice that these questions parallel the three direct question examples. The first indirect question—"How does your buying process work?"—gives the prospect an opportunity to save face because it doesn't question his buying authority. It asks how the buying process works in general. It offers the buyer a chance to volunteer the fact that he is or is not the decision maker. It gets the information in a non-threatening manner.

The second example avoids price altogether. It asks about *all* things that are important in this decision. It raises the buyer's awareness that there are considerations other than price. It doesn't presume that price is the only decision criterion. If price is important, it will come out in the answer.

The third question asks how many suppliers the buyer has. The intent is to get the buyer talking about all suppliers. This way, you discover what you really want to know: why this buyer purchases from a given supplier. It's a roundabout way of getting the information, but the buyer may be more open to the indirect approach.

The best time to use an indirect question is when you feel that the nature of the question is risky and warrants some caution. In such cases, broach the topic indirectly to get your information. If you perceive limited risk, ask the question more directly.

Leading and Neutral Questions

Another thing to consider when designing your questions is bias. Do you want an objective, fact-based response, or do you want the buyer to echo what you ask? Do you want the prospect to speak freely or just agree with you? Do you want to ask questions that encourage dialogue, or do you want to ask questions that lead the other person?

Your objective in the needs analysis is to engage and open up the buyer in order to gain maximum information. Leading questions discourage this give-and-take environment. A leading question suggests the answer you desire. It leaves no room for the buyer to voice opinions. Leading questions are seller focused.

A neutral question, on the other hand, offers no suggestion of what the response should be. Because it doesn't lead, the other person doesn't feel threatened.

Here are examples:

- Is price important? (neutral)
- Price is important, isn't it? (leading)
- Are you the decision maker? (neutral)
- You are the decision maker, aren't you? (leading)

A leading question may make buyers feel defensive because it forces a response. How do you feel when someone uses leading or biased questions on you? If you're like most people, you resent others telling you what to think and say. You feel cornered, manipulated, and controlled—none of which is conducive to building rapport or gaining information.

Sales trainers who advocate the use of leading questions in this phase of the sale mislead you. They're encouraging you to use techniques on others that you would resent being used on you. There is an incongruence here. Salespeople don't use skills that are philosophically incongruent with their own beliefs. Avoid bias in your questions during the needs analysis. Remember, your objective is to gather facts, not elicit canned responses.

STRATEGIC QUESTIONING AREAS

In addition to knowing *how* to formulate your questions, it's equally important for you to know exactly *what* to ask. The purpose of this section is to show you how to arrange your questions. First, ask questions that are level specific. For Level-I buyers, ask logistics questions. For Level-II influencers, ask technically oriented questions. For Level-III decision makers, ask profit-and-loss type questions. Asking questions in the order they are presented in this section will help you to capitalize on the logic of the needs analysis. Divide your questions into these three categories: situational, competitive, and projective questions.

Situational Questions

Situational questions probe the buyer's expectations. They elicit information about the buyer's world: needs, wants, decision process, and so forth. The buyer gives you information regarding all variables that influence the buying decision. Subdivide your situational questions into two groups: general information and specific need.

General-Information Questions

General-information questions are global, broad-based, nonthreatening questions that spark the conversation and provide a useful backdrop for focusing on the buyer's five areas of concern: industry, customer base, competition, company, and personal. The following general-information questions exemplify each of the five aspects:

- Tell me about your marketplace. (industry)
- What trends do you see in your market? (industry)
- Who are your customers? (customer base)
- What do your customers want from you? (customer base)
- Who is your competition? (competition)
- What competitive pressures do you face? (competition)
- How does your decision process work? (company)
- How long has your company been in this market? (company)
- How long have you been with the company? (personal)
- How does this decision affect you personally? (personal)

Notice that these questions are nonthreatening and serve as good conversation starters. You may not need to ask all the questions that are listed here. At least you want to ask, "Tell me about your business."

Specific-Need Questions

With specific-need questions, you ask for the prospect's needs, wants, requirements, and expectations from a product, a supplier, and a salesperson—the three dimensions of value. Get the necessary information to determine whether your company and product are a good match for your buyer's needs. Ask questions about specifications and delivery dates. Determine budget limitations. Probe for the buyer's quality needs. Ask questions in all three dimensions of value. For example:

- What are you looking for in a supplier? (company)
- What kind of technical support do you need on this project? (company)
- What availability does your project require? (product)
- What product specifications do you need? (product)
- What do you expect from me as your salesperson? (salesperson)
- How will you measure my effectiveness as your rep? (salesperson)

You are asking, "What do you need?" Situational questions make it easy for you to initiate the sales conversation. They are rapport building, nonthreatening, and fact oriented. You're asking the prospect to elaborate on his or her needs, wants, and fears.

Competitive Questions

Following situational questions, competitive questions are the second major category of needs-analysis questions. Competitive questions probe the performance of how and how well the buyer's needs are met. Answers to competitive questions give you information about your competitors and their performance. Most important, they help buyers understand the efficacy or lack of effectiveness in how they are attempting to satisfy their needs.

As buyers become aware of the gap that exists between their expectations and how they're attempting to meet their needs, they begin to feel some dissatisfaction with the status quo, which becomes the catalyst to change. Memorize this concept. Study it. Practice it on your sales calls.

How-Met Questions

How-met refers to how buyers *attempt* to meet their needs—via your competition. Notice the word *attempt*. True to the value-added philosophy, we believe there is always a better mousetrap to be built. The competition could be a past, current, or future supplier. It could also be an in-house solution that the buyer uses. Here are two examples of how-met questions:

- How do you currently handle your sulfuric acid needs?
- Who is your current supplier for sulfuric acid?

How-met questions help you identify the source of your competition for a specific customer. It includes questions about how the buyer meets the need and where she buys the solution.

How-Well Questions

As how-met questions identify the source of your competition, how-well questions are performance oriented. You're seeking information about the competition's performance. You want to determine what the buyer likes and dislikes about the current supplier as well as the competitor's goods and services. Are this supplier and product meeting the buyer's needs satisfactorily? The following are examples of how-well questions:

- How well does your current supplier meet your needs?
- What's been your experience with the sulfuric acid you're using?
- What type of feedback have you received from your people about this material?

Your objective is to raise the buyer's awareness level concerning his or her current way of *attempting* to meet his or her needs. In doing so, you want the buyer to realize that the competitor's solution may fail to satisfy those needs. Avoid anything that the buyer may view as sour-grapes selling, such as bad-mouthing the competition. The buyer made the decision to use that supplier. Walk softly with your competitive probes. At the same time, you do want to provide an accepting climate for the buyer to voice concerns about current problems. Create an opportunity for the buyer to discuss the problems that other suppliers have caused. Ask about the impact these problems have had on the buyer's world.

You may discover that buyers rationalize, deny, or exaggerate how well their current solution attempts to satisfy their needs. This type of defensiveness can be explained by loss aversion, cognitive dissonance, or simply, face saving. Who wants to admit their previous decision stunk? Some salespeople report that buyers respond flippantly to the how-well question. One of their concerns is that any positive response by the customer reinforces his or her previous buying decision. This is a legitimate concern. Some feel the how-well question may be too vague, general, or abstract. That, too, is a legitimate concern.

We have already established that buyers crave simplicity. This bias for keeping things simple may influence how the buyer responds to this question. If you were to ask an abstract question, the buyer may simplify it and respond with a predictable, "Everything's fine." If you sense from your probing that the buyer may simplify his response to the how-well question, you can use a technique we call *targeted probing*.

Targeted probing zeros in on areas where you know the competition is weak. You know this from your call preparation and competitive intelligence work. The Differentiation Matrix (Figure 12.1) provided you with this type of information. For example, you may have discovered that your competitor was vulnerable because it has fewer locations from which to serve, limited technical support, or insufficient inventory. Targeting these areas with questions spotlights these weaknesses without bad-mouthing the competition.

"Are you getting the convenience in locations that you need from your current source?"

"How is the technical support you receive?"

"Are you able to get all of the inventory you need when you need it?"

You may discover that targeted probing opens the door for the buyer to express his or her frustration and dissatisfaction. Beginning with these simple and specifically targeted probes makes the question easier for the reluctant buyer to answer. You may not need this with all buyers, but if you sense the buyer is overwhelmed by the how-well question, remember to use this technique.

Projective Questions

Projective questions follow situational and competitive questions to make up the final group of questions in the Needs-Analysis stage. Projective questions target the presumed gap that exists between the buyer's needs and how the buyer is *attempting* to meet those needs. You could call these gap questions. Your intent with projective questions is to spotlight this gap. This group of questions comprises two subgroups—ideal questions and the impact question.

Ideal Questions

Ideal questions are hypothetical "What if" questions. Encourage buyers to dream by asking questions that cause them to consider the ideal solution. Ask buyers about what changes or improvements they would like to make in how they are attempting to meet their needs. For example:

- If you could change anything about your current supplier, what would you change?
- What would be your notion of the ideal product?
- What would you like to see us do for you that your current supplier is not doing?
- If you were a supplier, what would you do differently?

In each case, you've asked the buyer to dream about the ideal solution to a problem. Projective questions encourage the buyer to maximize, not satisfice. When you ask projective questions, you are tinkering.

The Impact Question

Take the ideal question a step further and ask what effect the stated changes would have on the buyer's business: "If you could improve something about the service level you're receiving currently, what would you change? (Pause for answer) How would that help your business?" The latter is the impact question. The buyer is clarifying what your value proposition must do for them. The greatest strength you possess as a change agent relates to your ability to demonstrate the impact of your solution vis-à-vis the buyer's world.

The impact question encourages the buyer to elaborate on *why* he or she should change current suppliers. The logic of this question is that the buyer does all the selling; he or she convinces you and himself or herself that there may be a better mousetrap. The next logical comment from the prospect is, "What do you have available that could give me the things I need?" Now the buyer is open to change, and your task is to demonstrate how your solution can be the answer.

What happens if the buyer can't think of any changes or improvements to make? What do you do at that point? You suggest ideas and get a reaction to them. The ideas you suggest are coincidentally the unique strengths your company offers. The following scenario demonstrates how to do this:

> *Seller:* "Mr. Buyer, if you could change one thing about your current supplier, what would that be and how would it affect your business?"
>
> *Buyer:* "I'm not sure I'd change anything. We're happy with what we have right now."
>
> *Seller:* "Let me suggest a couple of ideas and get your feedback. How would you improve the delivery time and technical support from your current supplier?"

In this example, you draw attention to delivery and technical backup. Narrow your suggestions to two specific areas for the prospect to address. It's up to the prospect to tell you about some desired changes in these areas. By admitting that there are some needed improvements in these areas, the prospect opens the door for your presentation. Then describe the features and benefits of your delivery and technical support.

If you scrutinize the logic of the needs analysis, you discover how amazingly simple it is. You're asking three basic questions:

- What are your needs? (situational)
- How are you meeting those needs? (competitive)
- How can we better address those needs? (projective)

STRATEGIC PROBING OBJECTIVE

Forming strategic probing objectives allows you to put the needs analysis in motion as you ask questions in each of the three probing areas: situational, competitive, and projective. You can use the needs analysis, for example, to sell against price. You begin with strategic probing objectives, determining what you want to accomplish with your questions. One strategic probing objective is to gather facts. A second may be to sell your uniqueness. These can be part of your small-wins strategy. By asking the right questions of the buyer, you plant seeds in the buyer's mind for a potentially better mousetrap. Your questions spotlight areas where the buyer could find a better solution for root-canal-type problems.

One strategic probing objective is to preempt price resistance by focusing your questions on value added. You minimize its importance and underscore other variables a buyer must consider when purchasing. You might design the following questioning scenario for a sales call. Notice that the strategic questioning objective adds a sense of purpose to the questions.

Strategic objective: To gather facts and plant seeds regarding our value added (our strong technical department support and ability to customize).

Situational questions: "What are your needs?"
- How often do you find yourself in the position of needing additional technical support?
- Given the complexity of your process, how involved do a supplier's technical people need to be in your operation?
- I understand that many of your jobs are custom work. What do you need from a supplier in terms of customization?

Competitive questions: "How are you meeting these needs?"
- How have you handled your needs for customization and technical support in the past?
- What problems have you encountered in getting the support and flexibility you need?

Projective questions: "How can we better address these needs?"
- If you could improve the technical support and degree of customization you've received in the past, how would you change them?
- What effect would that have on your business?

Armed with information gathered from your needs analysis probing, you're able to advance to the Presentation stage, which is where you tell your story. Naturally, you tell how your technical support and ability to customize can satisfy the buyer's unmet needs. You sell proactively against price by highlighting important buying criteria that eclipse the acquisition price. This mitigates the importance of price by raising other relevant issues. Realistically, you have not eliminated the price issue totally, but if you arrange your questions around a strategic probing objective, you relegate price to its proper perspective, only one of many variables to consider.

SUMMARIZE NEEDS

Once you have thoroughly analyzed the buyer's needs, summarize your understanding of these needs in your own words. Feed back your understanding to the buyer for confirmation. When you summarize buyer needs, several things happen. First, you're demonstrating that you were listening. Second, you're verifying your understanding of the buyer's specific needs. Third, you're building commitment by getting the buyer to agree to the needs you've uncovered.

When summarizing, begin with a simple lead-in phrase and then recap what you've learned about the buyer's needs. When you get agreement to these needs, use it as a springboard to transition to the Presentation stage. For example: "Ms. Buyer, based on our conversation, I understand that you need better lead time, tighter quality control checks, and more flexible shipping hours. Does this cover it? (Yes.) Let's look at some ways that we can help you achieve these objectives."

TIPS FOR QUESTIONING

As you learned in the Opening stage in Chapter 21, begin by asking permission to probe. It's courteous, and the buyer commits to answering your questions. For example: "Would you mind if I asked a few questions to better understand your business?" These additional tips will help you conduct a thorough needs analysis:

- Ask one question at a time.
- Ask open-ended questions 80 percent of the time.
- Ask indirect questions to reduce a perceived threat.

- After you ask a question, pause to allow time for a response.
- Take notes. (You may even want to ask permission to do this.)
- Begin your needs analysis with a questioning objective. Know why you're asking questions. Generally, it's to achieve your small win for the sales call.
- If you sense that the other person has a problem in a specific area, pursue it with a follow-up probe. Dig deeper and drill down on the problem. Encourage the buyer to elaborate on the impact of this problem on his or her business.
- Interview, don't interrogate. You're not there to fill out a questionnaire. Your goal is to get the other person talking about problems. Too many closed-ended questions create this interrogation effect.
- When constructing your Needs-Analysis stage, make sure that you ask questions in each of the three strategic questioning areas: situational, competitive, and projective. Additionally, draw out needs for the three dimensions of value: product features and benefits, supplier value added, and salesperson commitments to serve.

VALUE-ADDED SELLING REVIEW AND ACTION POINTS

1. The Needs-Analysis stage is your fact-finding mission to direct the buyer's attention to his or her total needs, wants, and fears. As you ask more questions and actively listen to the buyer, you develop an in-depth understanding of how you must customize your solution to this person's buying position.

2. Top achievers spend 60 percent of their time listening to the buyer. Active listening is an important part of your needs analysis. You demonstrate your active listening skills as you patiently study and process the buyer's needs, wants, and fears. This enables you to formulate a strategy for meeting these needs.

3. Your questions will be either open-ended or closed-ended. Ask more open-ended questions than closed-ended questions when your objective is to draw the other person deeper into the conversation and encourage him or her to respond freely.

4. When soliciting information about a buyer's needs, probe in three specific areas: use situational questions that give you information on the buyer's expectations; competitive questions that provide information on how the buyer is attempting to meet these needs; and projective questions that spotlight the gap between the stated needs and how the buyer attempts to meet these needs.

5. Targeted probing is another way to highlight your solution over an alternative. Targeted probing spotlights the value of your differentiators. Buyers will compare your strengths to the competition.

6. Complete your Needs-Analysis stage with a summary of the buyer's needs, and get agreement to your understanding of these. This paves the way for the Presentation stage, the topic of the next chapter.

CHAPTER 23

The Presentation Stage

How good a storyteller are you? You know how to open the sales call; you've asked questions and listened patiently during the Needs-Analysis stage; you even summarized your understanding of the buyer's needs, and the buyer agrees to your assessment; now you follow the next natural step on the value-added sales call as you enter the Presentation stage. This is your time to talk during the sales call. You are the face and voice of your solution.

Top-achieving salespeople invest 56 percent of their time in the front half of the sales call opening and probing. They told us in our BSP research that they invest 27 percent of their time in the Presentation stage. Think about this: about one-fourth of their time is spent on the message. This means their message must be sharply focused on the buyer's needs and relevant to the outcome the buyer desires. This chapter is about building and presenting a compelling argument for your solution.

At the end of this chapter, you will be able to:

- Recite the rules of the Presentation stage
- Sell to the buyer's style
- Engage your buyer in your presentation
- Develop strong proof sources to reassure the buyer

RULES OF THE PRESENTATION STAGE

If buying and selling is an information exchange, the Presentation stage is your opportunity to give enough relevant information about your solution so that the buyer is more willing to buy than you are to sell. The ability to persuade is an important skill for value-added salespeople. You must be able to present a compelling reason for the buyer to choose your alternative.

The first rule of the Presentation stage is to customize your conversation to the level of decision maker you're addressing. If you're selling to a Level-I decision maker, discuss logistics and transaction issues: packaging, price, ordering, options, color, sizes, freight schedules, delivery information, lead times, terms, and the like. Remember, the Level-I buyer is a short-term thinker and looks to immediate gratification.

If you're selling to a Level-II decision maker, home in on usage, application, or resale: ease of use, training, technical support, safety, quality, convenience, compliance with specifications, marketing support, and so forth. Level-II's want you to make their jobs easier and safer. Technical types want lots of data. Compliance types want no surprises and tighter specs. Marketing types want something that is easy to sell. Maintenance people want something that is easy to repair and service. Their time focus is on the utility of the product. Remember, these folks are most affected by the changes you're proposing.

If you're selling to a Level-III decision maker, concentrate on results: increased profitability, cost control, efficiency and effectiveness, greater performance, higher productivity, competitive gain, and goals. Their time horizon is long term, and they view success as financial gain.

The second rule of the Presentation stage is to sell what's relevant. If the buyer spent a lot of time in the Needs-Analysis stage discussing quality problems, present your quality as the solution to the problems. If a customer has delivery problems, describe how your delivery will meet these needs. If the buyer tells you that product availability is paramount, emphasize your product availability and inventory policy.

Salespeople have standard ways to present their products and to discuss their company—this is their pitch. Value-added salespeople modify their presentations depending on what they discover in the needs analysis. You can prepare a message in advance based on what you know about the customer, and be prepared to be flexible in the way you present it.

The third rule of the Presentation stage is to determine how long your presentation should be. Settling on the appropriate duration is tricky. It should be long enough to convince but short enough to hold the buyer's interest. The formula is similar to that of a good sermon: it should have a strong beginning and a powerful closing, and the shorter the distance between the two, the better.

The most famous speeches in our history—the Gettysburg Address, Ronald Reagan's *Challenger* Address to the Nation, and FDR's Pearl Harbor Speech—share a common denominator. They were simple, short, and powerful. Reagan's speech was 648 words; FDR's speech was 518 words; and Lincoln's address was a scant 246 words.[1] What they lacked in length, they gained with substance and style. As Cicero wrote, "Brevity is a great charm of eloquence."

Your communication should be long enough to convince and short enough to hold the receiver's interest. The problem with most rhetoric is that it takes too long to make the point and suffers from clutter. Your message must be tight. Fewer words are better. Keep it short. Avoid clutter. Trim. The average attention span of workers is three minutes. The average television ad is between 15 and 20 seconds. The average movie scene is approximately 60 seconds. The average sentence length is 14.3 words, and the ideal length is 8 words or less for 100 percent retention. The average number of characters per word is 5.1 letters. You have precious little time to make your point. Keep it tight.

SELL ALL THREE DIMENSIONS OF VALUE

Don't you wish you had a dollar for every time you've read about the three dimensions of value: your product, your company, and you? This deliberate redundancy serves a purpose: overlearning. We want you to remember this concept.

Sell relevant features and benefits of your product. One problem salespeople have when discussing their products or services is that they use claims, not features and benefits. For example, "We're the biggest and the best!" Says who? You've made a claim. It's your opinion. Claims pump you up. They're fun. They're exciting. They build your enthusiasm and allow you to express your passion. Be prepared, however, to back up your claims.

Unlike claims, features are specific. Features are facts that describe. They include physical aspects: the size, color, weight, and other specifics. They also include operational or functional elements: the number of revolutions per minute, the speed of a computer, a description of how something works, and so on.

A second problem salespeople have when discussing their offerings is that they recite a litany of features without extending these features into benefits. Features answer the question "What is it?" Benefits answer the question "Why is that important?"

Benefits are *why* the buyer chooses your alternative. Collectively, benefits answer the question that all buyers ask, "What's in it for me?"

To determine the benefit of a specific feature, ask yourself, "So what?" "Why is that important?" or "What does that mean to the buyer?" The answers to these questions yield the benefit.

Link your feature-benefit statements with connectors such as "this means," "this assures you that," "why that's important," and "what this gives you." In this way, you make the feature-connector-benefit statement conversational, natural, and relevant.

The second dimension of value is your company and its value added. Explain your company's services. Discuss your company's commitment to the value-added philosophy. Present your qualitative and quantitative value added. Elaborate on the resources available from your company to the customer. Position your company as *the* value-added supplier.

The third dimension of value is you. It's what you personally do for the customer. In Chapter 5, "The Value-Added Selling Process," you learned how your role evolves as the sale progresses. Detail for your customer how you deliver value at every step along this path. Remember, the same product from the same company from two different salespeople represents two different solutions. Your commitment and knowledge are essential benefits to the customer, and you must let customers know how valuable you are to them.

SELL TO YOUR BUYER'S STYLE

Some buyers move quickly and intuitively, while others move slowly and methodically. Some buyers are more concerned with people issues, while others are more task oriented. The buyer's priority and pace make up his or her style. Your mirroring the buyer's priority and pace is called *pacing your buyer.*

Pacing is important throughout the entire sales call. You took your lead from the buyer in the Opening stage and asked questions in the Needs-Analysis stage in a way that made the buyer feel comfortable. In your Presentation stage, you must present your solution at a pace that mirrors the buyer's pace. Your features and benefits should reflect the buyer's priority: is it task or people?

For task-oriented buyers, ask yourself how your product or service enhances or improves any of the following measures:

- Profitability or cash flow
- Task performance
- Market image
- Credibility
- Productivity
- Operational efficiency
- Product quality
- Competitive advantage
- Lead time

Again, for task-oriented buyers, ask yourself how your product or service helps reduce, eliminate, avoid, or alleviate any of the following problem areas:

- Waste
- Rejection rates
- Mistakes/errors
- Inefficiency
- Downtime
- Quality glitches
- Back orders
- Profit piranhas

For people-oriented buyers, ask how your product or service enhances or improves any of the following priority areas:

- Comfort in use
- User-friendliness

- Ordering convenience
- Employee morale
- Safety
- Employee relations
- Employee benefits
- Service
- Training
- Employee satisfaction
- Employee retention

Another question to ask yourself for people-oriented buyers is how your product or service reduces, eliminates, avoids, or alleviates any of the following detractors:

- Risk
- Internal conflicts
- Employee stress
- Employee turnover/absenteeism
- Job-related hazards
- Morale problems
- Organizational silos

Presenting your solution in a way that your customer wants to buy is customer-oriented selling. This is the customer-value focus applied to a sales call.

ENGAGE YOUR BUYER

In the Needs-Analysis stage, your buyer played an active role in the process by being involved in answering your questions. This feedback helped you forge a solution that paralleled his or her needs. In the Presentation stage, you do more talking, which means the buyer will do more listening. Even though effective listening requires the buyer to be active in the process, there is a danger that the buyer will assume a passive role here. Your job is to keep the buyer actively engaged during your presentation.

- Ask involvement questions, those that draw the buyer into the conversation. Seek input on your discussion points. Ask these types of questions to engage the buyer: "Is this what you had in mind?" "Will this meet your needs?" and "Are these the results you had in mind?" You can open the conversation by asking, "How do you see this affecting your operation?"

  The added benefit of these opinion-seeking questions is that they are also trial closes. The responses you receive are an accurate indication of the buyer's interest in moving forward. Several positive comments signal that it's time to ask for a commitment.

- Project buyer ownership by using possessive words and assumptive statements to imply that the buyer has already purchased your product or service. For example, "One of the benefits *you'll* enjoy with *your* new computer is the data transfer speed. It will trim *your* online time by half."

  This projected-ownership statement, laced with possessive words and assumptive statements, puts the buyer in the frame of mind of having already purchased your product or service and begun to enjoy its benefits. Some buyers need this type of help to visualize ownership. They now own it, and once they own it, they won't want to lose it.

- Use *we* often throughout your presentation. Using the pronoun *we* draws the buyer into the presentation because it suggests teamwork and partnership. You and the buyer are working jointly to solve problems. The implication is that you will share the risk for an effective solution, assuaging the buyer's concerns.

- Involve the buyer by having him do something. Some buyers are visual processors. Others, however, are tactile processors; they learn better by hands-on involvement. The power of hands-on product or service demonstrations is that they engage buyers actively in the process; the buyer does something. Being involved makes it easier for the buyer to appreciate the value of your offering. Recent marketing studies have shown that buyers who handle products before purchasing them are willing to pay more because they have already formed an attachment.[2] Get the product in the buyer's hands.

- Give the buyer materials for selling internally. This includes VIP lists, one-sheets, and other collaterals that demonstrate your value. Enlist the buyer in your army of supporters who will help you fight your battle inside the company. The more buyers promote your cause, the more committed they are. Because they know the ins and outs of their company's politics, they weave through that maze more quickly than you can.

USE PROOF SOURCES

Support your case with credible sources. We covered this in Chapter 13, but it bears repeating. You reassure buyers when you demonstrate that others feel positively about your solution and are willing to go on record to prove it. Use testimonial letters and direct quotes. If your company has conducted customer satisfaction surveys, use the survey data to prove your point. Case studies have become popular in recent years. They allow buyers to read in-depth, real-life scenarios about the positive impact you have made on a customer's world.

Social media has become an increasingly more popular way for companies to establish credibility and popularity. This is especially true of younger buyers. They place great value on the opinions of their peers. You read about this in Chapter 7. Refer back to this chapter for ideas on how to use social media in your sales presentation.

Third-party endorsements are impressive. Endorsements speak favorably to buyers because the person giving the endorsement feels your product is a good buy. These include testimonials from trade magazines, Underwriters Laboratories (UL), *Consumer Reports*, and other well-known sources.

Warranties and guarantees offer a special kind of reassurance. Your warranties and guarantees signal to the buyer that you will stand behind your product or service. Remember to stress the positive aspects, not the remedies. Guarantee the buyer's satisfaction: "The benefit of our guarantee is that we work with you until you are *completely satisfied* with our solution." Complete buyer satisfaction is a powerful guarantee and an effective way to prove your worth to the buyer. Buyers want their money's worth, not their money back.

VALUE-ADDED SELLING REVIEW AND ACTION POINTS

1. Buying and selling is an information exchange. In the Needs-Analysis stage, you listened to the buyer's needs; in the Presentation stage, you discuss your solution to these needs. Your presentation should be long enough to convince the buyer, yet short enough to hold his or her interest.

2. Buyers move at different paces and have different priorities. Some buyers advance through the decision process quickly, while others move with caution. Some buyers are focused on task issues, while others concern themselves with people issues. Tailor your sales approach to mirror the buyer's style.

3. Buyers become more passive as sellers begin their presentations. Draw buyers into your Presentation stage with involvement questions and hands-on demonstrations so they are actively engaged in the buying process. Remember, your time is limited by the buyer's attention span. Be tight with your presentation.

4. Use proof to mitigate risk. This includes data, documentation, credible third-party sources, and social media content.

CHAPTER 24

The Commitment Stage (Closing)

You've opened the sales call, conducted a needs analysis, and presented your solution. Now, you're ready for buyer commitment on the next step—the point at which you achieve your action objective. Some people call this step the close. It is the logical next step in a series of events that lead to your securing the business. It generally involves detail work to finalize your arrangements.

Based on our Best Practices study of top-achieving salespeople, top achievers report spending 17 percent of their time at this stage of the sales call. They spend less time here than even in the opening. This tells us that if you invest the first 83 percent of your sales time wisely—probing, listening, and presenting—you will not need to spend as much time getting commitment from the buyer. This chapter is about gaining buyer commitment and closing the sale.

At the end of this chapter, you will be able to:

- Define closing and commitment
- Describe when to ask for the business
- Demonstrate several ways to ask for a commitment

CLOSING DEFINED

Some salespeople believe that gaining buyer commitment is anticlimactic because they anticipated fireworks that didn't go off. It was something less than amazing because there was no magic in it for them. Indeed, that's the way selling should be. There are no good clos-ers, just good salespeople.

If you've failed to do an adequate job of analyzing the buyer's needs and tailoring your presentation to these needs, it's difficult to resurrect interest during the Commitment stage. If you rely heavily on closing techniques to get the business, you offend buyers at the worst possible moment—when you're asking them for money.

We prefer the word *commitment* to *closing*, because closing indicates finality. Commitment indicates a strong relationship and two-way accountability for a course of action. In Value-Added Selling, you don't close sales; you build commitment to a course of action that brings value to the customer and profit to the seller.

Commitment isn't the end point that closing sounds like; it's the starting point for a course of action that solves a problem. Building commitment doesn't start at the end of the sale; it takes place through-out the presentation. As you study needs and propose alternative solutions, you're building commitment. You ask for commitments throughout the sales process. These were your limited sales objec-tives—small wins. The point at which the buyer makes the final decision is where you ask for the business.

WHEN TO ASK FOR THE ORDER

Asking for buyer action is a necessary step in the selling process. Noth-ing happens on your end until the buyer agrees to purchase, to write a check, or to sign a contract. This is what you're paid to do—gain business. Never assume the buyer will come forward and volunteer to purchase without your asking. It may happen occasionally, but don't depend on it. The buyer may be unaware that the sale is approaching the moment of action unless you say so. Ask for buyer commitment because without it, you're unable to provide the solution to the buyer's needs. Only a commitment to act brings the solution that the buyer desires.

Asking for the order is a two-step process. The first step is asking an opinion-seeking question—sometimes called a trial close. You're asking for an opinion about your proposal. If the customer's response is positive, ask for a commitment. It's simple, it's practical, and it works. Remember: seek opinion, then commitment.

Knowing when to ask the opinion question is crucial. Timing is everything in sales. It's just as essential for you to know *when* to ask for the business as it is for you to know *how* to ask. This section highlights some techniques you can use to determine if the buyer's interest level is sufficient to pursue a commitment. You're looking for two types of buying signals: verbal and nonverbal.

Verbal buying signals are comments made by the buyer that indicate a strong interest in owning your product. The message could also be in how the buyer says something: a vocal change in inflection or the sudden display of emotion. Here are some sample phrasings that indicate a strong interest in buying:

- I think it may cost too much. (The buyer is really saying, "Sell me.")
- How soon can you deliver? (The voice connotes a sense of urgency.)
- Who pays the freight charges? (It's a matter of working out the details.)
- Is there a guarantee? ("Reassure me that I'm making a good decision.")
- Is there an installation charge? (You're working out the details.)
- I'd like to buy, but . . . (Whatever follows "but" is what you need to address.)

The buyer may also show interest verbally by repeating strong benefits you've mentioned and by asking more questions—especially questions of a technical nature. When the buyer uses possessive words such as *mine* and *our* to describe your product, he or she is buying. Real estate salespeople listen for prospective buyers to use the word *home* versus *house*. When buyers say *home* they've mentally bought it. Be attentive to such changes in verbal behavior. Listen for subtleties that indicate psychological ownership has taken place. Sometimes, it's the nuances that tell you when the time is right.

Nonverbal buying signals—the other side of the coin—are anything the buyer *does* to indicate a strong interest in your product. Be sensitive to nonverbal cues. Nonverbal indicators include stroking one's chin, leaning forward toward the seller, hand rubbing, handling the product or the literature, smiling, giving a sigh of relief during the presentation, uncrossing of arms, and moving closer to the seller. All of these indicate that the buyer is seriously considering owning the product.

In Value-Added Selling, it's especially important to be sensitive to buying signals when you present nonprice factors. Watch for the prospect's interest level when you discuss freight, delivery, quality, technical support, or other such details. The buyer may *tell* you that he or she is not interested but verify interest through the nonverbal signs. If the nonverbal signals indicate strong desire, go with them.

HOW TO GAIN COMMITMENT

Commitment techniques describe how you ask the question that results in a buyer's agreement to act. Remember that a commitment to move forward doesn't necessarily mean that the buyer agrees to buy. The limited sales objective—small win—may be to get the buyer to agree to a product demonstration and trial. Practice these rules when asking for a commitment.

First, be alert to all of the verbal and nonverbal signals. Listen with your eyes and ears. Be prepared to seek commitment. Next, ask an opinion question to check the buyer's reaction to your ideas. Here are some sample opinion questions:

"What do you think?"

"Is this what you had in mind?"

"Will this do the trick for you?"

"How do you feel about this?"

These so-called trial closes are really the same involvement questions you asked during the Presentation stage. Their answers tell you if it's time to ask for a commitment. Opinion questions (trial closes or involvement questions) precede commitment questions. If you get a positive response to the opinion question, ask for a commitment. The buyer is ready to purchase, so go for it.

If you hear a pause or a hesitation from the buyer in response to your opinion question, pursue the reason. For example:

Salesperson: "How does this look to you?"
Buyer: "On the surface, it's OK."
Salesperson: "You sound hesitant." (Pause for response.)

At this point, the buyer elaborates on the reason for hesitating. Your job is to listen and respond to the resistance.

As you review the following commitment strategies, remember to always begin with an opinion question. Because you receive a positive response to your question, you feel confident asking for a commitment. Demonstrate this confidence in the action you ask the buyer to take.

Assumptive Technique

With this technique, take a matter-of-fact approach: assume the sale has taken place. Your assumption is implicit in the statement you make. You want to capitalize on the momentum you've established. Unless the buyer stops you, proceed because the sale has been made. For example: "If you feel this gives you the quality you need, let's schedule delivery for next Monday." Or, "Since this offers you the shipping flexibility you require, I can have this out here tomorrow afternoon if you'd like."

Each of the statements seems like the natural conclusion to the events that preceded it. Further, each one refers to a benefit. Anytime you can include a benefit with your request for action, you reinforce the reason why the other person should purchase your solution. It reminds the buyer of the advantage of going with you—the benefits he or she receives.

Summary Technique

With this technique, you recap the major benefits you offer and follow this summary with the assumptive technique. Use this strategy to refocus a conversation that has gone astray in the Presentation stage. For example: "Our next-day delivery reduces your lead time, and our product quality gives you the opportunity to be more competitive in your market. Let's schedule your first delivery for next week."

Immediate Advantage Technique

There are two ways to use this technique: the right way and the wrong way. The wrong way is more appropriately called the "doomsday" technique. With the doomsday, you try to intimidate and browbeat the other person into buying. You warn the customer that something bad will happen if he or she doesn't act now. You threaten limited inventory, price increases, or any other potentially negative situation. Because of its effectiveness, sales trainers have taught this strategy for years, and salespeople have abused it.

Consumers are desensitized to this approach and, in many cases, repelled by it. They feel backed into a corner to make a quick decision. For example: "If you don't give me an order right now for these goods, I can't guarantee you'll get them on time, because we have limited stock available."

The right way—the immediate advantage—demonstrates a more positive approach. With this, you explain why it's advantageous for the buyer to press ahead and make a decision to go with you. You're still capitalizing on a sense of urgency, but you're doing it in a more positive way. For example: "The real advantage of your moving on this right now is that, because we currently have inventory, we'll be able to guarantee you the delivery you want when you want it, so that you can stay competitive in your market."

With this technique, you're stressing the advantage of moving ahead now as opposed to the disadvantage of waiting. It's a much more positive approach for your buyer than the wrong way—the doomsday.

Alternate Choice Technique

With this commitment technique, you're asking the buyer to choose one of several options. Some people believe it's easier for buyers to select on a minor point (such as color or size) than to decide whether or not they're ready to buy. If the prospect is ready to buy, he or she will buy regardless of how you ask. Some salespeople have an easier time asking for the business with the alternate choice versus asking directly for a commitment. Here are some ways you can use this technique:

"Which would you prefer, the blue or green unit?"

"Would you want to go with the 90-day or 180-day certificate of deposit?"

"Do we need a written purchase order, or is your verbal commitment enough here?"

Your strategy presents an alternative, an either/or selection. Be sure to present options with which you can live. You don't want to offer a choice of items that would cause you difficulty.

Physical Action Technique

Some sales require the buyer to sign a contract, fill out an application, or complete a formalized purchase order. In these cases, handing the buyer a pen with the contract and asking for a signature is appropriate. Be careful with the wording you select. Try to avoid anything harsh that would turn the buyer off. For example, avoid this type of statement:

"I'll need you to sign your life away here."

"Put your John Hancock here, if you would."

Even though you're presenting both of these statements in good fun, treating the business and commitment lightly may irritate the buyer. Try for something softer:

"I'll need your OK for us to get the wheels turning on our end."

"We'll need your approval right here to begin your service."

Also, point out that it's a mutual commitment, because you've had to attach your signature to the document also, thus creating an atmosphere of teamwork.

Direct Technique

This technique is a straightforward request for action. There's no doubt what you want. You want the buyer to give you a commitment to act, and you make it plain because of your wording. For example:

"I'll need your purchase order number to ship these goods."

"Where would you like the material shipped?"

"Where would you like to go with this from here?"

Stall Technique

When you sense that the buyer is hedging or stalling, dig deeper. Discover the real problem by smoking out any hint of resistance so that you can answer the buyer's concerns. The stall technique gives you a systematic way to persist. When you ask an opinion question and receive a dubious answer, try these questions:

"You still sound hesitant . . ." (Pause and let the buyer respond.)

"What do you feel must happen on your end for you to go with us?"

"Do you see any reason at this point why you wouldn't go with us?"

If/When Technique

Whether you're following up with a customer or just trying to firm up a commitment on your call, this technique works well. Like the other commitment techniques for reluctance situations, this technique helps you identify the likelihood of your doing business with this person. Here's what your words sound like with this technique:

"Ms. Buyer, because we are interested in your business and would like to know where we stand, is it a question of *when* you're going to order, or is it still a question of *if* you're going to order?"

In this way, you can clarify whether or not the buyer has made a commitment. You're asking if the sale is just a question of time, yet you get one step closer to a firm commitment. If the sale is a matter of *when* and not *if*, determine your customer's timetable and find out what must happen from your customer's perspective for this sale to go through. Identify obstacles or potential barriers and try to do something about them. If it's still a question of *if*, dig deeper to identify unresolved questions or doubts.

VALUE-ADDED SELLING REVIEW AND ACTION POINTS

1. Closing is achieving your call objective, whatever that objective happens to be. It is accomplishing your small win. It's securing buyer commitment to the next logical step in the decision process, advancing the sale to its natural conclusion. Nothing happens until you ask.

2. Close when the buyer is ready to buy. He or she will send verbal or nonverbal signals indicating a desire to move forward. Ask two questions: an opinion-seeking question, sometimes called a trial close, and a commitment question, sometimes called a closing question.

THE VALUE-ADDED SELLING FORMAT

These are the four steps you go through on each value-added sales call. You can also use this outline to plan your calls.

Opening Stage
- Introductions (and pleasantries)
- State the purpose of your call
- Ask permission to probe

Needs-Analysis Stage
- Situational questions:
  - General information
  - Specific need
- Competitive questions:
  - How-met
  - How-well
- Projective questions:
  - Ideal
  - Impact
- Summarize needs

Presentation Stage
- Present specific features and benefits for all three dimensions of value
- Sell to the buyer's style
- Ask involvement questions
- Offer proof sources

Commitment Stage
- Opinion questions
- Ask for a commitment to action

CHAPTER 25

Handling Objections

The sale is never over until you or the buyer calls it quits. Top-achieving salespeople in our BSP research said they persist until they hear an average of 5.3 nos from the buyer. This is truly astounding when you consider that 75 percent of salespeople quit on the first rejection and another 5 percent quit on the second rejection. The goal is not to accumulate as many nos as you can. The goal is to gain commitment on a course of action.

Responding to objections does not necessarily mean reacting. Reacting implies a passive energy. Responding, on the other hand, means you wait for the objection to surface and then answer it. This describes time, not assertiveness. Being responsive doesn't mean that you're surprised or bushwhacked; it means that you respond *after* the objection surfaces. In most cases, you anticipated an objection and prepared a response.

This chapter is about prepared spontaneity—being ready for an objection. Readying yourself means projecting yourself into the rejection situation so that you're primed for whatever comes your way. Preparation builds your self-confidence to face the objection and to be persistent without being a pest.

At the end of this chapter, you will be able to:

- Recite several tips for handling objections
- Demonstrate a three-step communications model
- Discuss the root causes of price objections
- Name the three rules for discounting
- Design a powerful response to price objections

TIPS FOR HANDLING OBJECTIONS

Before delving into the mechanics of handling an objection, it's important to understand a few basic concepts that can make your life easier in this resistance situation:

- **Divorce your ego from the sale.** Remember that when the buyer rejects your product, it's not a direct assault on you. The rejection doesn't mean you're a crummy person and the buyer wants nothing to do with you. For one reason or another, this buyer is not sold on your product. Don't get defensive, and don't argue. You can defend without being defensive. We don't know any salesperson who won a sale by winning an argument with the client, though we do know several salespeople who won the argument and lost the sale. Be tactful with your responses. Objections represent tenuous situations.

- **Create an objections file.** One way to be prepared for an objection is to have an objections file that contains potential responses to possible objections. Being prepared builds your self-confidence. Your responses must reflect the uniqueness of the obstacle you face. Update your file regularly by adding new objections and responses. Review previously used responses and change the wording if appropriate. Why depend on your mind to store all this material?

- **Help the buyer save face.** If the objection indicates that the buyer misunderstands what you've presented, give the buyer an opportunity to save face. You may even want to assume partial responsibility for the misunderstanding by saying, "Maybe I didn't explain this fully enough." or "What if we go over a couple of things again? I could have missed something." Exonerate the buyer and give him or her a chance to bow out of a situation gracefully. The buyer will reward your tact.

- **Listen with all of your senses.** Be totally perceptive. Listen for what's being said as well as what's not being said. How does the buyer express objections? What is the buyer's mood? How tentative is his or her concern? Try to fully understand the emotion as well as the facts.

THREE-STEP COMMUNICATIONS MODEL

The dynamics of dealing with an objection are the same regardless of the nature of the objection. While you can use the model presented in this section for any objection you encounter, the major emphasis here is how to quell price objections. The process includes three steps: clarify, buffer, and answer.

Clarify

When you clarify an objection, you want the buyer to expound, elaborate, or discuss the concern more fully so that you can understand the objection and allow the speaker to ventilate emotion. If the buyer elaborates, it gives you time to think of a response, and the buyer may even talk his or her way out of an objection.

Clarifying generally involves one of two strategies. You can either ask an open-ended question about the objection or restate it in your own words, making the objection a question. For example:

> *Objection:* "Your price is much higher than the competition!"
> *Open question:* "When you say we're higher, could you be more specific?" or
> *Restate:* "Is it a question of why our pricing is different than the competition?"

When clarifying a price objection, probe to discover the underlying motivation. Be sure that the buyer is making an apples-to-apples comparison. Is the comparison product exactly the same as yours?

Is the buyer concerned with the total cost of owning your product or just the acquisition cost? The cost to own includes operating costs, the amount of money you can save a buyer, the amount of money you can earn for the buyer, and the life cycle of the product.

Determine if price is the buyer's only consideration in purchasing your product. Check the buyer's expectations. Unrealistic objectives may be driving this price objection.

Another variable is the availability of funds. Your price may not be too high for the value you deliver; it's just too high for the budget this person has available. Your price is fine; the buyer's budget is too low.

Some buyers want a cheaper price in order to be more competitive in the marketplace in which they operate. They may think the only way to compete is by offering their customers a lower price tag. You may be able to offer ideas on how to compete with nonprice value.

A final point of clarification is whether or not the person to whom you're selling actually has the buying authority. Can this person say yes and no? Is this person the decision maker or an influencer? Never accept a no from someone who cannot say yes.

Clarifying is digging deeper. It's probing to unearth any additional concerns. When you clarify, you want your counterpart to discuss objections openly. Clarifying means that you're in the *ask* mode versus the *tell* mode. When most salespeople hear an objection, they go to the *tell* mode and try to overwhelm the customer with prepared rebuttals. This reaction is not as effective as going to the *ask* mode, which gives the customer an opportunity to expound. Then, you respond.

Buffer

The second step in responding to an objection is to buffer it. This means acknowledging the other person's concerns. You're saying to the buyer, "I understand your concerns." Your empathy shifts psychological ownership of the objection. It projects the attitude, "We're in this together." Here are some examples for buffering an objection: "I understand your position," "I hear you," or "Yes, money is one concern."

Notice that I am not saying, "Don't buy, because our price is too high." Instead I'm saying, "Money is one concern, not the whole ball of wax—just one! There are other things to consider."

When you combine the clarifier and buffer, your dialogue flows smoothly. For example:

> *Objection:* "You're charging more than I thought we'd have
>   to pay!"
> *Clarify:* "What did you anticipate paying for this?"
> *Buyer:* "About 75 percent of what you're charging!"
> *Buffer:* "I understand your concern."

Here's an example of how to use the clarifier with the buffer in a nonprice objection:

Objection: "I don't like your delivery schedule!"
Clarify: "What is there about the schedule that you dislike?"
Buyer: "We need 24-hour delivery."
Buffer: "I understand. That is a legitimate concern."

One note of caution: Avoid the yes/but technique. When you use the word *but*, it negates anything preceding it. It's argumentative. Also avoid the words *however* and *although*; they're multisyllabic ways of saying *but*. Review the following *yes/but* buffers and consider how saying "but" negates the empathy.

"I understand your concerns, Ms. Prospect, *but* there is another way to view this!"

"I hear you, *but* look at it my way."

Both are argumentative and telegraph that you're preparing to slam-dunk the buyer. You can always use *and* versus *but*. For example:

"I understand your concerns, Ms. Prospect, *and* there is another way we can approach this."

"I hear you, *and* let's examine another option."

The *yes/and* technique is much softer, and it allows you to assert your position in a nonargumentative manner. Salespeople claim this is a tough habit to break. Don't despair; it's tough, *and* you can do it.

Answer
After you've clarified and buffered, answer the objection in one of four ways:

- **Inform the buyer.** State additional relevant features and benefits regarding your solution in order to either convince your buyer or correct a misunderstanding regarding your product, company, or service. In either case, your task is to provide additional information to establish that your solution is a good match for the buyer's needs.

- **Review the buyer's needs.** Buyers may object because they don't feel that they need what you sell. It makes sense at this juncture to review the buyer's needs and buying criteria. The review-needs strategy works well when the other person hesitates or stalls. When you review needs, ask buyers to reiterate what's important to them. Articulating one's own needs in this way increases the speaker's motivation to change.
- **Use the alternate-advantage overload.** If there's a particular feature that a buyer dislikes, overshadow it with features that he or she desires. Your objective is to demonstrate how the buyer is making a relatively small trade-off to get all of the other desired benefits. You in essence return to the Presentation stage and reiterate your description of these features, benefits, and value-added services to increase the buyer's desire enough to offset price.
- **Reverse the objection.** When you reverse an objection, you make it the reason to buy your product. For example: "Ms. Buyer, the fact that you are hesitating indicates to me that you want to make a good buying decision. If that's the case, that's exactly why I feel you need to go ahead with our product, since we've demonstrated its superiority relative to your needs." At this point, emphasize the specific features and benefits that are an advantage to the buyer.

Each of these four answer strategies requires you to retrace your steps to an earlier stage of the selling process. You'll either go back to the Needs-Analysis stage to generate additional motivation or return to the Presentation stage. If you view your answer strategy as reentry into a previous stage of the sale, the sales call flows smoothly. If you're unable to sell successfully on this call, your answer strategy may represent a follow-up call objective—the reason for your next sales call.

PRICE OBJECTIONS

"Your price is too high!" These are the five most dreaded words for salespeople—the number one problem that haunts them. Price objections are a daily reality in sales. You hear lots of them. You're not the first generation of salespeople to deal with price objections, nor will you be the last. The fundamental reality of price objections is that buyers have a closer eye on what they're giving than on what they're getting. They're thinking more about the money leaving their company than the solution they're receiving from you. They perceive an inequity in what they sacrifice for what they gain.

When you visit a doctor with symptoms of an illness, the terminology that medical professionals use to describe your condition is, "The patient presents with these symptoms." The symptoms are not the disease or the illness; they are indicators of the underlying problem. Likewise, when the buyer objects to price, it could mean a number of things.

"I can buy this cheaper online or from a competitor of yours." This sounds like a price objection. It presents as a price objection, but it's not. It's a lack-of-differentiation objection. The buyer is telling you that he or she does not see a dime's worth of difference between you and the competition.

"That's more than I want to spend." This is a low-expectations objection. The buyer did not plan on spending that amount. This doesn't make your price too high; it makes the buyer's expectations too low.

"I don't have the budget." This sounds like a price objection and presents that way, but it is really a lack-of-budget objection. This doesn't mean your price is too high; it means their budget is too low.

"I don't want to pay more than is necessary." No one does. This is an equity objection.

Before you decide to change your price, make sure you understand the real objection you're dealing with.

We surveyed 500 people to determine the most common reasons why they object to a price. Here's what we discovered. What masquerades as a price objection often has different concerns at its core. The number one reason people object to price is a perceived lack of equity—fairness. They feel they're giving better than they're getting. The second most common reason people object to price is fear. They are afraid of spending too much, or perhaps, they fear the unknown—that they may fail to achieve an equitable exchange for the money they spend. The third most common reason people object to price is limited resources, including budget. The fourth most common reason they object to price is a perceived lack of differentiation among buying alternatives. We determined that if salespeople demonstrated equity and fairness, alleviated buyer fears, pursued qualified leads, and differentiated, they would eliminate two-thirds of the price resistance that they face.

Three Rules of Discounting

Suggesting that you discount may sound odd in a book that teaches you how to sell value added. We know there are times when you will discount. The key to your discounting is that it must be strategic, not accidental.

Discount when it makes sense. If it fits your overall strategic plan and does not confuse the market, discounting could make sense. Discounting is a management and marketing decision, not a salesperson decision. Before you offer customer discounts, check with your management or marketing department to determine if the discount makes sense. When discounting, maintain your credibility by cutting something from your package to justify lowering your price. These guidelines will help you protect your margins.

Never discount a differentiator. This means that when you have a definable and defendable difference between you and the competition, do not discount this difference. Offering your difference at a reduced number discounts its value in the customer's eyes. You are tacitly acknowledging that it is no big deal.

Discount only with a firm commitment to buy. Otherwise, your buyer will shop your price with the competition. If the buyer is reluctant to give you this commitment, you didn't have the order to begin with. Never leave your discounts open-ended. Put a time limit on them so the buyer knows this will not be an ongoing situation. Convey the message that it's a special pricing action for a specific transaction.

Change the package with the price. If you decide to change the price, you must change the package that you deliver for that price. Otherwise, you are telling the buyer that you were not serious about the price to begin with and were only testing the waters.

THE PRICE OBJECTION REVERSAL

Money is always a better conversation to have with customers than price. Price is a product feature like the height, weight, color, packaging option, lead time, and so on. Money is a broader topic. Money is more about the total financial impact you have on the customer's business. If you're talking money, you can sell your value.

How many ways can your solution provide a positive financial impact on the customer? Price affects one thing—the product. Money is every way you affect their business. That is why it is a better conversation to have with customers. You affect money (i.e., their bottom line) with your product, your company, and you.

When customers raise price objections, reframe the conversation as a discussion about money. You can say to the customer, "Mr. Customer, the fact that you have raised money (not price) as your primary concern is a positive thing. It tells me that you will be open to all the ways our company will help you drive money to the bottom line. Is that true?" (Who can say "No" to that question?) Follow with this statement, "Let me share with you all the ways that our solution helps you grow your bottom line." Then, explain how your solution has a positive financial impact on their business.

Price is a top-line issue. It affects the acquisition cost. Money is a bottom-line issue because it affects the total profitability of your customer's business. Money is always a better conversation to have with customers. The following example demonstrates how one of our clients built a response using this concept.

Mr. Buyer, the fact that you have raised money (not price) as your primary concern is a good thing. It tells me two things. First, it means you are taking a long-term view to capture the most value. Second, you will be open to all of the various ways that we can help you drive more money to your bottom line. Is that right? (Pause) Good, that is the most compelling reason why you should give our solution another look. Here is why I say that:

First, the depth and breadth of our large local inventory and our same-day delivery policy will help you liberate your current inventory dollars, which can be reinvested in other areas of your business.

Second, our technical training makes sure that your equipment is installed right the first time, every time. This means no costly call-backs, do-overs, or dissatisfied customers. This savings goes directly to your bottom line.

Third, our forward and backward compatibility means that you only install the replacement components that are needed, saving you time and money.

Fourth, our online tech support multiplies your staff by allowing for quicker installations. In your business, time is money.

Fifth, the reliability of our systems lowers your service costs. That savings translates into profit for your company.

Sixth, our Made-in-America products mean that your dollars go to work for our economy, and that is good for your business and your family.

So, when you study these financial advantages of our solution, doesn't it make sense to choose our solution if your goal is to drive more money to your bottom line?

Notice the sixth reason to buy, Made-in-America. A 2016 study by a Rice University researcher found that buyers do in fact demonstrate regional loyalty when they purchase items, and this was tested on a global audience.[1] What is the price premium for locally made, owned, and operated? It varies, but the differential is enough to warrant your mentioning it in this era of globalization.

Mastering this response requires some preparation and planning on your part. The potential return on your time investment makes it worth the effort. You may find that this is the only response to a price objection that you will ever need.

VALUE-ADDED SELLING REVIEW AND ACTION POINTS

1. Objections represent a break in your forward momentum. The objection could be a legitimate concern or hidden resistance masked by an excuse. Your challenge is to root out the reason behind the objection and resolve it to the buyer's satisfaction.

2. Prepare a list of rebuttals to the more common objections you may encounter. This simple preparation activity will boost your confidence and competence in dealing with sales resistance.

3. You learned a three-step communications model to help you persist when buyers resist: clarify, buffer, and answer.

4. Price objections pose a special challenge for salespeople. Review the answer strategies in this chapter and select three ways to respond to price resistance, making the responses sound like you. The key to handling price objections effectively is to be better prepared to respond than the buyer is to give you an objection.

5. The most powerful response to a price objection is to demonstrate the bottom-line impact of your solution on the buyer's business by listing these impact areas and reversing the objection.

CHAPTER 26

Postcall Activities

Spanish philosopher and poet George Santayana wrote, "Those who cannot remember the past are condemned to repeat it." Pity those who fail to learn from their successes or failures.

You planned and executed a value-added sales call. Now it's time to enter the third and final phase of the tactical side of Value-Added Selling: postcall analysis and follow-up. Our friend, a retired U.S. Air Force officer and pilot, told us that the U.S. Air Force discovered 50 percent of what pilots learned came from postflight debriefings. The rest came from preflight (30 percent) and in-flight learning (20 percent). The U.S. Army has a similar process called the after-action review. Salespeople can benefit from this review as well. You learn a lot by slowing down the process and investing some time in postcall analysis.

This chapter is about all of the activities that value-added salespeople engage in once they have met with prospects and customers.

At the end of this chapter, you will be able to:

- Conduct an in-depth postcall review
- Discuss the rules for effective follow-up

POSTCALL REVIEW

What do you do when you finish your sales call? If you're like most other salespeople, you hop into your car and drive frantically to your next sales call. You may spend that travel time checking voice mails or text messages, checking social media, returning calls, reflecting casually on your sales call, or mentally preparing for the next call. Consider these ideas when reviewing your efforts.

Review your performance in the parking lot before leaving the customer's location. Why? Because at that point, everything is fresh and clear in your mind. Writing your postcall analysis at the end of the day means you may forget something or run all of your calls together. You can become your own sales coach and improve your performance. Ask these questions about your performance before moving on to your next call:

- **Was I focused?** Did I stay on track? Did I wander all over the place with my presentation? Being focused is targeting the buyer's needs with relevant solutions and resisting the temptation to meander by telling the buyer everything you know about your product and company.
- **Was it a good information exchange?** Buying and selling is a dialogue, not a monologue. The buyer gives you information prompted by your questions, and you process that information to feed back a solution. The back-and-forth flow of your conversation produces a nonthreatening climate for the buyer to tell you what's on his or her mind. The buyer can do that only when you're listening. Who did most of the talking on this call? Was there balanced participation?
- **How was the chemistry between the buyer and me?** Did we click? Did we hit it off? Chemistry is one of the most important dynamics in selling. It's how well you interact with your buyer. Do you get along well with the other person? Even though chemistry is one of those intangible forces that operate beneath the surface, you can feel it in your gut and see it in the buyer's nonverbal signals. You know when you're in sync with the buyer.
- **Did I achieve my objectives?** Chapter 20 stressed the importance of setting call objectives, especially limited sales objectives. Achieving these objectives moves the sale along the intended path and provides you with a yardstick to measure your success. This is especially true with your action objectives—what you wanted the buyer to do or say at the end of the call. Again, these are your small wins. Asking if you achieved your call objectives relates directly to the first postcall

analysis question about focus. How can you achieve your objectives without being focused? How focused can you be if you don't achieve your objectives?

Ask yourself the preceding questions to help you understand the effectiveness of your efforts. Being busy is not enough. You must use your sales time productively.

Schedule the next action step for this buyer before you leave his or her office. This practice is a great time saver, and few details slip through the cracks. Write the answer to the following question in your planner or your digital calendar: "Where do I go from here?" or "What's my next step?" If you make the time to record it somewhere, you're likely to remember to do it.

As you review your performance on this sales call, reflect on your successes as well as your failures. More than half of all salespeople perform an autopsy on a dead sale to study their failures. They ask, "What killed the sale?"

More astounding is that few study their successes. Few salespeople ask, "Why did we get the business in spite of our price, delivery, and specifications?" If you don't know what you're doing right when you're doing it right, how will you know what to do right when you're doing it wrong?

Have you heard salespeople and their managers say, "The best time to make a sale is right after you make one"? They generally use passion, enthusiasm, or some other emotional energy as the reason. Enthusiasm is contagious, and passion sells, but success cuts deeper than that.

Everyone has a unique success profile and style that works just for him or her. Some salespeople are successful because they came from the service department and understand their business inside out. Some salespeople are successful because of their charisma; customers love them. Some salespeople are successful because of their strategic thinking and planning abilities; they are master strategists. Other salespeople possess incredible product knowledge; customers are drawn to do business with them.

Why are you successful when you're successful? Why do you make sales in spite of the obstacles you encounter? Study your successes.

Learn from them. Feel the excitement, and leverage this passion and knowledge into greater successes. Nothing breeds success like success.

REILLY'S RULES FOR FOLLOW–UP

In 1981, Tom commissioned a study to identify what salespeople did that frustrated buyers. Number one on that list was a lack of follow-up. Today, our latest buyer survey found that poor follow-up by salespeople is still the buyer's greatest frustration.

A basic principle of Value-Added Selling is follow-up, follow-up, and follow-up. Buyers rate follow-up as one of the most important things a salesperson can do, yet it is one of the areas in which salespeople remain weak. This inverse relationship presents you with a golden opportunity. Follow up consistently, and you'll be ahead of the pack. Our BSP top-achievers and their sales managers revealed that delivering on their promises and following up was the number one way these salespeople earned the trust of their customers. These guidelines will help you improve at follow-up:

- **Whatever time frame the buyer tells you, cut it in half.** How often have you discovered that buyers often exaggerate how long it takes to make a good decision? The times that you waited the full duration, you probably discovered that they had already taken action with someone else. If they say, "Call back in four weeks," call back in two weeks.
- **Always seek permission to follow up.** Asking permission has several benefits. First, the buyer knows you will call again and feels obligated to treat you fairly. At the same time, it demonstrates your willingness to serve even without any current business. In addition, when the buyer gives you permission to follow up, you feel less intrusive. You're not a pest. You've been told, "Sure, call me back if you like."
- **Call back for a different reason.** Tell the buyer you want to follow up for another reason. For example, you want to follow up to see if he or she has any questions or to check if things change.

- **Call back when it's convenient for the other person.** Find out the best time to call, and you'll feel even less intrusive. Combine this rule with the previous two to ask one follow-up question: "Mr. Buyer, because I am interested in your business, I'd like to follow up to see if you have any questions before making the final decision. When is it most convenient for me to call—early morning or late afternoon?" When the buyer answers, you have permission to follow up and the best time to do it. You're not a pest; you're delivering a value-added service.

  If you sense that the buyer is becoming uneasy with your persistence, explain that the reason you are persistent is that you are interested in his or her business and want an opportunity to prove it, even when you haven't received any business yet. Tell the buyer your persistence is actually a benefit, and that if a problem surfaces after the sale, you'll be equally persistent in finding a solution.

- **Establish how many unsuccessful callbacks you'll accept before calling it quits.** Don't be a prisoner of hope. Effective salespeople know when to hold 'em and when to fold 'em. At some point, you must change your strategy for dealing with a buyer who continues to string you along. Leverage your sales time effectively.

- **Be innovative with your follow-up ideas.** Send news articles of interest (about your company or the customer's company); send premium incentives or giveaway advertising items with your name on them; or do something thoughtful for your buyer's office or staff. For example: send flowers, bring doughnuts, or have a lunch catered.

VALUE-ADDED SELLING REVIEW AND ACTION POINTS

1. Postcall review is an integral part of the tactical side of Value-Added Selling. In postcall review, you reflect on your performance and learn from it. Ask yourself the coaching questions listed in this chapter. You also use this time to schedule your next action step to ensure nothing slips through the cracks.

2. Buyers rate follow-up as a top priority, but salespeople woefully underperform in this area. In fact, a lack of salesperson follow-through on promises is a top complaint by buyers. Seek buyer permission to follow up, and deliver on your promises. If you deliver on your promises and follow up appropriately, you will earn the buyer's trust.

PART IV

SPECIAL TOPICS

To help you understand the flow of Value-Added Selling, Part I introduced you to the core value-added philosophy and presented you with supporting data to capture your buy-in. Part II described, in strategic terms, the Value-Added Selling Process and detailed the 11 strategies that value-added salespeople use. Part III explained the tactical side of Value-Added Selling—the how-to application of the strategies. Here, you learned how to plan, execute, and evaluate your efforts. Part IV is real value added. The chapters in this final part deliver tangible value added for your sales efforts.

Chapter 27, "Managing Multiple Decision Makers," explains how to compete in a group decision-making environment. More and more decision makers are getting involved in the process. This new dynamic presents a challenge for some salespeople and opportunities for others.

Chapter 28, "Competing in an Amazon World," focuses on the challenges facing salespeople with online retailers, like Amazon. In this chapter we explore why Amazon is such a formidable competitor. We also provide salespeople and organizations with ideas to compete with Amazon.

Chapter 29, "Value-Added Inside Sales," highlights the changing structure of sales. Organizations are hiring more inside salespeople than outside salespeople. In this chapter, we highlight key development areas for value-added inside salespeople.

CHAPTER 27

Managing Multiple Decision Makers

Our internal research found that the average B2B buying decision includes 5.8 people. If selling one person on your value-added solution is challenging enough, 5.8 people complicate the process. This means 5.8 problems to solve, 5.8 separate purchasing biases, 5.8 individual expectations to exceed, and 5.8 individual definitions of value. No wonder group decision making is one of the greatest challenges salespeople face.

Salespeople sell across multiple departments, at different levels, and in multiple locations. Influencing a group of decision makers is challenging but doable. The complexity of group decision making is so discouraging that some salespeople give up before they start.

Like buyers, salespeople have an immediacy bias. Salespeople also want what they want, and they want it now. What they want is an order. Given this, the time lapse of group decision making frustrates salespeople. A CEB study revealed that group decisions take twice as long as expected and are twice as difficult to make as individual decisions are.[1] If B2B decision makers view the process as long and complex, salespeople must feel the same impatience and frustration.

Even though group decisions take longer and are more difficult, decision makers prefer a group for several reasons. Group decisions are safer and insulate against individual risk. Groups prefer consensus, safety, and the status quo. In a group setting, you're competing against other suppliers while dealing with the group's dynamics. Although this presents a greater challenge for some, it can also create a great opportunity for salespeople who understand group selling. A long, complex sale has the potential for roadblocks and distractions. Some may view these roadblocks as failure and prematurely give up on the sale.

Salespeople who are unfamiliar with group dynamics rely on familiar selling methods. They sell to each person the same way. Selling the same way to everyone is seller-focused thinking. Value-Added Selling is a customer-focused approach. This means customizing your approach to each decision maker and influencer.

In this chapter, we address the dynamics of group decision making and how to adjust your selling strategy for group decisions. At the end of this chapter, you will be able to:

- Describe how group dynamics impact decision making
- List three strategies to overcome group biases
- Name three ways to generate momentum in a group setting
- Discuss how to customize a group presentation
- Detail how to gain consensus

DYNAMICS OF GROUP DECISION MAKING

Have you ever noticed that people act a certain way one-on-one, but they're different around a group? In a group setting, people act and think differently. A group setting influences decision making. There are several group biases and dynamics that impact a buying decision. In this section, we'll analyze these dynamics and how they impact decision making.

Groupthink

Irving L. Janis, a research psychologist at Yale and University of California, Berkeley, spent much of his career studying groups and how they make decisions. Janis's curiosity led to his most notable discovery. He wanted to determine why a group that makes one good decision could go on to make an obvious bad decision. He discovered that people prefer consensus and team cohesion. People in a group often conform to the group's decision, even if they know the group is wrong. He also discovered that people in a group setting are reluctant to share opposing ideas or views. An individual's desire to conform trumps his or her desire to be right. People prefer conformity. Janis wrote about this phenomenon in his book titled *Groupthink*.

Decision-making groups want conformity. Their need to conform can trump logic and self-interest. For example, an internal champion may buy in to your value-added solution, but if he is outnumbered, he'll conform to the group's decision. A strong-willed, persuasive leader can use the group's desire for cohesiveness to drive home his preference.

Social psychologist Solomon Asch is known for his research on conformity in a group setting. Asch conducted a famous conformity experiment in which participants had to match a set of lines based on length.[2]

In his experiment, the first set of participants were asked which line matched the line on the left (See Figure 27.1). Individually, the participants selected the correct answer, C, nearly 100 percent of the time.

FIGURE 27.1 **Asch Experiment**

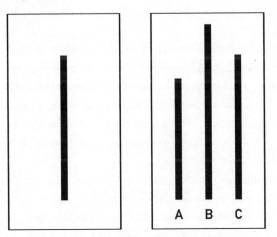

In a group setting, Asch used seven accomplices and one real participant. Asch instructed the accomplices to provide the same wrong answer. Each accomplice responded with the same wrong answer, and the unknowing, real participant gave her response. Seventy-five percent of the time, the real participants agreed with the accomplices and gave the wrong answer. The real participants' need for conformity was stronger than her need to be right. How often do your buyers choose conformity over the right solution?

To combat groupthink, first identify all the key decision makers and their preferences. Before the decision goes to committee, identify who is for and who is against your solution. Engage each decision maker individually and gauge their commitment. Address any individual concerns before the group decides.

Group Polarization

Group polarization hardens an individual's attitude or belief. It explains why moderate individuals become extreme when surrounded by people of the same beliefs or attitudes. Political groups are a good example of this. These groups listen selectively to what is said within their group. They anchor to opinions that are congruent with their beliefs. When a group of conservatives discuss politics, their individual attitudes and beliefs become more conservative. When a group of liberals discuss politics, their individual attitudes and beliefs become more liberal.

Group polarization intensifies an individual's attitude and affects the decision. For example, several decision makers have a moderate concern about your company's ability to deliver. Initially, one person expresses his concern, then another, and another. Initially, the group is moderately concerned, but group polarization intensifies that belief. The group is now extremely concerned about your ability to deliver. Their beliefs feed on each other.

This dynamic also works in the reverse and can represent an opportunity. If the group is moderately optimistic that your solution will fix their problem and one decision maker expresses her optimism, then another, and another, the group's optimism intensifies.

Loss Aversion

Groups are more concerned about avoiding the wrong decision than making the right decision. You read about loss aversion in Chapter 6. To review, losses loom greater than gains. Pain is a more powerful motivator than gain. People hate losing more than they like winning.

Loss aversion impacts all decision making, not just group decision making.

Since attitudes and beliefs can intensify in a group setting—group polarization—that means loss aversion can also intensify in a group setting. For example, a group of decision makers is choosing between three suppliers. One option is to stay with the incumbent supplier. The group doesn't want to lose what they have with their current supplier. One decision maker expresses her concern, then another, and another. Even if the other options are marginally better, it may not be enough to overpower the group's loss aversion. The group's aversion to loss is more compelling than the potential gain of a marginally better supplier.

So, how much potential gain is needed to balance a potential loss? Daniel Kahneman, in *Thinking Fast and Slow*, mentions a "loss-aversion ratio." Most people need the option to gain 1.5 to 2.5 times as much as they would lose. The gain must be approximately twice as much as the loss.

For example, if you have an opportunity to win money or lose money, the gain must be 1.5 to 2.5 times greater than the potential loss for you to take the chance. If you have the chance of losing $10, most people need an opportunity to gain $15 to $25 to take the risk.

According to this theory, if you are trying to dislodge an incumbent, this means your gain must be at least 50 percent greater than the value of the incumbent supplier. It follows that if you are the incumbent, your competition must offer a solution that contributes at least 50 percent more value than your solution. All of this hinges on the dynamics of a specific group. The real takeaway from this point is that if you attempt to create 50 percent more value than the field of competitors, it strengthens your position.

Loss aversion fuels other cognitive biases such as the endowment effect and the status quo bias. You read about these in Chapter 6. The endowment effect is the tendency to place more value on things already owned. This applies to ideas, too. People place higher value on their own ideas. Consider the implications of the endowment effect on group decision making. Since a group of decision makers places higher value on their own previous ideas, they naturally defend their previous buying decisions.

Understanding the group's decision-making history is critical to assess the endowment effect. Use these questions to guide your effort:

- Who owns this previous decision?
- How instrumental was this group in designing the current solution?
- Did this group select the current provider, or did they inherit this provider?
- Did this group establish the buying criteria, or were the criteria established for them?
- What would this group do differently this time around?

These questions help you understand the intensity of the endowment effect. If the group designed, selected, and implemented the previous solution, they place a higher value on that solution. A group will not give up a highly valued solution they created, unless you can help the group come up with a better idea.

GROUP DECISION-MAKING STRATEGIES

Incumbent suppliers have a significant advantage. Their strategy is more defensive than offensive. Being an incumbent supplier is similar to a winning competitor having a lead at the end of a game. Winning teams manage the game differently. They still try to score, but their primary objective is to protect what they have. They assume a more defensive position. For example, in soccer, many coaches will reposition an offensive striker to play as a defensive fullback. Football teams focus on low-risk running plays to exhaust the clock. They protect the lead.

New entrants to a market or account—a new supplier—need a different strategy. The approach is more aggressive and offensive. The entrant is battling the status quo as much as a competing supplier. It is like trailing at the end of the game. When losing, the losing competitor must be more aggressive and take more risk. For example, hockey teams pull their goalies, and football teams throw Hail Mary passes. They are in attack mode.

Your position determines your strategy. In this section, we explore the different techniques based on your position.

Defensive Selling—The Incumbent Advantage

"It was amazing I won . . . I was running against
peace, prosperity, and incumbency."
—George W. Bush

George W. Bush was caught on tape explaining to the Swedish prime minister how he won his first presidential election, one of the closest elections in U.S. history. Al Gore was a tough opponent. What made him so formidable was incumbency—Gore had already been in the White House for eight years. Politicians understand the power of incumbency. That's why George W. Bush was so amazed by his victory. He knew that people like to stick with what they know.

In politics, voters are more likely to stick with the devil they know versus the devil they don't. In 2014, Congress had one of the lowest approval ratings in history, roughly 11 percent. Despite this, roughly 96 percent of Congress was reelected. People like to stick with what they know.

As the incumbent supplier, you are in a powerful position. Due to loss aversion, the group doesn't want to give up what they have. Before you consider discounting or matching a new supplier's aggressive offers, remember loss aversion. The group's desire for a cheaper price is trumped by their aversion to loss. Here are some tips to help you manage the process as an incumbent.

Value Reinforcement

Decision makers view giving up your value added as a loss. Therefore, remind the buyer of all the value added you deliver. Detail the impact your value added has on their business. Buyers can only fear losing what they are made aware of.

A competitor's cheaper price is not as compelling as your value added. You offer experiential value added. Your value added is known, they have experienced it, and they own it. It is a known outcome that they receive. The competitor's solution is unknown. People stick with what they know versus what they don't unless there is an overwhelmingly compelling reason to change.

There are roughly six people who need to be aware of your value added. Each decision maker must be aware of your value added. Reinforce the value added relevant to each type of decision maker. When reinforcing your value, review the level-specific value added that had the most impact for each person. For example, if a Level-II engineer is part of the process, reinforce the value added that is important to her group such as engineering support, compliance to specification, or design ease. Reinforce your high-level value added for a Level-III business owner by emphasizing profit impact and efficiency. When you are reviewing value added for a Level-I procurement manager, reinforce deliverability, invoicing, and consistency.

Identifying, dollarizing, and presenting your value added should happen before the group starts its decision-making process. If you are bidding on business every year, document and dollarize your value added throughout the year.

Value reinforcement reduces the group's cognitive dissonance. Cognitive dissonance appears when there are conflicting attitudes, behaviors, or beliefs. These conflicting attitudes increase the likelihood of regret. Cognitive dissonance is commonly referred to as buyer's remorse. Your challenge is to reinforce the group's decision to buy and own. You are promoting consonance and avoiding the remorse that comes from dissonance.

The risk of buyer's remorse increases when the decision is critical and there are several attractive options. You want the group of decision makers to feel great about the decision they made. Provide the group with verbal reinforcement. Tell them, "Your team made the right decision to partner with our organization. Here's why I say that . . ." Give the group the tools they need to justify the decision to other members of the organization.

Every employee can help reinforce the group's decision, not just salespeople. When your service department is maintaining your equipment, have them reassure the end users about the decision. When your technical department is providing support, compliment the customer on his decision. From the very first purchase, reinforce the group's buying decision. If the group already made a great decision, why would they overturn it this time?

Negotiating as the Incumbent

A group of decision makers can make salespeople feel like they have to sell their solution more than the decision makers need to buy it. Buyers do this to gain a negotiating edge. Whoever feels the most pressure makes the most concessions. This is a fundamental negotiating principle. That's why skilled decision makers attempt to conceal any pressure they feel.

Negotiating as the incumbent favors the seller, not the buyer. The group is less willing to give up what they already have. This is why loss aversion is a critical dynamic of group decision making. When you are the incumbent provider, price is less of an issue.

Researchers conducted an experiment for a major electric utility.[3] They asked consumers about their preferences for reliability or lower energy costs. They offered greater reliability for a 30 percent premium or a less reliable alternative for a 30 percent cost reduction. The current system's reliability was the status quo. In both cases, the majority of consumers chose the existing power solution regardless of price or reliability because it was the status quo. That is the power of incumbency.

Remind customers that you are the incumbent, and make them aware of their other pressure points. Remember that losses loom greater than gains. Frame the conversation in loss terms. The buyer's aversion toward loss is more compelling than a cheap price. If you are creating value as the incumbent, you don't need to be the cheapest.

Offensive Selling Strategy

Whether you are the incumbent or new entrant, you'll need some offensive strategies to win the business. In this section, we dive deeper into offensive selling techniques and how they apply to group decision making.

Group Consensus

Too many salespeople focus on just closing the sale. They believe a signed contract is the only measure of success. Although securing the business is a goal, it's not the most immediate goal. The immediate goal is consensus, not contract.

Our internal research on group decision making shows that 48 percent of decision makers said gaining agreement and consensus among themselves was their greatest frustration. Although gaining consensus is the decision maker's greatest frustration, it is the salesperson's greatest opportunity.

Your immediate goal—small win—is to gain consensus early in the process. Help the group discover their needs and agree on those needs. Once the group agrees, discuss possible solutions and options to satisfy their needs and solve the problems. Gain consensus on how to solve a problem or satisfy the need.

For example, a group is considering a new piece of capital equipment. Your initial goal is to help the group understand their needs and confirm agreement. You could ask the group questions to draw this information out: "What is the pressing need for this new equipment?" "What's important to your team when making this decision?" "As a group, what outcomes are important to you?" "As a team, how will you define success on this project?" Frame each question from the group perspective, not the individual.

Consensus early in the decision-making process makes it easier to gain consensus later in the process. Cohesive teams are more likely to conform. Early consensus in the process paves the way for team cohesiveness during decision making.

People with common goals work together. Throughout the end-to-end experience, common goals unite groups and generate momentum. Early in the process, establish common goals and timelines. Timelines keep the process moving forward. Parkinson's law states, "Work expands so as to fill the time available for its completion." When a group is given more time to complete a task, they take more time. If the group is struggling to agree, suggest shorter timelines to motivate the group.

If individual decision makers prefer your solution and the group is unaware of their consensus, their individual preferences matter less. Individual decision makers need to be made aware of their collective agreement. Buyers are more likely to promote your solution if they are aware of everyone's buy-in. To gain collective buy-in, make the group aware of individual buy-in.

One of Paul's college roommates was the master of group consensus. He knew that individuals needed to be aware of their shared intentions. One specific example illustrates this point. On a Wednesday evening, Sean started recruiting a group to go out. He went to one room and asked, "Does anyone want to go out?" Most responded with moderate interest. He went to the next room and asked the same question and got a similar response. He repeated the process, going room by room. At each room, he got the same response, moderate interest. Although there was moderate interest, Sean knew that wasn't enough. He then went back to each room and made each person aware of everyone else's interest. Once everyone was made aware of the others' buy-in, everyone formally committed. Everyone had a great night. Sean made everyone aware of the shared interest, and that was all the social proof needed to get the party started.

In group decision making, it's not enough for each individual to buy in to your solution; other decision makers have to be aware of the buy-in. One CEB survey showed that willingness to advocate for a purchase more than doubled as perceived organizational support for a supplier increased. Knowing that other people support an individual's decision provides social proof.

Another benefit of sharing this information is that groups operate in fear of making the wrong decision. Making the wrong decision is a form of loss aversion—loss of money, personal status, or market standing. Making individuals aware of everyone else's buy-in can alleviate some of that fear. It reassures members that the group is moving in the right direction.

Group consensus can only happen if decision makers feel like part of the team. If individual decision makers have the right attitude and want the best team outcome, then you are on the right track. However, organizational silos can divide a group of decision makers. It's harder to generate consensus in a divided, siloed group of decision makers. You read about silos in Part I, Chapter 4. Silos separate groups of people.

Every company deals with organizational silos. As the salesperson, you're trying to connect with the group of decision makers, some of whom operate in silos. The way to sell across organizational silos is to first break down the silos.

You can only break down silos that you know exist. Early in the process, it's critical to identify what silos are present. Once you identify the organizational silos, develop a plan to break them down. A simple and easy way to break down silos is to get people talking to one another. Facilitate interaction between departments. Arrange joint meetings and conference calls. Encourage open communication and discussion in these meetings. Help each department understand how this decision impacts other departments. Once the group communicates, begin establishing common goals they can work toward.

When you break down silos, you are adding value to the customer's business. Uniting a siloed group positions you as a value-added partner. A collaborative group is a productive group. High-level decision makers view your silo-busting activity as value added that differentiates your solution.

Consensus is key throughout the buyer's decision-making process. Help the group agree on their needs and how to satisfy their needs. It's not enough to have individual buy-in; make the group aware of their shared buy-in. A siloed group struggles to gain consensus. A house divided will not stand. Break down organizational silos through communication and common goals.

Building a Web of Relationships

A LinkedIn study revealed that 65 percent of customer relationships rely solely on one person, and only 9 percent of relationships are multilayered.[4] You can't build group consensus with six people if you're only engaging with one of them.

Salespeople need to focus on building a web of relationships. A web has multiple connection points. Salespeople need multiple contacts to generate support and consensus. The web should also be connected on both sides. The salesperson is the initial contact, but the next step is facilitating symbiotic relationships between your organization and the customer. Connect your engineers with your customer's engineers. Connect your inside sales team to the company's procurement department. Connect your high-level decision makers to its high-level decision makers. This web of relationships strengthens and protects the bond between your organization and the customer.

Building a web of relationships means going beyond procurement. If you are just meeting with procurement, you are selling to the department least likely to buy your value-added solution. Unfortunately, salespeople spend most of their time selling to Level-I buyers. In a recent study, we asked salespeople, "What type of decision maker do you spend most of your time with?" Salespeople indicated that most of their time was spent with procurement managers or professional buyers. Although procurement's primary function is buying product, different decision makers are getting involved. Each decision maker is another strand in the web.

Level-I buyers are more accessible. Their contact information is available to salespeople. They may even initiate contact with you. Procurement dedicates time to meet with salespeople. When it comes to initiating contact with an opportunity, procurement represents the path of least resistance. That's why salespeople start with procurement and spend most of their time with procurement.

There's a downside to initiating contact with Level-I buyers. Procurement departments intentionally block salespeople from other departments. In our seminars, this is a common frustration. Procurement will directly tell salespeople, "Don't call on operations; don't call on engineering; you only need to interact with me." You are now stuck selling your value-added solution to the department least likely to buy your value-added solution. To get beyond procurement, start with a different department.

Here are some ideas to help you initiate contact with other decision makers:

- **Make joint calls with your teammates.** If you're trying to meet with an operations manager, ask *your* operations manager to join you. If you're meeting with the customer's technical team, ask *your* technical people to initiate the request.
- **Initiate contact with sources of influence.** If you are selling an automation solution that increases operational efficiency, then initiate contact with the operations team. It might take longer, but it prevents you from getting stuck in procurement.
- **Ask for a referral from another decision maker.** A referral increases the likelihood of scheduling an appointment, and it builds instant credibility.
- **Offer value-added training.** Training is a nonthreatening way to initiate contact with a group of influencers. Training is a

great way to bring different departments together and break down silos.

- **Request field visits.** One of the best ways to understand your customer and meet multiple decision makers is getting into the field. Level-II decision makers will give you the unfiltered version of their needs. Seeing the problems they experience in the field will help you develop a better solution for their team.
- **Participate in trade shows.** Trade shows are great opportunities to initiate contact with high-level decision makers and influencers. People attend trade shows expecting to network and meet new people.

Understanding the Group's Organizational Needs and Personal Wants

Imagine sitting in a meeting with a group of your peers. The person who called the meeting is only conversing with one person. He doesn't ask you any questions, and you feel neglected. You feel as though it's a waste of time and there is no reason for you to be there. How often do decision makers feel this way?

Conducting a group needs analysis is more in-depth than when you're dealing with one decision maker. In a group setting, you help the group uncover their common needs. However, you need to understand the group's needs, wants, and fears. In a group setting, individuals are less likely to focus on their personal needs and wants. They don't want to appear selfish or self-serving. Therefore, you must assess the needs of the group in a group setting, and personal needs and wants individually.

During the Needs-Analysis stage, consensus is important. To generate consensus, individual decision makers need to understand how this decision impacts other departments. To invoke empathy among the group, have individuals describe the needs of the other department. For example, have the procurement buyer answer the question, "What does the operations team expect from this solution?" Have the vice president of finance answer the question, "What outcomes are important to your engineering team?" By answering these questions, the team gains an in-depth understanding of the different departmental needs. This exercise connects the individuals to each other.

Remember, individuals will veil their true intent so they don't appear self-serving or selfish. Answer these questions to help you understand the group's needs. If you're unsure about the group's needs, then probe deeper:

- How much pressure is this group experiencing to make the best decision?
- Have there been any highly visible failures caused by the current provider?
- What represents a win for this decision-making group?
- What is the team trying to avoid?
- What are the common goals the group is trying to achieve?
- Who is the most persuasive and dominant voice in the group, and how are you positioned with this individual?
- How will this group be evaluated on their decision?
- What represents a personal win for each decision maker?
- Are there any conflicting personal wins among this group?

Presenting to a Group of Decision Makers

Nobody wants a canned presentation. Buyers prefer a solution hand-crafted to satisfy their unique needs. Since today's buying groups include 5.8 decision makers, you can't just present one solution, you must present 5.8 solutions—one for each decision maker and influencer. Yes, there will be overlap. Your solution doesn't change, but how you satisfy the individual needs of each decision maker does change. Personalize for each decision maker.

Prepare a summary statement showing how your solution satisfies the group's agreed-upon needs. Then, present the level-specific needs for each decision maker. In your presentation, clearly present how your solution meets individual needs. For Level-III's, stress profitability. For Level-II's, stress ease of use. For Level-I's, stress logistical support.

Stress group benefits more than individual benefits. Individual decision makers are more likely to accept their individual benefits if the group benefits as well. If one decision maker personally gains but the others do not, that one is viewed as selfish or self-serving, not a team player. Stressing the personal gains of one decision maker creates tension among the group. You can have those conversations in private.

In your presentation, reassure the group that you will deliver on your promises. In our recent Buying Study, we asked decision makers, "What's your greatest fear in switching suppliers?" The number one response was the ability to deliver on promises. To alleviate this concern, you must provide proof. If you're the incumbent supplier, your end-to-end experience is proof positive. For the new entrant, your proof has to be more compelling than the value delivered by the incumbent.

In a group setting, attitudes and beliefs can be intensified. If several individuals express concern about your ability to deliver on promises, this belief is intensified. For that reason, it's critical to provide proof to support your claims. Here are some additional proof ideas for your presentation:

- **Arrange a visit with a current customer.** A customer who has a positive experience is unbiased proof that you can deliver on your promises.
- **Provide case studies that demonstrate success.** Document success stories that emphasize your ability to deliver on promises.
- **Use third-party, independent endorsements.** Independent tests and agencies provide unbiased support. Third-party endorsements substantiate your claims.
- **Include level-adjacent testimonials.** Different decision makers have different concerns. If an operations manager requests a testimonial, get a testimonial from another operations manager. A level-adjacent testimonial is more compelling.

VALUE-ADDED SELLING REVIEW AND ACTION ITEMS

1. Group decision making is complex. Each decision maker adds another dynamic. To sell to a group of decision makers, you must understand the group's dynamics—the need for conformity, groupthink, group polarization, and loss aversion. These dynamics influence the group's decision.

2. If you are the incumbent, play defense. If you are a new entrant, play more offense. Incumbency is a powerful position. The group will feel pressure to maintain the status quo. As the incumbent, you reinforce your value added and the buyer's decision to partner with you.

3. Whether you are the incumbent or the new entrant, you must generate consensus among the group. Unite the group by uncovering their common needs and gain consensus on how to satisfy the group's needs. Make the group aware of their joint buy-in. Building a web of relationships will further bond the customer to your organization. Facilitate symbiotic relationships between your team and the customer's team. Building up relationships means breaking down silos.

4. Understand the group's and individuals' needs. Discuss group needs as a group, but individual needs privately. Individual decision makers are hesitant to share their personal needs and wants in a group setting. Once you identify group and individual needs, present your custom solution to satisfy those needs. Tailor your presentation to focus on group and individual need satisfaction.

CHAPTER 28

Competing in an Amazon World

Goliath stood nearly 10 feet tall. His armor weighed nearly 125 pounds. The tip of his spear alone weighed 15 pounds. The sheer size of Goliath was enough to deter any opponent. Goliath taunted the Israelites for days, shouting, "Send me your best warrior!" After several days, a brave shepherd emerged to fight Goliath. His name was David.[1]

King Saul, ruler of the Israelites, was surprised at David's willingness to fight Goliath. King Saul also had his doubts. Goliath was a giant, and David was an average-sized man. Goliath was a seasoned, battle-tested warrior. David was a simple shepherd. David reassured Saul that protecting his flock from bears and lions prepared him for this battle. Although Saul was doubtful, he allowed David to fight. Saul even gave David his armor and sword.

David put on the armor, took a few steps, and removed the armor and dropped the sword. "I can't fight in these," he protested to Saul. "I'm not used to them." Then David grabbed his sling and found five smooth stones. Rather than battling the world's greatest warrior with the unfamiliar sword and shield, David approached Goliath with his familiar sling.

From a distance David engaged Goliath. David reached into his shepherd's bag for a stone. He then armed his sling and launched a stone at Goliath. The stone hit Goliath in the forehead rendering him unconscious. While Goliath lay there motionless, David unsheathed Goliath's sword and used it to cut off his head.

This biblical story has served as a business metaphor for decades. Any time there is a larger-than-life competitor and insurmountable odds, we call it a David-and-Goliath-type battle.

In today's sales environment Goliath is armed with one-click ordering, cheap prices, and free two-day shipping. This behemoth is called Amazon, and its astronomical size has many organizations, especially wholesale distributors, feeling as though they are battling Goliath when they are competing against it.

The biblical account of David's victory over Goliath provides several parallels for organizations battling Amazon. Too many organizations try to "out-Amazon" Amazon. David did not try to "out-Goliath" Goliath. David didn't fight Goliath with armor and a sword. He knew that he couldn't defeat Goliath by trying to beat Goliath at his own game. Instead he fought Goliath by leveraging his own tactical strengths. Prior to fighting Goliath, David battled lions and bears as a shepherd. He learned to thwart lurking predators from his flock with a sling—the same skill that rendered Goliath motionless. Businesses constantly face Goliath-type battles. Every battle you face strengthens a new set of skills for the next battle.

David didn't rush in to fight Goliath face-to-face. He knew that rushing Goliath head-on at a close proximity only favored his opponent. Instead he protected himself from Goliath's sword by keeping his distance. From a distance, David was able to fight before Goliath knew the fight had started. David proactively initiated and finished the battle instead of waiting for the battle to come to him. In your business, how can you proactively sling rocks instead of swinging swords?

In this chapter, we explore the Goliath-type battles facing today's sales organizations. You will learn why online retailers like Amazon are successful, and you will also learn how to compete in this environment. At the end of this chapter, you will be able to:

- Understand the "Amazon effect" and how it impacts your organization
- Describe the underlying reason for Amazon's success
- List three ideas to compete in an Amazon world
- List three ways not to compete with Amazon

THE AMAZON EFFECT

Amazon disrupts industries. For many companies, disruption causes confusion, creates stress, and clouds judgement. In disruptive times, competitors adopt a wait-and-see approach. These organizations wait for Amazon to enter, see how it will disrupt, then choose to respond. These organizations often attempt to beat Amazon at its own game, a game they cannot win. For most organizations, disruption can be painful. But value-added organizations view disruption as an opportunity.

Amazon's recent entrance into the grocery industry illustrates how it disrupts industries. Consider the progression of events:

- Amazon purchased Whole Foods and announced a 30 percent discount on hundreds of items.
- Investors reacted to the news by selling off their grocery stocks.
- With the promise of cheap prices coupled with curious consumers, Amazon noticed an immediate 25 percent increase in foot traffic.
- Kroger responded by slashing prices. Kroger investors started selling off their stock.
- Walmart has responded to the Amazon effect by beefing up services, online growth, and reestablishing its position as the low-cost provider. Walmart customers can order groceries online and pick them up at more than 1,000 Walmart locations.
- Walmart is also testing a service where it will deliver groceries and place milk, eggs, and meat directly in the fridge.

It's hard to read any newspaper without Amazon being mentioned. It commands a lot of attention and publicity. Amazon's success and disruptive reputation have left consumers curious about its next move. The Amazon effect lures competitors into playing Amazon's game. Mere rumblings of Amazon entering an industry can impact financial markets and cause organizations to rethink their strategies. This is the Amazon effect.

High consumer expectations are another aspect of the Amazon effect. Amazon has established extremely high benchmarks. In less than one minute, you can research a product, compare pricing, place an order, and secure two-day delivery with free shipping. The Amazon experience sets the expectation of convenience, cheap prices, and free delivery. Amazon initially created these expectations in the B2C retail environment. But B2C buyer expectations transfer to B2B customer expectations. Whether buying personal items or business items, people want the Amazon experience. This is the Amazon effect.

B2B sellers are expected to provide an Amazon experience even if Amazon is not a direct competitor. Research shows that any recent experience shapes expectations for other customer service experiences. For example, you could go to Starbucks and have a great experience. With high expectations, you enter a Macy's expecting an equally great experience. Amazon has raised the bar for every aspect of the customer experience. Your best customer experience becomes the benchmark by which the competition is judged.

Frame of reference means that customers compare current experiences to previous good and bad experiences. If a buyer experienced your excellent postsale technical support, you have set the benchmark. In this example, it's difficult for Amazon to compete with your postsale support. If you deliver strong postsale support, Amazon is less of an issue.

Amazon encourages buyers (and their competitors) to focus on the transaction versus the end-to-end experience. Most of the value Amazon delivers happens at the transactional level: free shipping, one-click ordering, additional product suggestions, low prices, and so on. In a purely transactional sale, Amazon wins. Change the interaction from a transaction to an experience.

The end-to-end customer experience begins long before customers place an order, and it continues long after the product is delivered. In Chapter 4, we discussed the Critical Buying Path. This is the series of benchmark steps customers go through from the moment a need exists through complete satisfaction and disposal of a solution. The transaction is just one small aspect of the broader end-to-end experience. The customer has broad, complex, and different needs throughout the Critical Buying Path. Value added is delivered at every step along the customer's buying path, not just during the transaction.

Amazon has disrupted the B2B industry. But what if traditional B2B sellers were also disrupting Amazon? What if Amazon starts adopting more traditional approaches to be successful in the B2B world? Amazon's recent moves show it is becoming more traditional. By purchasing Whole Foods, the world's largest online retailer proves that brick-and-mortar retailers are still important. Also, Amazon recently partnered with Kohl's and Sears. Kohl's will accept Amazon returns at select stores. Some Kohl's stores are also offering Amazon retail space. Sears will also be selling select Amazon items in its stores. Amazon Business is also expanding its services to include same-day delivery options, customer support, warranty support, and manufacturer-provided technical support.

The Amazon effect can be simplified into one word: *disruption.* Amazon disrupts the status quo, customer expectations, the stock market, and the competitive landscape. Although Amazon's success is undisputed, there is a misunderstanding as to why Amazon is so successful. Amazon's ability to disrupt goes beyond its technology, algorithms, and cheap prices. There is something more fundamental that enables Amazon to disrupt every industry it enters. Until you understand this fundamental, you will struggle to compete in the Amazon world.

WHY AMAZON IS SUCCESSFUL

> *"If you're competitor-focused, you have to wait until there is a competitor doing something. Being customer-focused allows you to be more pioneering."*
> —Jeff Bezos, founder of Amazon

Amazon's success is not due to the millions of products, the online experience, prime membership, or low prices. The root cause of Amazon's success is its obsession with customers. Amazon's mission is to be Earth's most customer-centric company where people can find and discover anything they want to buy online. It lives its mission. That's why Amazon disrupts every industry it enters.

Most organizations are competitor obsessed, not customer obsessed. Focusing your time, energy, and effort on the competition limits you to your competition's ability. Again, consider the grocery industry example. Walmart and Kroger responded to Amazon, not their customers. The only way to compete in an Amazon world is to obsess over the customer, not the competition. What if you were competing for the customer rather than against any one competitor?

When Amazon enters a new industry, it triggers a series of "me-too" strategies. Companies vie to offer better delivery, cheaper prices, or improve their online experience. Companies try to out-Amazon Amazon. If you weren't willing to make drastic changes pre-Amazon, why make them now? This is seller-focused thinking. Many are losing sleep because they ask themselves, "How can we compete with Amazon?" The better question would be, "How can we create more value for our customer?" If your entire organization asked and answered this question, you'd sleep a little easier.

Competing in an Amazon world goes beyond tactics. Tactically, you can't compete with Amazon on price or technology. Before competing tactically with Amazon, you must compete philosophically. Use Amazon's entrance as a trigger event to think differently, dream bigger, and act boldly. Amazon doesn't focus its energy and effort on its competition, it focuses on the customer. Initially, the best way to compete with Amazon is to ignore Amazon. Obsess over the customer, not the competition. What if you spent more time obsessing over the customer instead of the competition?

HOW TO COMPETE IN AN AMAZON WORLD

You are not doomed to pick up the crumbs that spill from Amazon's table. You can compete aggressively and profitably by using the principles of Value-Added Selling.

Set Expectations Early

Customer expectations are the true benchmarks of satisfaction. Amazon has created some high expectations. The best way to manage the buyer's expectations is to get there early in the process and establish your value-added criteria as the buying criteria.

Our latest buyer survey showed that decision makers need salespeople to add more value in the beginning of the process. Forty-one percent of decision makers surveyed indicated that salespeople could add more value by providing meaningful insight at the beginning of the buying process. If you're not providing that meaningful insight, the buyer is going to find it somewhere, perhaps at Amazon.

At the beginning of the buyer's process, it's easier to shape buyer expectations around your value-added solution. Emphasize the value-added services important to your customer and uncover new opportunities to add value. Discuss budgetary procedures and timelines. You're better off using your price and timeline instead of Amazon's to establish expectations.

Salespeople are fed up providing customers with free consulting. Salespeople uncover the buyer's needs, solve her problem, and suggest a product solution. Then, the buyer goes online and shops for the same solution. How often do you do all the up-front work only to have the customer buy from Amazon?

Equity plays a major role in Value-Added Selling. The sale must be equitable for both parties. You've read earlier that putting the customer first doesn't mean putting yourself last. Early in the process, set the expectation of reciprocity. Let the customer know that you are not in the free-consulting business. As a salesperson, you deliver maximum value to the customer with the expectation of capturing maximum value from your customer. Your value added is part of a bundled package. To experience your value-added extras, the customer has to purchase your value-added solution.

Differentiate Your Value-Added Solution

What are your definable and defendable differences? Few salespeople have a compelling response to this question. Depending on the benchmark, it's a tough question to answer. Many organizations offer similar services, the same products, and have similar value propositions. Differentiation is challenging, except when you are competing against Amazon.

Consider all the value added you offer that Amazon does not: technical expertise, retail locations, after-market support, field-level support, on-hand inventory, product knowledge, industry expertise, and so on. This is an empowering exercise for your next sales meeting. Have the group list on a flipchart all the value-added extras and special requests that your customers want. Then, go through this list and note which ones that Amazon does not offer. This will embolden your sales efforts. Now, you can proactively steer the conversation toward the value added that Amazon cannot deliver. You begin this conversation with *targeted probing* (Chapter 22) and complete it with your presentation of your value added.

Size can be a compelling differentiator. Sometimes bigger isn't better. Bigger also means more rigid, slower to change, and more bureaucracy. Smaller organizations are more flexible and nimble. Your ability to customize and offer additional value-added services is a significant advantage. Amazon can't do this. If you're a small-to-medium-sized business, use size to your advantage.

Differentiation is an offensive Value-Added Selling strategy that can help protect the business you have. Reinforce your value-added differences. In this context, reinforce the value-added differences that Amazon cannot deliver. If customers are unaware of your differentiated value, then any supply partner will do. Buyers don't like giving up value-added services they are accustomed to. Since losses loom larger than gains, buyers who are considering a switch to Amazon must be made aware of what they are giving up—the sacrifices they make for the Amazon gain.

Differentiate by offering unique solutions. Salespeople unintentionally commoditize their solution by focusing on products with well-established demand. They focus on selling products for which there is always a need. Just selling these products positions you as a commodity supplier. Customers are more likely to source these products using an e-marketplace like Amazon. Our internal research shows that 60 percent of customers prefer to purchase standard stock items online. Focus on uncovering unique customer problems and satisfying complex needs. Where there is frustration and complexity, there are opportunities to add value.

Sell the Personal Value

Have you given the buyer a good enough reason to buy from you versus Amazon? This is a gut-check question. Salespeople have the opportunity to deliver 25 percent of the total value. Salespeople represent a unique dimension of the total solution. Selling your personal value spotlights a gap in Amazon's offering. If you're not selling your personal value, then your presentation is missing 25 percent of the reason a buyer should work with you.

We have the privilege of training great salespeople. One of these salespeople illustrates the power of selling personal value. We were discussing the challenges facing salespeople today: Amazon, availability of information, pricing pressure. He shared an example of how he sells his personal value. He was meeting with a large prospect. The salesperson was familiar with the prospect's needs because he worked with several of this prospect's competitors. This prospect was buying products from another supplier. The salesperson didn't try to sell products. Instead he focused on the unique aspects of his solution. During the meeting he told the prospect, "We provide an advantage over your current supplier." The prospect asked, "What does your company have that our current supplier doesn't?" The salesperson responded, "Me." Then the salesperson steered the conversation toward the unique personal value that he as a salesperson creates.

A buyer saying, "I can buy this for 10 percent less online" is equivalent to him or her saying, "You are not worth 10 percent to me." Are you creating enough personal value? Are you delivering the 25 percent of the total value buyers expect?

Focus on the Right Business

There is business you pursue and business you attract. Some organizations are drawn to your value-added solution. These customers appreciate your value added and are willing to pay for it. These customers are HVTs. Other customers are more interested in cheap prices. These high-aggravation, low-margin, slow-pay customers are called price shoppers or PPs (profit piranhas). Which type of customer do you attract?

Which type does Amazon attract? Amazon attracts customers that want a big selection, easy online experience, and cheap prices. There are some customers that you want Amazon to have. Amazon's entrance into your industry is the catalyst to weed out low-margin, high-aggravation customers. Amazon is helping you to purge PPs from your portfolio. If Amazon can somehow figure out a way to make money on these customers, more power to it; but these drains on your profitability will no longer be a problem for you.

There is also a slice of the market Amazon is not attracting. Identify customer segments that have unique needs and purchase specialty, complex solutions. Price is less of an issue when customers have complex needs. These customers also tend to focus on more profitable niche segments. Use Amazon's entrance as an opportunity to identify and forge a new customer segment. These questions will help you uncover new opportunities:

- What unique segments have we not approached?
- What customer segments are underserved in our industry?
- What segments have unique, complex needs?
- What external factors (i.e., technological advancements, government regulations) have created opportunities for different segments?
- What segments are currently being ignored by Amazon?

Use this disruption as an opportunity to weed out price-shopping customers and focus on new, niche segments.

Focus on Service

All customers are not created equal. Certain customers are more important to your business. Certain customers require higher levels of service. These customers are special, and they deserve more. These customers pay more for value added. Amazon understands this concept. Even Amazon offers a higher level of service to certain customers. Prime members receive free two-day shipping, streaming videos, exclusive prime-only deals, book borrowing for their Kindle, and more.

Offering tiered levels of service will build loyalty and protect business that you have. Many organizations we train will offer qualifying customers a higher level of value-added services. Customers who meet a volume threshold, margin threshold, or product-line threshold qualify for additional value-added services. Offering tiered value-added services is another way to ensure you are taking care of your most important customers first.

Tiered value-added services give the buyer a goal to reach for. Airlines have leveraged this concept to build loyalty and increase share of wallet. Toward the end of the year, many business travelers will add additional trips to maintain or gain status with airlines. What if your customers bought more products to gain the tiered level of service?

A fierce competitor like Amazon forces you to get better. When Amazon enters a new industry, survival instincts kick in and companies look for ways to adapt and evolve. Use Amazon's entrance as a trigger event to create new and innovative ways to serve customers. This is tinkering to protect your business. Jeff Bezos famously said, "Your margin is my opportunity." Are you offering enough value-added services to protect your margin? Here are some questions to uncover new, additional value-added services. Discuss these questions at your next meeting. Ask your best customers for their input:

- What value-added services are missing from our current offering?
- What additional services can we offer that Amazon can't or won't?
- What are the fundamental needs that Amazon satisfies?
- What value-added services can we offer to satisfy those fundamental needs?
- What do our customers hate doing that we can do for them?
- Throughout the end-to-end experience, what frustrates our customers, and what value-added services can we offer to alleviate their frustration?

Who's doing a better job of answering these questions, you or Amazon? Customer-obsessed organizations always look for ways to improve the end-to-end customer experience.

If You Can't Beat 'Em, Join 'Em

One organization we had the privilege of working with was facing extreme pressure from a low-cost provider in the industry. The CEO of the organization made a bold move. He decided to create a flanking organization that would directly compete with this low-cost provider. There were two reasons the CEO made this strategic move. First, the company could compete without jeopardizing its reputation as the value-added partner. Second, it could gain an in-depth understanding of how a low-cost provider competes. The CEO explained the decision, "This is our chance to walk on the dark side and see how they actually compete."

E-commerce will continue to grow. Millennials prefer e-marketplaces more than other generations. However, a recent *Industrial Distribution* survey revealed that only 57 percent of distributors indicated that they generate web-based revenues.[2] Some companies are still hesitant to make the e-commerce leap. Perceived cost and complexity are the deterrents. But what's more expensive, building an e-commerce platform or sending your customers to Amazon?

Many small-to-medium-sized businesses are reluctant to launch an e-commerce platform. Owners and executives believe it's expensive and complex. Remember when companies debated over whether they should develop a company website? Fundamentally, this is the same debate. Initially, building a website was expensive. Today, you can build one for free.

Large organizations are investing heavily in their online experience. However, many smaller organizations don't have the budget to compete with Amazon. Build the platform for the purpose of satisfying your customers' needs and not to compete with Amazon.

Some companies prefer to offer customers the Amazon experience. If you can't beat Amazon, join it. Fulfillment by Amazon (FBA) allows you to sell the product, but Amazon will pick, pack, and ship it. FBA provides smaller businesses an opportunity to compete. By partnering with Amazon, you could leverage its resources and global reach. This is another opportunity to "walk on the dark side."

New competitive pressures create new opportunities. Amazon could be the catalyst to help you create an e-marketplace. You can also leverage Amazon's global reach and technology through FBA. E-commerce is here to stay. Expand this offering with the intent to serve customers, not compete with Amazon.

WHO IS MAKING A BIGGER DEAL OUT OF AMAZON

In 2013, *Modern Distribution Management* surveyed distributors and manufacturers, and only 1 percent of participants acknowledged that AmazonSupply (now Amazon Business) had any impact on their business.[3] AmazonSupply was barely on the radar. Four years later,

92 percent of wholesalers view Amazon as a competitive threat.[4] In just four years, AmazonSupply became one of the greatest competitive threats facing wholesalers.

Amazon enters a new industry and creates excitement, curiosity, and headaches. Amazon's size, reputation, and publicity is enough to cause many organizations to freak out. Consider Kroger's moves when Amazon entered the grocery industry.

Amazon's entrance into the industrial space has caused a similar reaction from many B2B sellers. Before you completely change your direction in response to the Amazon effect, ask yourself, "Who is making a bigger deal out of Amazon, me or the customer?"

Before answering this question, consider the following data taken from a group of over 50 decision makers. We surveyed multiple types of decision makers from procurement buyers to business owners and everyone in between. This research helped us gain an in-depth understanding of buyer decision making. Here are some of the questions we asked decision makers:

- "Which best describes how you will research a potential supply partner or service provider?" The number one response was, "Meet face-to-face with the salesperson."
- "When choosing between multiple suppliers, why do you choose one supplier over another?" The top three responses included "better service, hard cost savings, and the relationship with the salesperson."
- "How can salespeople provide greater value for you and your organization?" The number one response was, "Provide more after-market, value-added services."
- "Why would you choose one supplier's solution over another?" Out of 11 different options, online ordering ranked eleventh. This group of decision makers indicated that there are 10 things more important than online ordering. Buyers were asked: "Why would you choose one supplier over another?" Their responses are listed in rank order.

   1. Better quality product or service
   2. Ease of doing business

3. More knowledgeable staff and salesperson
4. Availability of product
5. They provide the lowest total cost
6. Better customer service
7. Strong relationship with the salesperson
8. Lower acquisition price
9. Problem solving ability
10. I'm already working with the supplier
11. Online ordering capability

Along these dimensions, compare your end-to-end solution to Amazon's. In these key areas, you outperform Amazon. When you are competing in an Amazon world, remind your customers (and yourself) of the advantages of your total value-added solution.

Amazon is also still the new kid on the block. Amazon has only been in existence since 1994—23 years. Most Fortune 500 companies last about 45 years. Amazon's rise has been unfettered. It has yet to face competition that challenges its ever-growing customer base. There will always be a new competitor that disrupts your status quo. Use each disruption as an opportunity to adapt and evolve. Take Jeff Bezos's advice: obsess over the customer, not the competition.

VALUE-ADDED SELLING REVIEW AND ACTION POINTS

1. **Amazon disrupts industries. For many organizations, disruption can be painful. For value-added organizations, disruption creates opportunities.**

2. **Amazon is successful because it obsesses over the customer, not the competition. If you only focus on the competition, you limit your strategy to the competition's capabilities. Look for better ways to satisfy your customers' needs, not just to beat the competition.**

3. **You can't "out-Goliath" Goliath, and you can't "out-Amazon" Amazon. Competing in an Amazon world requires thinking differently and acting differently. Choose to compete on your battlefield, not Amazon's.**

4. **Sell your differentiated value that Amazon cannot provide. Consider all the value added you offer that Amazon does not. Offer value-added customers more services.**

5. Focus on the right business. Some customers buy on price; others choose value. Target business that Amazon ignores. Find a way to serve these niche customers.

6. Have you given the buyer a good enough reason to buy from you versus Amazon? Are you worth the 25 percent differential that buyers say salespeople represent? Focus on delivering the personal value that Amazon cannot.

CHAPTER 29

Value-Added Inside Sales

Your company is sitting on a gold mine of sales opportunities. Your company has established credibility, delivered value, and captured value. And there are hundreds of these unmined opportunities waiting for you to deliver and capture more value.

These opportunities come from the dozens of customer touch points your inside sales team has every day with customers. Every touch point is an opportunity to create value for the customer and differentiate your value-added solution. You read in Chapter 19 that outside sales professionals average only 11 face-to-face sales calls per week. Their average sales call lasts 45 minutes. That's just over eight hours of face-to-face selling time per week.

Organizations are growing their inside sales teams. Steve W. Martin emphasized this point in his article "The Trend That Is Changing Sales" in the *Harvard Business Review* (November 4, 2013). Martin's research showed that organizations are hiring twice as many inside salespeople as outside salespeople. Expanding inward makes economic sense because these companies are leveraging their resources. Because of the logistics of inside sales, inside salespeople can efficiently contact and process more sales opportunities.

Although selling principles are similar, there are tactical differences between outside and inside sales. These tactical differences can create confusion, misunderstanding, and unique challenges.

In this chapter, we address the challenges and opportunities facing inside salespeople. This chapter provides a framework for training and developing the inside sales team. At the end of this chapter, you will be able to:

- List three challenges facing inside salespeople
- List three ideas to more effectively communicate value
- Describe three ways to improve communication between departments
- Detail the importance of team selling

KEY CHALLENGES FACING INSIDE SALESPEOPLE

In a recent survey, we asked over 250 salespeople the following question, "Think of your largest revenue-producing customer. If the customer said, 'I want a 10 percent discount, or I will bid this out,' would you give the customer a discount?" Ninety-seven percent of inside salespeople were willing to discount. Inside salespeople are 42 percent more likely to discount than outside salespeople. Inside salespeople are either more candid about their discounting tendency, or they are more likely to focus on price.

If the inside salesperson has not communicated value, the price is always going to be high. In a separate study, we focused on how salespeople communicate value. Only 21 percent of inside salespeople believe they offer a solution that is meaningfully different. If you don't believe your solution is meaningfully different, neither will the customer. If all solutions are similar, the customer is more likely to focus on price.

Inside salespeople also struggle to communicate their value proposition—the downline outcome of their end-to-end customer experience. Only 31 percent of inside salespeople clearly understand their company's value proposition. This is a compelling reason why communicating value is a greater challenge for inside salespeople than outside salespeople.

As companies grow their inside sales teams, higher expectations are placed on inside salespeople. Here are three relevant questions to ask about your company's commitment to inside sales:

1. Are inside salespeople prepared to meet these new and shifting demands?
2. Have they been properly trained?
3. How clearly has management created and communicated its expectations for inside salespeople?

Inside salespeople cannot be expected to sell value if they have not been coached and trained to do so. Our research found that outside salespeople receive 10 times more training than inside salespeople receive. How much training do your inside salespeople receive? Every year, the American Association of Inside Sales Professionals studies the top challenges and trends facing inside sales professionals. Since the inception of its "Top Challenges of the Inside Sales Industry" study,[1] training remains a top concern for executives and inside salespeople. Like any other profession, inside salespeople require training to be successful.

Failing to train inside salespeople devalues their role to the organization, which has a profound motivational and profit impact on the organization. A failure to train is tantamount to a company's underutilizing production equipment in a plant. We have met few executives who permit capital equipment to remain idle when it could be used to grow profits.

KEY AREAS OF DEVELOPMENT

Some believe that the best salespeople are outspoken, gregarious, and aggressive. But we have found that the most successful salespeople are humble. Humility is a foundational principle of Value-Added Selling. If you embrace humility, you believe that you can always improve your skills. Every salesperson has room for improvement.

This section focuses on the key areas of development for inside salespeople. These areas were selected through a meta-analysis of several studies that included participation from inside salespeople.

Transactional Selling
Consider the following data:

- Inside salespeople are more likely to discount than outside salespeople.
- We asked salespeople, "What's the best way to grow your sales with a current customer?" Inside salespeople said, "Asking for more projects to quote." Outside salespeople said, "Looking for problems to solve."

- Compared to outside salespeople, inside salespeople understand less about the customer's budgeting process and timeline.

There is an underlying theme. Inside salespeople view the customer experience as a transaction. A transactional mindset is short term. It means viewing each customer interaction as a single, stand-alone event instead of a broader, end-to-end experience. This transactional mindset is likely fueled by the transactional nature of inside sales. The traditional role of inside salespeople is to process orders. However, the role of inside sales is changing. Many organizations expect the inside sales team to be more consultative versus transactional.

Every interaction is not a stand-alone event. Inside salespeople need to view each interaction as part of the end-to-end experience. In Chapter 4, we discussed the Critical Buying Path. The CBP is the end-to-end experience. Inside sales plays a critical part in the buyer's process. To illustrate this point, detail the steps in the customer's CBP, and answer the question, "What value-added extras does our inside sales team offer from the very beginning, during the transition, and during the usage phase?" In a transactional sale, the salesperson (and the buyer) focuses on short-term, transactional needs. This short-term view can lead to price conversations.

To further understand your value added, follow an order throughout your organization. An inside salesperson shared an example at one of our seminars. The salesperson processed the buyer's purchase order, then followed the equipment from final assembly to packaging, delivery, staging, installing, equipment training, and postsale usage. The inside salesperson said, "The first time I performed this exercise, I was amazed at the amount of value we offer buyers. I had no idea we do all these things." Inside salespeople cannot sell value if they are unaware of their value.

In a recent survey, we asked salespeople, "What are your greatest challenges as a salesperson?" Inside salespeople indicated that understanding the buyer's needs was their greatest challenge. In a transactional sale, the focus is on quantities, lead times, and other logistical needs. Although these transactional needs are important, there are deeper needs and concerns that drive decision making. In a value-added sale, the salesperson (inside or outside) takes the time to uncover and understand the buyer's greatest needs.

In a transactional sale, buyers often initiate contact and dictate the products they want to purchase. Salespeople should be cautious when a customer tells them exactly what they need. Customers don't always know what they don't know. Use this as an opportunity to dig deeper. Review Chapters 10 and 22 on customer-izing and needs analysis. Develop a list of go-to questions. Ask customers these go-to questions to gain an in-depth understanding of the buyer's needs.

Communicating Value

A scant 21 percent of inside salespeople believe they offer a meaningfully different solution. That means four-in-five inside salespeople have a commodity view of their solution. This fuels their tendency to cut price. If salespeople perceive nothing meaningfully different, buyers will not perceive a meaningful difference. This paves the way for buyers to focus on price.

We have found that only 31 percent of inside salespeople clearly understand their company's value proposition. If the inside salespeople don't understand their value proposition, how will they communicate it to customers, and how will customers understand it? Customer messaging is about the ongoing conversation you have with customers. Customer messaging is an opportunity to predispose your buyer to your message of value. Effective customer messaging is compelling and consistent across multiple channels.

When was the last time you analyzed what makes your solution different? One of the toughest questions to answer in sales is, "What makes you different from everyone else?" Review Chapter 12 on differentiation and complete the Differentiation Matrix in Figure 12.1. Involve other team members to gain their perspective. Some salespeople ask their loyal and well-tenured customers, "What makes us different from other vendors?" Some customers may better understand your differences. Sometimes your key differences and value added hides in plain sight.

Inside salespeople are literally surrounded by their company's value-added extras. They share an office with engineering, operations, technical support, and so on. It would make sense that they have a grasp on the organization's value added. That is not necessarily true. People immersed in tasks often lose sight of their surroundings. The following example illustrates this blindness.

Would you notice a gorilla walking through a group of basketball players? Daniel Simon and Christopher Chabris studied this perceptual phenomenon and published their findings in a report titled *Gorillas in Our Midst: Sustained Inattentional Blindness for Dynamic Events.*[2]

In this study, participants were asked to watch a video showing a group of students passing a basketball. Observers were instructed to count the number of times the players passed the basketball. During the game on the video, a gorilla walked across the scene, paused to beat his chest, and then exited. After watching the video, participants were asked if they noticed the gorilla. Only 54 percent of the participants noticed the gorilla. This is *inattentional blindness.* (You can see the video on YouTube at https://www.youtube.com/watch?v=vJG698U2Mvo.)

As inside sales focuses on other priorities, it's understandable that they are perceptually blind to all of the value added happening around them. Like gorillas in their midst, value added hides in plain sight. Conducting a value audit, reviewing differentiation exercises, and following an order will help inside salespeople understand and communicate value added to the customer.

Proactively Generating More Business

Traditionally, inside sales is more reactive and responsive than proactive. This has proven to be one of the great challenges for managers as they struggle with this question: How and where do we find salespeople who are proactive but can operate in a sedentary setting?

Customers call inside sales to check pricing or process an order. Customers call when they have an issue or they need additional information. In most cases, the customer initiates contact. Even when prospecting for new business, inside salespeople are more reactive than proactive. In a recent survey, we asked salespeople, "What percentage of your leads are generated proactively (where you make initial contact with the prospect)?" Outside salespeople indicated that 57 percent of their leads were generated proactively. Inside salespeople indicated that 42 percent of their leads were generated proactively. This environment creates a wait-and-see approach. It's more challenging for an inside salesperson to proactively sell a value-added solution.

Organizations are growing their inside sales teams expecting them to proactively sell versus just take orders. As inside salespeople focus more on prospecting, it's critical to define the ideal prospect and then focus on those prospects. We asked inside salespeople to what extent they agreed with this statement: "I have an established profile for the ideal prospect." Just 9 percent of inside salespeople strongly agreed with the statement. We also asked about this statement: "I focus my time and energy on pursuing ideal prospects." Just 7 percent strongly agreed with this statement. How can an inside salesperson focus on the right business if he or she hasn't defined the ideal prospect? Review Chapter 8 and work with management to develop a list of ideal prospects that fit the criteria for good business.

Breaking Down Silos

You have read in multiple places in this text (see Chapters 4 and 27) about organizational silos—the tendency for different departments or members of an organization to feel compartmentalized or separate from other groups, departments, or individuals. When silos are present, individuals will act without considering the impact of their actions on the rest of the group. Organizational silos often exist between outside sales and the "inside." If these phrases sound familiar, then silos exist in your organization:

- "Why does the outside sales team always overpromise?"
- "Why can't the inside sales team get this order sent out sooner?"
- "Corporate doesn't have a clue what it's like in the field."
- "Inside sales doesn't understand how it works in the field."
- "Outside salespeople just entertain and glad-hand our customers."

We have found that top inside salespeople play a major role in breaking down silos and bridging the gap between the field and the office. They are the communication pipeline between the two. Additionally, because of the volume of calls they field during the day, top inside salespeople are lead generators for outside sales. Nothing tears down a silo quicker than lead sharing between inside and outside sales.

Customers today expect a consistent experience, whether it's face-to-face or over the phone. A consistent experience can only happen if inside and outside salespeople are communicating. Outside salespeople need to communicate customer expectations inside, and the inside team needs to communicate ongoing needs to the outside team. Customer satisfaction (and dissatisfaction) is determined through a customer's cumulative experiences over time and through multiple channels. A consistent experience is a result of consistent communication through multiple sales channels. Here are some tips to help break down silos between inside and outside:

- Establish common goals that unite inside and outside salespeople.
- Establish joint accounts to encourage open communication.
- Schedule regular team conference calls or video conferencing meetings.
- Schedule frequent, face-to-face meetings.
- Conduct cross-functional training to gain perspective.
- Schedule networking times for inside and outside salespeople.
- Conduct meetings that include inside and outside sales management.

The Need for Team Selling

Typically, salespeople are given a territory or a certain number of accounts to manage. Their number of accounts and prospects remains about the same every year. Whether salespeople know it or not, every year their territory is getting bigger, even if their number of accounts stays the same. Research shows that the number of decision makers is increasing. Based on the number of accounts, the territory stays the same. But based on the number of decision makers, the territory could double without the salesperson's (or the company's) knowledge. As decision makers increase, salespeople cannot effectively manage the same number of accounts.

Selling is relationship management. You can outsell your quota, but you cannot effectively manage more than a certain number of relationships. Consider Dunbar's number. Robin Dunbar is an anthropologist who studies human relationships. Dunbar's number refers to the number of stable social relationships we can manage. This study was popularized by Malcolm Gladwell's book *The Tipping Point*. Based on Dunbar's research, people can effectively manage relationships with approximately 150 people. The fundamental argument is simple: People can only manage so many personal relationships. The same is true for business relationships. The only way to manage more accounts is to get some help.

Every year, more decision makers are getting involved. Whether you're aware of it or not, every year your territory is getting bigger. Currently, the average number of decision makers is approximately 5.8 people per buying group. That number is on the rise. If a salesperson manages 25 top accounts, she is currently managing 150 relationships. If the number of accounts stays the same but more decision makers are added, the salesperson is forced to manage more relationships. Have we reached the point where one person can no longer manage the sale? What if the sale is becoming so complex and crowded that a team is needed to support the process and relationships?

Team selling unites organizations, breaks down silos, and leverages resources. The future buyer is collaborative and prefers insight from additional decision makers. Since Value-Added Selling is customer focused, it makes sense that we mirror the customer's team buying approach with a collaborative selling approach. Work with management to define a team selling process. Review the customer's CBP and determine each salesperson's role and responsibilities in the process.

The burden of building, strengthening, and maintaining relationships should not rest squarely on the shoulders of the outside salesperson. Customers' needs transcend the capabilities of an individual salesperson. That is why teams exist. There is incredible power in the synergy of inside and outside sales working together to design and deliver value-added solutions.

VALUE-ADDED SELLING REVIEW AND ACTION POINTS

1. Companies are growing their inside sales teams. Several challenges face inside salespeople as this shift is made: discounting, communicating value, and transactional selling. Focus your training and development efforts on helping inside salespeople overcome these challenges.

2. Traditionally, the role of inside salespeople has been more reactive. They respond to customer cues. The inside sales team must become more proactive in selling and serving customers. This means asking more questions to discover additional needs, reaching out to customers earlier in the buying process, and developing a list of opportunities to proactively pursue.

3. As the number of decision makers increases, there will be more relationships to manage. Outside salespeople are limited in the number that they can manage effectively. Team selling can help. Team selling means that inside and outside sales work together to understand and satisfy the customer's needs. The synergy of these teams creates value for the customer and the company.

CHAPTER 30

Final Thoughts

Value-Added Selling is a content-rich message of hope. It is a book to study, not just to read through. To extract the most value from this book, you must read it again and again, study its principles, take notes, and practice what you've learned.

As people complete our Value-Added Selling seminars, they, too, want to apply what they have learned, but they want it to sound like them, not the text. And that is great advice. For a smoother transfer of skills, you must internalize the Value-Added Selling themes coursing through the preceding 29 chapters and apply them strategically, tactically, and personally, using the models we provide. In short, use the ideas here, but make them sound like you.

In this final chapter, we will review key fundamental themes of the value-added philosophy and the strategies and tactics of Value-Added Selling and discover follow-up tips for using this material:

- **First: Life is bigger than I am.** This attitude paves the way for an empowering humility. We call this the *humility paradox.* This dynamic makes us willingly subordinate our egos for the greater good of serving others—to embrace the attitude that *serving is a privilege, not a pain.* Because of this empowering humility, we are able to share in the value that we help create for other people.

  This selfless attitude of service does not mean that we ignore our interests; in fact, the opposite is true. We pursue equity in our relationships with customers. We want them to get as good as they give; we want to get as good as we give also.

The outcome of our win-win sales efforts result in a mutually rewarding experience for both of us.

Subordinating our egos makes it easier to view life from another's perspective, to understand what is important to this person. This bird's-eye view from the customer's perspective makes it easier to find win-win outcomes. This customer value focus gives you the ability to view your value added as value received.

Value-Added Selling is a team sport. This synergy recognizes that salespeople may get the business initially, but it is the customer's total experience with a company that determines repeat business. Salespeople can only sell what operations delivers. Value-Added Selling is an integrated sales and operations model to design and deliver value-added solutions.

- **Second: My mission is to add value, not cost.** From this grows the following attitude: do more of that which adds value to your life and less of that which adds little or no value. This attitude applies to all areas of your life—health, relationships, time management, career, and spiritual and emotional well-being. When you're in the value-added mode, you're part of the momentum of life, not the resistance of life.

- **Third: I can achieve major victories with small wins.** The small-wins strategy for creating change plays a powerful role in Value-Added Selling. Understanding the next best outcome you want to achieve means that you break down success into manageable steps that create momentum for your ultimate goal—to create value for your customer and to share in that value. This philosophy of incrementalism has been used to create some of the most powerful historical movements.

- **Fourth: Price shoppers demonstrate predictable attitudes.** They operate from a short-term perspective, narrowly focusing on a single product feature—price. Achieving small wins, like teaching them to think long term and to view a total solution, are fundamental to improving the viability of these shoppers. One-in-six will always shop price. That leaves a huge segment of your market for Value-Added Selling.

PREPARATION

Preparation encompasses both personal and collateral preparation. Personal preparation is continuous investment in your own research and development. Study. Invest in your knowledge base. Increase your personal brand equity for the customer. Become an expert in your field. Become the standard against which all other salespeople are compared.

Value-added salespeople are serious students of their profession. After you have garnered all that you want to take from this book, buy another book on sales. Read and apply what you learn in that book. Enroll in seminars. Sign up for company product training sessions. Attend factory schools. Seventy-six percent of the value added that buyers receive comes from knowledge-based activities.

Collateral preparation means creating sales tools to support your customer messaging campaign. Create an elevator speech, design a VIP list, build a customer bill of rights, know your value proposition and unique selling proposition, and combine these ideas into a one-sheet. Your messaging campaign must include a strong social media dynamic. Buyers rely on online sources and social media sites to gather information about prospective sellers. Make sure your content aligns with your buyers' search parameters.

STRATEGIC PRESCRIPTIONS

Ideally, you have a sales coach. That's good. In some cases, you must become your own sales coach. The following coaching questions review the strategic side of Value-Added Selling while directing you to apply them in your territory. Ask yourself these questions to remain focused on the Value-Added Selling philosophy and process:

- Am I chasing the right business?
- Am I talking to all the right people?
- Do I understand my customer's needs, wants, and fears?
- Am I projecting the image of a value-added supplier?
- Have I differentiated our status as a value-added supplier?
- How compelling is my argument for our solution?

- How painless have we made it for the customer to implement our solution?
- How is my personal and professional relationship with the customer?
- Are we working as hard to keep the business as we did to secure the business?
- Are we getting credit for all of our value added?
- Are we maximizing our value?

TACTICAL PRESCRIPTIONS

When you make sales calls, use the tips in this section to direct your calling efforts. Be sure to have a specific objective for every call.

Precall Planning

Prepare for every call by asking these six questions:
- What do I want to accomplish on this call?
- What questions will I ask?
- What will I present to the buyer?
- What collateral pieces do I need?
- What resistance may I encounter?
- At the end of the call, what action do I want from the buyer?

Plan your sales call by using the Call Planning Guide (see Figure 20.1). Ten minutes of pencil-and-paper preparation reaps huge dividends in confidence and competence.

During Your Sales Call

- Open the call by telling the buyer why you're there—state your objective.
- Take your lead from the buyer on small talk and socializing.
- Spend the first half of the call probing and listening to the buyer's needs.

Ask more open-ended questions than closed-ended questions. Probe deep for "root-canal-type" pain.

- Present relevant sales messages that mirror the buyer's concerns and pace. Include all three dimensions of value in these sales points: product features and benefits, company value-added services, and personal commitments from you, the value-added salesperson.
- Prepare for price resistance. Being prepared does not mean that you will create resistance or that it is inevitable. Have a list of six ways you help contribute to the buyer's bottom line. Weave these into a response that uses a reversal technique to argue your case.
- Close the sales call by agreeing on your next step to advance the sale along your path. Get some commitment from the buyer that reflects your call objective.

After the Sales Call

Review every sales call immediately after you make the call, and ask yourself these questions:

- Did I achieve my objectives?
- How was the chemistry between the buyer and me?
- What is the next action step? Schedule it before you leave the parking lot.
- Why was I successful in spite of any obstacles I faced?

This last point is critical to your long-range success. To maintain your success momentum, you must understand what works best for you so that you can go out on your next sales call and do it all over again.

ADDITIONAL THOUGHTS

You will be selling to multiple decision makers—5.8 according to the latest research. This includes Levels I-II-III decision makers. Buying committees share common dynamics with other group decision-making bodies: groupthink, polarization, and loss aversion have significant influence on how these committees work.

You can compete in an Amazon world. Tens of thousands of small companies have figured out a way to compete that gives them an advantage in the David-and-Goliath battle. You and your salesperson peers are a significant advantage. Wield this advantage to increase your competitiveness.

Inside sales is an important part of your company's go-to-market strategy. Too many companies underutilize this valuable resource. Work with your inside team to create more value for your customers.

Again, thank you for purchasing this book. We appreciate your passion for the Value-Added Selling message and your faith in the messengers. Congratulations on completing your reading of this book. Your commitment to buying and reading *Value-Added Selling* says a great deal about your commitment to our profession. We're proud to share that with you and wish you great continued success.

You can stay abreast of updates for *Value-Added Selling* by visiting this website: www.TomReillyTraining.com. We'll leave you with some words from Thomas Wolfe: "If a man has a talent and cannot use it, he has failed. If he has a talent and uses only half of it, he has partly failed. If he has a talent and learns somehow to use the whole of it, he has gloriously succeeded, and won a satisfaction and a triumph few men ever know." You have the talent; you have the opportunity—the rest is up to you. God bless.

Notes

Introduction

1. Marissa Levin, "Reading Habits of the Most Successful Leaders That Can Change Your Life Too," Inc.com, August 13, 2017, https://www.inc.com/marissa-levin/reading-habits-of-the-most -successful-leaders-that.html.
2. Michael Simmons and Ian Chew, "What Entrepreneurs Can Learn from Tesla Founder Elon Musk," Fortune.com, August 11, 2016, http://fortune.com/2016/08/11/how-to-think-like-elon-musk/.
3. Karl Smallwood, "Theodore Roosevelt Could Read a Book Before Breakfast," Factfiend.com, July 15, 2014, http://www.factfiend .com/theodore-roosevelt-read-book-breakfast/.
4. José Ángel Manaiza Jr., "Speed Reading," Huffington Post, updated December 6, 2017, https://www.huffingtonpost.com/josa -angel-manaiza-jr/speed-reading-a-proven-sy_b_9052412.html.
5. Marissa Levin, "Reading Habits of the Most Successful Leaders."
6. Jim Probasco, "10 Habits of Successful People," Investopedia, updated August 29, 2017, https://www.investopedia.com/articles /personal-finance/092515/10-habits-successful-people.asp.
7. Jonathan Segura, "Print Book Sales Rose Again in 2016," *Publishers Weekly*, January 6, 2017, https://www.publishersweekly.com /pw/by-topic/industry-news/bookselling/article/72450-print-book -sales-rose-again-in-2016.html.
8. Jim Milliot, "The Bad News About E-books," *Publishers Weekly*, January 20, 2017, https://www.publishersweekly.com/pw/by-topic /digital/retailing/article/72563-the-bad-news-about-e-books.html.
9. Wall Street Journal U.S. Dollar Index, March 21, 2018.
10. Aaron Smith and Monica Anderson, "Online Shopping and E-Commerce," Pew Research Center, December 19, 2016, http:// assets.pewresearch.org/wp-content/uploads/sites/14/2016/12 /16113209/PI_2016.12.19_Online-Shopping_FINAL.pdf.
11. U.S. Department of Commerce, *Quarterly Retail E-Commerce Sales 4th Quarter 2017*, U.S. Census Bureau News, February

16, 2018, https://www.census.gov/retail/mrts/www/data/pdf/ec _current.pdf.

12. Lauren Thomas, "Amazon grabbed 4 percent of all US retail sales in 2017," CNBC, January 3, 2018, https://www.cnbc.com/2018/01 /03/amazon-grabbed-4-percent-of-all-us-retail-sales-in-2017-new -study.html.

Chapter 1

1. Amy Adkins, "Majority of U.S. Employees Not Engaged Despite Gains in 2014," Gallup, January 28, 2015, http://news.gallup.com /poll/181289/majority-employees-not-engaged-despite-gains-2014 .aspx.

2. Mario Natarelli, "How Emotion Drives Brand Choices and Decisions," *Branding Strategy Insider*, November 14, 2017, https:// www.brandingstrategyinsider.com/2017/11/how-emotion-drives -brand-choices-and-decisions.html#.WrPLXYjwZPY.

3. Teresa M. Amabile and Steve J. Kramer. "What Really Motivates Workers," *Harvard Business Review* 88, nos. 1/2 (January–February 2010): 44–45. (#1 in Breakthrough Ideas for 2010.)

4. Spherion Workforce survey, "Corporate Culture Penetration," as reported in USA Today Snapshots, January 4, 2006.

Chapter 3

1. Teresa Amabile, Steven Kramer, *The Progress Principle* (Boston: Harvard Business School Publishing, 2011

Chapter 4

1. Herbert A. Simon, "Rational Choice and the Structure of the Environment," *Psychological Review* 63(2) (1956): 129–138.

2. "AMA 2002 Survey on Internal Collaboration," American Management Association (New York), June–July 2002.

3. Tim Stevens, "View from on High," *IndustryWeek*, December 21, 2004, http://www.industryweek.com/companies-amp-executives /view-high.

4. Gallup report, "State of the American Workplace," February 2017, http://news.gallup.com/reports/178514/state-american-workplace .aspx.

5. John Simpson and Eric Winquist, "Eliminate the Top 3 Productivity Killers," JavaSoftware.com, September 15, 2009, http://provisor.jamasoftware.net/media/documents/Central_Hub _Product_Intelligence_Jama.pdf.

Chapter 6

1. Adrian Wooldridge, "Schumpeter: Corporate Short-Termism Is a Frustratingly Slippery Idea," *The Economist*, February 16, 2017.
2. Ibid.

Chapter 7

1. Wendy Cole, "Please, Go Away," *TIME* magazine, October 3, 2004, http://content.time.com/time/magazine/article/0,9171,709054 ,00.html.
2. "What Is Industry Value Added?," Department of Commerce, Bureau of Economic Analysis, ID 184, March 10, 2006, https:// www.bea.gov/faq/index.cfm?faq_id=184.

Chapter 9

1. Patrick Spenner and Karl Schmidt, "Two Numbers You Should Care About," CEB Blogs, B2B Sales and Marketing, March 31, 2015, https://www.cebglobal.com/blogs/b2b-sales-and-marketing -two-numbers-you-should-care-about/.

Chapter 10

1. CEB Marketing & Communications, "Market Insights: The Power of a Customer Journey Map," May 15, 2017, https://www .cebglobal.com/blogs/market-insights-the-power-of-a-customer -journey-map/.

Chapter 11

1. Shama Hyder, "How B2B Buying Decisions Really Get Made in the Digital Age," Forbes.com, February 21, 2017, https://www .forbes.com/sites/shamahyder/2017/02/21/how-tech-buying -decisions-really-get-made-in-the-digital-age/#5d9f4d5f3b01.
2. Mark Fidelman, "Study: 78% Of Salespeople Using Social Media Outsell Their Peers," Forbes.com, May 19, 2013,

https://www.forbes.com/sites/markfidelman/2013/05/19
/study-78-of-salespeople-using-social-media-outsell-their-peers/
#29adc178a39e.

3. Tom Reilly, "Persuasion and Influence," white paper (2011), https://
tomreillytraining.com/wp-content/uploads/2017/11/Persuasion
-and-Influence-whitepaper-VAS-header.pdf.

4. "Social Selling," Research Brief, Aberdeen Group, February
2013.

5. Jim Keenan, "Social Media & Sales Quotas: The Impact of Social
Media on Sales Quota and Corporate Revenue," A Sales Guy
Consulting, http://info.asalesguyconsulting.com/social-media-and
-sales-quota-attainment.

6. "The 2016 B2B Buyer's Survey Report," Demand Gen, https://
www.demandgenreport.com/resources/research/2016-b2b-buyer
-s-survey-report.

7. "Ultimate Guide to Sales Prospecting: Tips, Techniques and
Tools," Techniques for Successful Prospecting/LinkedIn Sales
Solutions, https://business.linkedin.com/sales-solutions/b2b-sales
-prospecting/techniques-for-successful-prospecting#.

Chapter 12

1. http://www.nytimes.com/1997/10/19/us/roberto-c-goizueta-coca
-cola-chairman-noted-for-company-turnaround-dies-at-65.html.

Chapter 13

1. Tim Colter, Mingyu Guan, Mitra Mahdavian, Sohail Razzaq,
and Jeremy D. Schneider, "What the Future Science of B2B Sales
Growth Look Like," McKinsey & Company, January 2018,
https://www.mckinsey.com/business-functions/marketing-and
-sales/our-insights/what-the-future-science-of-b2b-sales-growth
-looks-like.

2. Doug Hall, Innovation Engineering Leadership Institute, offered
by University of Wyoming, August 25–27, 2010.

Chapter 14

1. Colonel Bradford K. Nelson, "Defeating the Threat to Sustain-
ment Operations," *Army Logistician*, PB 700-08-02, vol. 40,

issue 2 (March–April 2008), http://www.alu.army.mil/alog/issues /MarApr08/defeatthreat_susop.html.

2. Aaron Smith and Monica Anderson, "Online Shopping and E-Commerce," Pew Research Center, December 19, 2016, http://www.pewinternet.org/2016/12/19/online-shopping-and -e-commerce/.

3. 2017 Global Online Consumer Report, "The Truth About Online Consumers," KPMG (2017): 27, https://assets.kpmg.com/content /dam/kpmg/xx/pdf/2017/01/the-truth-about-online-consumers .pdf.

Chapter 15

1. "Guide to Customer Centricity: Analytics and Advice for B2B Leaders," Gallup (2016), http://news.gallup.com/reports/187877 /b2b-report-2016.aspx.

2. Carl R. Rogers and Richard E. Farson, "Active Listening," in *Communicating in Business Today*, eds. R. G. Newman, M. A. Danzinger, and M. Cohen (D.C. Heath & Company, 1987).

Chapter 16

1. Jeremy Goldman, "13 Insightful Quotes from Intel Visionary Andy Grove," Inc.com, March 21, 2016, https://www.inc.com /jeremy-goldman/13-insightful-quotes-from-intel-visionary-andy -grove.html.

Chapter 17

1. Andreas Hinterhuber and Todd C. Snelgrove, eds., *Value First Then Price* (London and New York: Routledge, 2017), 61.

Chapter 18

1. Manta Press Release, "Money vs. Happiness," Manta /Dell Survey, April 22, 2014, https://www.manta.com/resources/press /money-vs-happiness-manta-dell-study-reveals-unique-insights -into-small-business-ownership-and-the-life-of-an-entrepreneur/.

2. W. Edwards Deming, from *Out of Crisis* (Cambridge/London: The MIT Press, 1982), http://quotes.deming.org/authors/W._Edwards _Deming/quote/4749.

3. Fred Reichheld, "Prescription for Cutting Costs," Bain & Company, http://www.bain.com/Images/BB_Prescription_cutting_costs.pdf.

4. Amy Adkins, "Biggest Driver of B2B Success: Meaningful Customer Impact, *Business Journal*, March 31, 2016, http://news.gallup.com/businessjournal/190400/biggest-driver-b2b-success-meaningful-customer-impact.aspx.

5. Charles Atkins, Maria Valdivieso De Uster, Mitra Mahdavian, and Lareina Yee, "Unlocking the Power of Data in Sales," McKinsey & Company, December 2016, https://www.mckinsey.com/business-functions/marketing-and-sales/our-insights/unlocking-the-power-of-data-in-sales.

6. Julie T. Johnson, Hiram C. Barksdale Jr., and James S. Boles, "Factors Associated with Customer Willingness to Refer Leads to Salespeople," *Journal of Business Research* 56 (2003): 257–263.

Chapter 19

1. D. J. Dalrymple, W. L. Cron, and T. DeCarlo, *Sales Management*, 8th ed. (Hoboken: John Wiley & Sons, Inc., 2004), 124–125.

Chapter 20

1. Dartnell Corp., "Benchmark Must-Have Selling Skills," Chicago, December 1992.

Chapter 21

1. The Brooks Group, "The 21 Biggest Myths in Sales," https://brooksgroup.com/sales-resources/whitepapers/21-biggest-myths-sales-download.

Chapter 22

1. Adrian F. Ward, "The Neuroscience of Everybody's Favorite Topic," *Scientific American*, July 16, 2013, https://www.scientificamerican.com/article/the-neuroscience-of-everybody-favorite-topic-themselves/#.

2. Ken Dooley, "The No. 1 Reason Why Customers Stay or Leave," *Customer Experience Insight*, June 10, 2013, http://www.customerexperienceinsight.com/the-no-1-reason-why-customers-stay-or-leave/.

3. Carl R. Rogers and Richard E. Farson, "Active Listening," in *Communicating in Business Today*, eds. R. G. Newman, M. A. Danzinger, and M. Cohen (D.C. Heath & Company, 1987).

Chapter 23

1. National Archives, https://www.archives.gov/.
2. Benjamin Bushong, Lindsay M. King, Colin F. Camerer, and Antonio Rangel, "Pavlovian Processes in Consumer Choice: The Physical Presence of Good Increases Willingness-to-Pay," *American Economic Review* 100 (September 2010): 1–8, http://www.rnl.caltech.edu/publications/pdf/bushong2010.pdf.

Chapter 25

1. Jeff Falk, "Why Do Consumers Pay More?," Rice University News & Media, October 25, 2016, http://news.rice.edu/2016/10/25/why-do-consumers-pay-more-rice-research-finds-the-surprising-effect-of-consumer-local-identity/.

Chapter 27

1. Karl Schmidt, Brent Adamson, and Anna Bird, "Making the Consensus Sale," *Harvard Business Review*, March 2015, https://hbr.org/2015/03/making-the-consensus-sale; Nicholas Toman, Brent Adamson, and Cristina Gomez, "The New Sales Imperative," *Harvard Business Review*, March–April 2017, https://hbr.org/2017/03/the-new-sales-imperative.
2. S. A. McLeod, "Asch Experiment," Simply Psychology, 2008, www.simplypsychology.org/asch-conformity.html.
3. Daniel Kahneman, Jack L. Knetsch, and Richard H. Thaler, "Anomalies: The Endowment Effect, Loss Aversion, and Status Quo Bias," *Journal of Economic Perspectives* 5, no. 1 (Winter 1991): 193–206.
4. "LinkedIn's Definitive Guide to Selling to Multiple Decision-Makers," LinkedIn, accessed November 2017, https://business.linkedin.com/content/dam/me/business/en-us/sales-solutions/resources/pdfs/linkedins-definitive-guide-to-selling-to-multiple-decision-makers.pdf.

Chapter 28

1. *Every Man's Bible*, New Living Translation (Carol Stream, IL: Tyndale House Publishers, Inc.), 1 Samuel 17:32–51.
2. Mike Hockett, "ID's 70th Annual Survey of Distributor Operations, Pt. 2," May 18, 2017, https://www.inddist.com/article/2017/05/ids-70th-annual-survey-distributor-operations-pt-2.
3. Jenel Stelton-Holtmeier, "Survey: AmazonSupply's Impact on Distributors Low, but Curiosity High," *Modern Distribution Management*, accessed November 8, 2017, https://www.mdm.com/blogs/1-management-strategy/post/30132-management-strategy-2013-04-19-survey-amazonsupplys-impact-on-distributors-low-but-curiosity-still-high.
4. Edwin Lopez, "Report: 92% of Wholesale Distributors See Amazon as a Competitor," Supply Chain Dive, July 19, 2017, https://www.supplychaindive.com/news/wholesale-distributor-amazon-competition-technology/447372/.

Chapter 29

1. "Top Challenges Of The Inside Sales Industry 2017," AA-ISP Research, May 17, 2017, https://aa-isp.org/development/693
2. *Perception* 28 (1999): 1059–1074, http://www.chabris.com/Simons 1999.pdf

Index

Page numbers followed by *f* refer to figures.

About the Authors

Tom Reilly is the founder of Tom Reilly Training. His pioneering work in Value-Added Selling sparked a revolution in sales training. In addition to *Value-Added Selling*, Tom is the author of fifteen other books including *Crush Price Objections*. Tom has written over 400 journal articles on sales, service, and management for major business publications. His client list reads like a Who's Who of global business. After enjoying success as a salesman and business owner in industrial chemicals, Tom decided to pursue a speaking and sales training career in 1981. He has a BA/MA in Psychology and has earned the prestigious Certified Speaking Professional designation from the National Speakers' Association. Tom lives in St. Louis, MO with his family.

Paul Reilly is the president of Tom Reilly Training and the co-author of Value-Added Selling. Paul spends most of his professional time speaking and training on the Value-Added Selling message. Paul works with world-class sales organizations to help them compete more profitably. Paul writes for several business publications. Prior to joining Tom Reilly Training, Paul spent over ten years in professional sales. Paul is a faculty member at the University of Innovative Distribution and has an MBA from Webster University-St. Louis.